SOCIETIES BEYOND OIL

ABOUT THE AUTHOR

JOHN URRY is a Distinguished Professor of Sociology at Lancaster University. Educated at the University of Cambridge (B.A./M.A. Economics, Ph.D. Sociology), he is the editor of the *International Library of Sociology*, co-editor of *Mobilities* and director of the Lancaster Centre for Mobilities Research. His recent books include *Automobilities* (2005), *Mobilities, Networks, Geographies* (2006), *Mobilities* (2007), *Aeromobilities* (2009), *After the Car* (2009), *Mobile Lives* (2010), *Mobile Methods* (2011), *The Tourist Gaze* 3.0 (2011) and *Climate Change and Society* (2011).

SOCIETIES BEYOND OIL

Oil Dregs and Social Futures

JOHN URRY

Zed Books
LONDON | NEW YORK

Societies beyond Oil: Oil Dregs and Social Futures was first published
in 2013 by Zed Books Ltd, 7 Cynthia Street, London N1 9JF, UK
and Room 400, 175 Fifth Avenue, New York, NY 10010, USA

www.zedbooks.co.uk

Designed and typeset in Monotype Bembo Book
by illuminati, Grosmont
Index by John Barker
Cover design by www.roguefour.co.uk
Cover image © Stockphoto.com/kristaweber
Printed and bound by CPI Group (UK) Ltd, Croydon CRO 4YY

Distributed in the USA exclusively by Palgrave Macmillan, a division of
St Martin's Press, LLC, 175 Fifth Avenue, New York, NY 10010, USA

A catalogue record for this book is available from the British Library
Library of Congress Cataloging in Publication Data available

ISBN 978 1 78032 169 1 hb

CONTENTS

ACKNOWLEDGEMENTS

Many colleagues around the world have helped me in developing the ideas and arguments for this book. I am especially grateful for suggestions or collaborations with Andrew Curry, Jørgen-Ole Baerenholdt, Mike Berners Lee, Thomas Birtchnell, Lucy Budd, Monika Büscher, Javier Caletrio, Rachel Cooper, Saolo Cwerner, Tim Dant, Kingsley Dennis, Pennie Drinkall, Anthony Elliott, James Faulconbridge, Bianca Freire-Medeiros, Tony Gatrell, Anthony Giddens, Margaret Grieco, Michael Haldrup, Kevin Hannam, Mark Harvey, Christa Hubers, Michael Hulme, Paola Jiron, Peter Jones, Roger Kemp, Sven Kesselring, Jonas Larsen, Scott Lash, Glenn Lyons, Phil Macnaghten, James Marriott, Cary Monreal Clark, Colin Pooley, Satya Savitzky, Heiko Schmid, Mimi Sheller, Mark Stoddart, Bron Szerszynski, David Tyfield, Tom Urry, Claire Waterton, Brian Wynne, and especially Amy Urry and Sylvia Walby.

I am indebted to the Sociology Department at Lancaster University for much support and encouragement over an exceptionally long time. I am also grateful for inspiration from those groups and experiments that are seeking to innovate what I term here a low carbon civil society.

Lancaster

August 2012

THE PROBLEM OF ENERGY

Energy

Overall how societies are 'energized' is crucial for understanding how they work, how they are 'powered'. This powering of societies depends upon systems of energy production, distribution and consumption. These vary enormously, from muscle power, wood, wind, water and sun to coal, gas, oil, hydroelectric, geothermal and nuclear, from small-scale localized production to huge global systems. Until the eighteenth century energy derived from muscle power (80–85 per cent), wind, wood for burning and water. Now the fossil fuels of coal, gas and oil account for over four-fifths of the world's current energy.[1]

Energy systems are incredibly important. They 'generate' very varied and often highly unequal economic, social and political patterns. Such powering of society often takes a long time to change. And yet if they do change this has huge consequences for economies, cities, inequalities, mobilities, gender relations, foreign policies and levels of income and well-being within and across societies. As energy use became larger and more large scale, so inequalities tended to increase and greater divisions of interest arose between major social groups with regard to their energy production and use.

Energy and its consequences are central to almost all aspects of contemporary life. There is little activity that does not involve substantial energy supplies. The exploitation of energy is moreover doing something that many had thought impossible, namely changing the climate through global warming.[2] There are also huge insecurities in future supplies of energy. There are often many local and global risks involved in the processes through which energy resources are produced, distributed and used. Energy rarely involves a 'free lunch', although the bill is often paid by those not actually consuming the lunch.

These effects are most pronounced in those energy resources which power tools, buildings, machines and especially 'mobile-machines'. These are responsible for ordering and reordering physical, economic, social and military worlds. Especially significant has been the coal-based steam power that developed in the 'West' during the eighteenth and nineteenth centuries. This set societies, first in Europe and then North America, onto a quite different path of development. Nobel prizewinner Paul Crutzen argues that these innovations initiated a new geological period of human history, the 'anthropocene'. Matthew Boulton's first factory and James Watt's steam engine were central to this new fateful era beginning in England in the second half of the eighteenth century. James Boswell in 1776 commented on visiting the world's first factory, owned by Matthew Boulton: 'I shall never forget Mr Bolton's [sic] expression to me: "I sell here, Sir, what all the world desires to have – POWER."'[3]

From then on the paths of the 'west' of the world and the 'east' diverged. These coal-fired steam engines in the west with their new kind of power generated novel workplaces, new industries and products, huge factories, new cities, and machine-based movement, the railway, which transformed much of the physical world. These all depended upon the fossil fuel of coal extracted from shallow and open-cast coalmines.[4]

Coal enabled the production and consumption of various large systems, generating the horsepower of millions of people. Societies came to be organized around new production, transportation and communications, whole new patterns of living. The anthropocene period stemmed from developing immensely powerful systems using coal which remade the world. Coal was the energy resource initiating the anthropocene. This was significant for many reasons but especially for its transformation of human movement.

Prior to the nineteenth century, people's movement had been slow, by foot, sedan chair, riding an ox or horse, sailboat and carriage. These were all non-mechanical. So although people moved, they did not move fast and their forms of movement did not involve huge transformations of the physical world. The main exception to this was the eighteenth-century building of canals, which pioneered techniques of bridge-building and cuttings subsequently significant in the building of railways during the second half of the nineteenth century, beginning first in Britain.

Railways were especially significant, the first 'mobile-machines', as they restructured physical and social worlds. In 1901 H.G. Wells predicted that future historians would take 'a steam engine running on a railway' as the nineteenth century's central symbol.[5] For the first time in history people and objects, including coal itself, travelled faster than any galloping horse. A commentator at the time suggested that the new railways were 'compressing' people's sense of time and space. As distances were annihilated, so 'the surface of the country would, as it were, shrivel in size until it became not much larger than one immense city'.[6]

J.W.M. Turner's iconic painting *Rain, Steam and Speed*, first exhibited at the Royal Academy in London in 1844, captured this providential event, with the colour and shape of life changing as a black speed machine sliced through a pre-industrial landscape. Karl Marx too thought that the circulation of commodities via new forms of transport and communications (train, mail, telegraph) represented a huge upward shift in the annihilating of space by time. Capitalist production increasingly rested upon speeding up exchange through mechanizing the movements of people, food, coal, iron ore and manufactured goods.[7]

Towards the end of the nineteenth century coal power was thought of as possibly powering not just trains travelling along fixed tracks, but smaller machines travelling more freely and flexibly along roadways. There was a very significant contest to develop the first 'horseless carriages' or what we now call cars. This contest occurred between advocates of steam power, of electric batteries and of petrol. This was a contest between developments occurring in France, Germany and the USA. Britain, which initiated the railway age, little appreciated the potential of horseless carriages. It was wedded to the railway, demonstrating how the 'first shall be last, and the last first'. But then oil transformed this contest.

Oil

Social philosopher Slavoj Žižek wrote about the origins of oil: 'Nature is one big catastrophe. Oil, our main source of energy – can you even imagine what kind of ultra-unthinkable ecological catastrophe must have happened on earth in order that we have these reserves of oil?'[8] Ancient fossilized organic materials came to settle on the bottom of seas and lakes and were buried. As further layers settled on top, so intense heat and pressure built up, causing the organic matter to change into a waxy material called kerogen. And then, with more heat, it turned into liquid and gaseous hydrocarbons, oil and gas. This enormously rich resource was laid down mostly below the earth's surface beginning some 400 million years ago. Such oil consisted of long hydrocarbon chains taking an unimaginably long time to develop. Oil is in effect 'preserved sun'.

A few pre-industrial societies used oil when it bubbled up to the surface but its qualities were hidden from view for most of human history.[9] Oil was not deemed to be a significant resource, although only the sun exceeds oil in its energy. When oil was first discovered in Pennsylvania in the 1840s, it was thought of as a potential fuel for lighting and hence might replace whale oil. Research was undertaken to see whether this new oily substance could be used for lighting. Refined oil stemming from the first oil well established in Pennsylvania in 1859 did indeed provide fuel for lighting people's houses.

But the really significant oil event was the first gusher in 1901 at Spindletop, Texas. This gusher established the era of cheap plentiful oil. Such oil rapidly came to be used to power cars, steamships and aeroplanes. The use of oil for transportation energy rather than for lighting was utterly significant for the modern twentieth century. Virtually free energy spurting out of the ground led many to believe that there really was a free lunch. There was (black) gold at the end of the rainbow. One only had to drill in the right place and, with very little energy expended, vast amounts of more or less free energy were enabled. As the novelist Upton Sinclair described such gushers in *Oil!*: 'The inside of the earth seemed to burst through that hole; a roaring and rushing, as Niagara, and a black column shot up into the air, two hundred feet, two hundred and fifty – no one could say for sure – and came thundering down to earth as a mass of thick, black, slimy, slippery fluid.'[10]

This was a unique gift but finite and irreplaceable. It is calculated that the total value of the worldwide oil industry is now greater than all banks. At $100 a barrel the world's known oil reserves are worth $104 trillion or forty times the value of the UK economy.[11] Oil is central to 'Western civilization'. The systems of twentieth-century capitalism came to depend upon this exceptional oiling of the wheels of society. Oil as much as money makes the world go round. Oil is energy-dense, storable, mobile, versatile, convenient and for most of the twentieth century exceptionally cheap. The oil currently used each year is equivalent to the energy that would be annually produced by 2,500 nuclear power stations or 5,200 coal-fired power stations.[12]

As a result oil provides almost all transportation energy in the modern world (at least 95 per cent), powering cars, trucks, planes, ships and some trains. It is the single resource which makes possible in today's world friendship, business life, professions and much family life. These all presuppose 'mobile lives' as there is increasing separation of where people live, work and engage in their leisure. Oil also transports components, commodities and food around the world in trucks, planes and vast container ships.[13] Almost all activities that presuppose movement now rely upon oil; and there are few activities that are significant in the modern world that do not entail movement of some kind. As peak oil analyst Thomas Homer-Dixon writes, 'oil powers virtually all movement of people, materials, foodstuffs, and manufactured goods – inside our countries and around the world.'[14]

Oil is also an element of most manufactured goods and much packaging and bottling worldwide (95 per cent). Increasingly especially plastics production is now occurring in the Middle East. About 2 per cent of oil is used in manufacturing and yet produces an astonishing range of material objects.

Oil is also crucial to at least 95 per cent of food production and distribution for a rising world population through providing power for irrigation/drainage, for pesticides and fertilizers and moving food to market.[15]

Also oil is used for much domestic and office heating, especially in oil-rich societies, and is crucial in providing backup power and lighting when other energy sources fail (as in hospitals or nuclear power stations). Overall oil generates well over a third of all carbon emissions and is a major category of such emissions currently increasing around the world.[16]

Moreover, there are few systemic alternatives to oil. This commodity is like no other. It has been available, mobile and flexible for the past century. The global economy and society became dependent upon this one source of power, products and provision. All alternative fuels to oil have a much poorer ratio of energy returned on energy invested, or EROEI. Furthermore, as oil's price rises there is not necessarily more produced and delivered to the marketplace. Currently its supply seems relatively fixed, and intermittent rapid increases in price are almost certain. Until the last few years there had been an annual average growth rate of oil production of more than 2 per cent; since when its supply has more or less stabilized.

Much of this book is concerned with the economic, political and social implications of how oil is energy-dense, storable, mobile and non-renewable. I examine how oil has been used up and especially burnt as fuel. It seemed in the twentieth century that there was unlimited energy from oil and that it was going to cost decreasing amounts to produce as more and more huge fields were coming on stream.[17] It has normally been presumed by economists that since energy accounts for only about 5 per cent of national income this is what its 'real' contribution is to an economy. Energy did not have to be especially factored in to 'economic calculations' since it was apparently plentiful and did not appear to be directly responsible for economic growth.[18]

However, many now calculate that the price of oil should have been very much greater than that actually charged, both because of oil's exceptional functionality and because of its finite supply. If it had been much more expensive it would have been seen as a valuable resource to be carefully deployed and used over a much longer time period.

In particular if one rewinds to 1901, the very last thing that should have been done with this oil was to burn it up in powering cars, trucks, trains, ships and planes. Jeff Rubin notes how 'there is a lot more value in producing products like plastics from oil than there is from turning oil into gasoline or diesel … You can make five times as much by turning oil or natural gas into a petrochemical as you can from selling it as a transport fuel.'[19] And if it had been used far more slowly, then the resulting carbon dioxide emissions would have been very much lower. This might have avoided what Nicholas Stern terms the world's greatest ever market failure, of global climate change generated by the burning of fossil fuels over the last two centuries.[20]

Leading social analyst Zygmunt Bauman famously described the twentieth-century development of all this movement as a 'liquid modernity'. But what he did not examine was how there was in fact a literal liquid – oil – that made this modernity, oiling the wheels of a globalizing society.[21] It seemed that the modern world had struck 'black gold'. Its supplies of oil powered up societies in many novel ways and this high carbon pathway would move onwards and upwards, developing and reinforcing Western modernity as both 'business as usual' and as 'natural'.

Urbanist David Owen refers to this twentieth-century development as 'liquid civilization', a mobile civilization based on the very cheap liquid of oil and for which there are no significant alternatives.[22]

Many policies and prototypes are being developed worldwide to produce alternative forms of energy, especially nuclear, solar and wind. But most of these do not replace oil, with its more or less total monopoly in transporting people and things. Moreover, most energy innovations take a very long time to develop, often decades. An energy transition from one type of fuel to another happens once a century or so, with momentous consequences.[23] Switching from this oil civilization is thus no simple and quick task and may take getting on for a century to occur.

During the twentieth century people's lives in the rich north were thus based upon increasing incomes, wealth, security, well-being, movement and fossil fuels. These increases made the modern dream, which looked like it was here for good, especially as the only rival to Western capitalism, state socialism in Eastern Europe, mostly disappeared around 1989. High-carbon modern production and consumption seemed to have 'no borders', no 'limits to growth' and no likelihood of going into reverse.[24] Although there were some disruptions, there was little appreciation of the historic contingency of the model.

So we should not think that 'Western civilization' is inherently superior to the rest of the world. Rather, it was the contingent carbon resources and especially the small discovery of 'oil' that enabled 'the West' to dominate the long twentieth century. It was not only the Enlightenment or Western science or liberalism that secured Western civilization; it was also its carbon resources and especially the mobile energy resource of oil lying just beneath the ground, and especially below US territory, during the first half of the twentieth century. As J. Paul Getty once wrote, 'The meek shall inherit the Earth, but not its mineral rights.'[25] As oil gushed to the surface, so it helped to generate an exceptional 'modern, mobile' civilization. This enabled the West to consolidate its power and influence in the world over the 'modern' period.

This oil civilization began in the USA. Cheap plentiful oil became central to twentieth-century American economic, cultural and military power. The USA now accounts for one-third of global wealth, 22 per cent of world energy consumption and one-quarter of total carbon emissions (its population is 5 per cent).[26] The USA drives almost a third of the world's cars (and still most of the bigger ones) and produces nearly half of the world's transport-generated carbon emissions.[27] It would be impossible for the rest of the world to share this American Dream. If the American Dream was indeed experienced by all the world's population, it would take at least five planets to support it.[28]

American production and consumption got there first, especially because the USA initiated and monopolized the manufacture and use of 'large independent mobile machines', or LIMMs. And with LIMMs the machine carries its own energy source; given the denseness and historic cheapness of oil, this was a highly efficient system, helping to generate the USA's 'addiction to oil'.[29]

Globally there are nearly one billion cars and trucks and almost one billion international air journeys undertaken a year. It is a huge problem for a single resource to be the basis of all these modern systems and societies. The future of oil is the future of modern societies set upon their pathway during the momentous twentieth century. This had the dramatic effect of overexploiting the earth's resources. David Nye reports how 'We have deployed more energy since 1900 than all of human history before 1900.'[30] The twentieth century used as much as the previous hundreds of centuries of recorded human history. And in consuming those resources that century generated carbon dioxide emissions that will remain in the atmosphere for hundreds of years. This book explores the implications of this exceptional energy use and especially how the twentieth century created a vision of the future unsustainable into even the medium term. The energizing of society may go into reverse. The modern mobile dream is not so set in stone.

Twentieth-century energizing was based upon coal, gas and oil. And these fossil fuels still account for over 80 per cent of CO_2 emissions. They cause major problems. Coal produces far too many emissions. As climate scientist James Hansen argues, 'If we want to solve the climate problem, we must phase out coal emissions, period.'[31] World coal-energy production is likely to peak in 2035 but it is being increasingly used rather than being left in the ground.[32]

Gas and oil also generate greenhouse gas (GHG) emissions, at about half the figure for coal, but they are running down. Globally there is no large-scale plan B that would enable societies to be energized and mobilized on the global scale that the twentieth century had set in place. The twenty-first century will be very different from the previous century.

This is especially because the supply of oil seems to have peaked. The problem with oil is, as M. King Hubbert, the geologist who raised the issue of 'American peak oil', expressed it, that 'you can only use oil once … Soon all the oil is going to be burned.'[33] As a result, we get left with the 'oil dregs'. A dreg is 'the worst and lowest part of something'.[34] This book examines what an energy descent would be like. In policy terms this is known as 'de-carbonizing', as set out in the EU's 2020 plan. What lessons can be learnt from the past about de-energized societies, how would conflicts over resources be resolved, what are likely levels of income and well-being, how will markets allocate scarce energy, and how will societies be organized as scarce energy resources are central? If we are really down to the oil dregs, then what kinds of societies are likely after oil?

Summarizing the argument

Part I establishes the main features of the problem of oil. The next chapter tells the story of the economic and financial crash of 2007–08. Oil and its rapidly rising price during the 'noughties' are key to understanding this crash. Oil shortages were connected with subprime mortgages and they both came to grief in distant American suburbs built during the previous couple of decades. Resources can 'bite back', since energy lies at the heart of much social life, hidden from view, but on occasion having dramatic consequences. The crash of 2007–08 onwards was not simply an economic crash but an oil crash; thus oil and its shortages have already had dramatic effects. The future has arrived.

Chapter 2 examines how the twentieth century formed around an array of novel 'systems', including automobility, suburbs, homes full of electric-powered consumer goods, and national systems of food production, distribution and consumption. Central in many of these was oil, which until the early 1970s was cheap, accessible and plentiful. It was more or less vital to everything that moves on the planet. Oil also helped to develop US hegemony as it fuelled speedy travel by car, truck and aeroplane by civilians and, especially, by the US military. American hegemony presupposed plentiful cheap oil.

Chapter 3 examines some aspects of oil dependence. One was the development of places of excessive consumption for those in the rich north of the world. Increasingly central to twentieth-century lives were places of high-carbon living. The speculative development of such places involved large infrastructural projects necessitating the profligate consumption of water, power and building materials. Norms of behaviour within these places were less regulated by family or neighbourhood. Many became known for excess, providing models of high-carbon living that were then circulated across the world's media and displaying what the 'good high carbon life' could and should be like.

This twentieth-century carbon dependence also stemmed from the organized interests of 'carbon capital'. This consists of oil companies, auto companies, state oil corporations, various states and governments that protect and enhance the interests of oil-based mobility and production systems. Chapter 4 examines how this interest wielded global power throughout the twentieth century. Carbon capital organized against regulation and intervention in energy markets and prospecting; it funded various foundations and think-tanks to engender climate change scepticism; it denied the finite nature of carbon resources; and it bent foreign policies to its interests. It has probably been the world's most powerful 'interest'.

Chapter 5 demonstrates that oil does indeed seem to be running out. The peak occurs when around half the potential oil has been extracted, after which further oil is increasingly difficult to produce. The largest oilfields in the world were discovered over half a century ago, with no very significant discoveries since the 1970s. The peaking of oil in the USA occurred forty-two years ago, and recently in China. Oil supplies are concentrated among a few countries, which led to a political peaking of oil before its literal technological peaking around 2006, according to the International Energy Authority. The last century was an interlude of easy oil, gas and coal. In this century there will be frequent shortages of oil, especially with the world's population continuing to soar and high levels of insecurity within oil-producing states.

In Chapter 6 this peaking is shown to be even more significant on account of oil's increasing use within China. If China reaches the USA's per capita car ownership there would be nearly one billion cars, more than the current world car fleet. At the current growth rate China will in ten years consume all the available world exports of oil according to one estimate! If people in China acquire 'Western' forms of car-based mobile lives, then this will transform domestic transport infrastructures, road safety, global fuel resources, the environment and the global climate. China's effort to sustain its rate of growth of 'energizing' dwarfs developments occurring elsewhere with regard to energy futures.

Chapter 7 examines some centres of oil and gas production. Many energy-producing societies are places of untold wealth, huge inequalities, autocratic government, militarization, corruption and intermittent protest and resistance. Oil can generate very large 'rents'. The more a society depends upon oil (and gas), the greater the chances it will be autocratically governed and local populations will suffer deprivations, including paradoxically a lack of oil itself. Overall the chapter explores the 'global curse' of oil (and gas); while the counter-case of a democratic governance of oil within Norway is examined.

In light of these intersecting processes, four futures for societies around 2050 are examined in Part II. It is shown just how important 'societies' are. The problem of oil is not just a technical or economic issue. The first future for societies is set out in Chapter 8. This involves the possibility that a viable, global magic bullet is discovered which offsets the problem of oil decline. This new 'high-tech system' substitutes for the energy descent of oil and other fossil fuels, without worsening GHG emissions. Fast travel and high-carbon social lives continue with the scale and intensity of contemporary globalization further enhanced. Twentieth-century patterns of economy and of 'mobile' social lives spread throughout the world. The possibility that hydrogen power could be this magic-bullet high-tech future is assessed.

The second model, examined in Chapter 9, is also a 'high-tech' future. Here widespread developments in the scale and impact of digital worlds substitute for much physical travel. Co-present conversations will be a 'luxury' since they presuppose high energy costs. Production systems also change through three-dimensional 'printing'. Digital travel significantly replaces the physical transport of people and things. This future significantly substitutes the energy costs of oil and is part of a broader shift, with 'digital capital' becoming the dominant interest in the world, displacing carbon capital. Some major costs of digital lives are examined.

The third future, presented in Chapter 10, is the continuing shift from easy oil to a new century of tough oil. The oil dregs require increasingly more resources to extract the oil and to offset global temperature rises. Such energy resources are fought over by countries and corporations. Resource wars involving many different forces and periodic economic crises are commonplace. Especially significant are the USA and China 'fighting' over diminishing oil reserves (and related resources of food and water given 'peak ecological water'). Oil, food and water shortages forcefully 'localize' economic production and social lives.

The fourth future, explored in Chapter 11, is that there is a planned powering down to low-carbon lives and systems. Societies plan to cope with reduced energy yet sustain some of the pleasures of contemporary wealthy societies. There is a global transition to lower oil and other energy production and consumption systems. States, NGOs and corporations all engineer low-carbon systems through what some term reduced 'demand'. The chapter examines what would be necessary for powering down to occur, as well as some green shoots of such a future in the rich north. Various movements to think, design and innovate low-carbon alternatives are examined.

The final chapter considers recent literature that draws upon historical accounts of how previously 'dominant' civilizations collapsed. They collapsed because they no longer ensured that they had systems to guarantee sufficient energizing of their societies and their rising populations. I examine whether these historical experiences have lessons for the present. Are contemporary societies so locked into systems of energy, producing the need for ever more energy, that there is no way to get off such a treadmill without 'collapse'? There are many difficulties in reversing existing systems. The book ends with a bleak vision of the future as oil dependence, oil decline and the power of finance bring about likely de-globalization, resource wars and de-democratization, unless the low probability is realized of a low-carbon civil society taking root very fast and with sufficient traction around the world.

The problem of oil is 42

I end this Introduction by noting how in Douglas Adams's *The Hitchhiker's Guide to the Galaxy* the number 42 represents the secret of the universe.[35] What no one has noted is that 42 also refers to the secret of oil. If total proven reserves of oil are divided by current annual consumption, 42 years of oil are left from now. This assumes no increase in consumption, the full ability to extract what remains of conventional oil and no political difficulties in exploiting these reserves. Well before then oil will be many times more expensive than now and there will be frequent and abrupt shortages, increased competition and more wars to access remaining supplies. Also 42 years have passed since 1970, often referred to as the 'year of the environment', a previous high moment when the carbonizing of society was significantly critiqued. 1970 saw the founding of Greenpeace, the first Earth Day with 20 million demonstrating in the USA, the forming of the USA's Environmental Protection Agency, the peaking of US oil supplies and Joni Mitchell singing: 'They paved paradise and put up a parking lot.'[36] At the time the world's population was slightly more than half that of today and there were a little over one-fifth of today's motor vehicles. There are also, curiously, 42 gallons in a barrel of oil.[37]

This book is about how the greatest energy resource apart from the sun got exhausted after a century and a half. How did oil and society strike up such a deadly embrace? Can't live with it, can't live without it, we might say of oil. What, then, of the societies lying beyond oil?

PART I

OIL DREGS

CHAPTER I

OIL AND THE CRASH OF 2007–08

Oil and money

It is often said that money makes the world go round. And there is something in this as trillions of dollars, euros, yen, renminbi and the major currencies circulate around the world at dizzying speed. Although once that money was physically moved, most movement now is virtual, taking place on computer screens located in banks, insurance companies, trading rooms, multinational companies, accountancy firms and so on. This digital movement of money dwarfs the income and resources available to individuals, most companies and even most countries. So there is a very powerful force central to the 'globalizing' of the contemporary world.

But this book shows that there is another powerful force in the world, that of oil. This chapter is concerned with how money and oil intersect. First, the oil exploring, producing and using industries are a huge economic enterprise containing many of the world's largest and richest companies. This 'carbon capital' consists of Western-based oil 'super majors' (such as ExxonMobil, which grew out of Rockefeller's Standard Oil), state oil companies mainly found in producing countries (such as the world's most valuable company, Saudi Aramco), car and truck producing corporations (Toyota being the world's largest up to 2011), huge engineering and road construction companies (such as Bechtel), and the wide array of corporations providing services to car drivers and passengers (such as Holiday Inn or McDonald's).

Further, there is much intertwining of new kinds of finance with supplies of oil. Oil is a key commodity speculated upon in financial markets. Its price movements stem as much from this speculation as from changes in the supply and demand of oil for transportation and manufacturing. A major report for Lloyds of London shows that speculation destabilizes supply and price and further reduces energy security.[1] There are now over seventy-five crude oil financial derivatives where there was one just fifteen years ago. A derivative is a financial instrument whose value depends on other, more basic, underlying variables such as, in this case, the future price of oil. This report suggests that the extensive growth in financial trading in oil is driving oil prices higher and making them more unstable.[2] Oil prices are exceptionally sensitive to even small changes in demand.

It might be thought that the oil problem is something for the future. However, this chapter shows that oil supplies are already having major economic and social consequences. The world economic crash of 2007–08 onwards was partly brought about by oil shortages and price increases. The speculative building and risky funding of extensive tracts of 'marginal' suburbs and related shopping and leisure developments within the USA depended upon cheap land, mortgages and petrol, which made it seem that the continued upward movement of house prices was inevitable. But these began to unravel when oil prices dramatically soared in the mid-2000s. How did cheap oil and cheap mortgages produce such an economic and social nightmare, first on Main Street, USA, then on Wall Street, and then throughout much of the world?

Neoliberalism

Crucial here is neoliberalism. This became the dominant if not universal global orthodoxy of economic and social policy from around 1980. The doctrine spread from its birthplace within the Economics Department at the University of Chicago through the huge influence of what are sometimes known as the 'Chicago boys'.[3] Even as early as 1999, Chicago School alumni included twenty-five government ministers and more than a dozen central bank presidents scattered around the world.[4]

Neoliberalism is a doctrine and set of practices that assert the power and importance of private entrepreneurship, private property rights, the freeing of markets and the freeing of trade. These objectives are brought about by deregulating private activities and companies, privatizing previously 'state' or 'collective' services especially through low taxes, undermining collective powers of workers and professionals, and providing conditions for the private sector to find ever-new sources of profitable activity. Neoliberalism especially minimizes the role of the state, to re-address the balance as it sees it between the 'bad' state and 'good' markets. Matt Ridley, the former boss of UK bank Northern Rock, which had to be rescued by the UK state in early 2008, writes of how government is 'a self-seeking flea on the backs of more productive people of this world'![5]

Neoliberals hold that states are always inferior to markets in 'guessing' what should be done. States are seen as inherently inefficient and easily corrupted by private interest groups. Markets are presumed to be 'natural' and move to equilibrium if unnatural forces or elements do not get in the way. Neoliberalism elevates market exchanges over and above other sets of connections between people. The 'market' is the source of value and virtue. Any deficiencies in markets are the result of their imperfections.

However, states are often important in eliminating 'unnatural' forces, destroying sets of rules, regulations and forms of life that slow down economic growth and constrain the private sector. Sometimes that destruction is exercised through violence and attacks upon democratic procedures, as with the first neoliberal experiment in Augusto Pinochet's Chile beginning in 1973. Thus on occasion the 'freedom of the market' is brought about through what its architect Milton Friedman terms 'shock treatment', the creation of an 'emergency' which enables the state to wipe the slate clean and impose sweeping free-market solutions.[6]

These occurred from 1973 onwards in Latin America, Reagan's USA, Thatcher's Britain, post-communist Russia and eastern Europe, 'communist' China, post-apartheid South Africa and much of the world. The state is central to what global analyst Naomi Klein terms 'disaster capitalism'. This includes the use of warfare to force through massive compulsory privatization in Iraq in the aftermath of the Allied invasion in 2003. Klein describes how the disaster of Hurricane Katrina in New Orleans in 2005 provided conditions for the large-scale privatization of the New Orleans school system.[7] Never let a good crisis go to waste is sometimes said to be a neoliberal mantra. This can be seen in the

2011 eurozone crisis where democratic governments have been forced to accept public-sector cuts and almost a coup by 'finance' to roll back the state and notions of the public interest.

Klein evocatively writes how 'only a great rupture – a flood, a war, a terrorist attack – can generate the kind of vast, clean canvases they crave. It is in these malleable moments ... that these artists of the real plunge in their hands and begin their work of remaking the world.'[8] 'Crises' provide a clean slate, a shock treatment, a 'creative destruction' enabling the work of remaking the world for fresh rounds of private-sector investment.

Economic geographer David Harvey summarizes how neoliberalism involves 'accumulation by dispossession'.[9] There are many examples. Peasants are thrown off their land, collective property rights are made private, indigenous rights are stolen and turned into private opportunities, rents are extracted from patents, general knowledge is turned into intellectual 'property', the state forces itself to sell off or outsource its collective activities, trade unions are undermined, and new less regulated instruments and flows redistribute income and rights towards finance and away from productive activities.

Since 1980 neoliberalism has thus become the dominant global discourse, albeit significantly contested. It is written about and acted upon within most corporations, many universities, most state bodies and especially international organizations such as the World Trade Organization, the World Bank and the International Monetary Fund. Harvey summarizes how neoliberalism was 'incorporated into the common-sense way many of us interpret, live in, and understand the world'.[10]

Such neoliberalism is significant for energy. Neoliberalism promotes the notion that only markets and the private sector should develop solutions to what economists term the external diseconomies of economic growth. Some neoliberals simply expect the market to generate solutions without needing extra measures or state encouragement of any sort. The recent growth in various generations of biofuels is the kind of market solution favoured by neoliberalism in response to the dramatically rising price of oil.

Neoliberalism also involves the light regulation of banks and financial institutions and the resulting trillion-dollar growth in financial securitization. There has been the undermining of the distinction between commercial and investment banking with the lowering of lending standards and the proliferation of innovative or risky business models. There was the 'macho' domination of financial services and a privileging of competitive individualism implemented through a bonus culture that rewarded indebtedness and dangerous risk taking. Hedge funds, which are private investment funds investing in a hedged portfolio to protect the fund's investors from market downturns, have mushroomed.

There has also been the extensive offshoring of earned revenues that ought to be taxed and used for providing collective services and benefits. Nicholas Shaxson describes the growth of tax havens or what he calls 'treasure islands'. These various islands and other centres of power involve jurisdictions facilitating tax avoidance (legal) and tax evasion (illegal). There are around seventy or so secrecy jurisdictions or 'treasure islands' making up this offshoring world. 'Offshore is how the world of power now works', says Shaxson.[11] These treasure islands include the City of London, Delaware, Switzerland, Jersey, Manhattan, the Cayman Islands, Monaco, Panama, Gabon, the Netherlands, Liechtenstein, Singapore, Hong Kong, Gibraltar and so on.

This offshore world reduces the capacity of states to tax revenues in locations where companies and individuals generate their income and wealth. More than half of world trade now passes through tax havens, including much oil revenue. Eighty-three out of the USA's top hundred companies have subsidiaries located in one or more tax havens. A quarter of all global wealth is held 'offshore'. This offshore money uses the same kinds of accounts, instruments and devices as deployed by corrupt, laundered, terrorist and criminal monies, which are easily able to evade weak regulation, often depending upon banks themselves for implementation.[12] Poachers make bad gamekeepers we might observe.

This offshoring within secrecy jurisdictions generated the enormous shadow banking system and the overwhelming imbalance between 'financialization' and the 'real economy', so much so that almost all of the world economy is now 'financialized'.[13] By September 2008 the global value of financial assets was $160 trillion, more than three times world GDP.[14] By April 2010, the average *daily* turnover in global foreign exchange markets exceeded $4 trillion. These huge flows of finance result in the 'dictatorship of financial markets'.[15] Such a dictatorship redistributes income and rights away from the 'real economy' and creates a significantly untaxed, ungovernable and out-of-control 'casino capitalism', much more like gambling than banking according to Roubini and Mehm.[16] Finance generates about 30 per cent of all operating profits in the USA, although it accounts for less than 10 per cent of value-added in the economy.[17]

In recent years finance has especially flowed not into manufacturing industry but into many kinds of property development, so generating various housing and real-estate 'bubbles'. In order for property to get built the private sector often cajoles national or regional states to create and pay for related infrastructure such as motorways, high-speed rail links and airports. Property development is undertaken by firms borrowing finance, with the properties built then being purchased by buyers who also borrow to make the purchase. Loans are made to property purchasers who would not otherwise be able to buy such properties. Thus there is the speculative funding of highly leveraged new developments leased or sold with escalating indebtedness. Property developments include here suburbs, apartments, second homes, hotels, leisure complexes, gated communities, sports stadiums, office blocks, universities, shopping centres and casinos. These are all built on the indebtedness of governments, developers and purchasers. And the greater the reliance on debt and leverage, the more fragile will be the macroeconomic system.[18]

Central in neoliberalism is this speculative intertwining of finance and property development. This involves new forms of 'finance', which is another way of referring to debt. The debts incurred are themselves turned into commodities or 'securitized'. The debts are parcelled up, sliced and diced, into financial packages that are sold on, with huge markets developing throughout the world for many of these 'products' which presuppose that property can only be worth more. This creates a financially complex 'house of cards' resting upon the 'bet' that property rises in value. This is the most recent version of what Nouriel Roubini and Stephen Mihm say is typical; that is, 'capitalism is not some self-regulating system … rather it is a system prone to "irrational exuberance" and unfounded pessimism. It is … extraordinarily unstable.'[19] There is 'systemic risk in banking ecosystems'.[20]

And capitalism is especially unstable because of the problem of debt, not something typically analysed by conventional economics, which is thus poor at anticipating this fundamental instability. During the 2000s an unsustainable 'bubble' of private, corporate and national indebtedness developed, initially within the USA. It was this bubble that then burst during 2007–08, bringing down householders, banks, financial institutions and property developers, first in the USA and then worldwide. This was the worst financial collapse since the Great Crash of 1929. How is this sorry story of chronic instability related to the supply and price of oil?

Sprawltown

From the 1980s onwards many new suburbs in the USA were built distant from city centres. They were not connected to their city centres by mass or public transit. Such *Sprawltowns* depended upon car travel and hence plentiful cheap oil to enable their newly arriving residents to commute to work and drive about for leisure and social life.[21] Only half of US suburbs have access to public transport and hence residents depend upon car travel and thus on the price of oil.[22]

Especially from 2005 onwards, much suburban housing was 'sold' to people with 'subprime' employment, credit and housing histories, involving new financial 'innovations'.[23] Although subprime housing is 'central' to the events that 'triggered' the crash of 2007–08, it has not been recognized how many subprime suburbs were driven to the brink by oil dependence *and* oil price spikes in the few years beforehand. Even Joseph Stiglitz's dissection of the American 'mortgage scam' does not fully grasp how energy resources could bite back and reverse what seemed at the time irreversible.[24] How did oil reverse what appeared inevitable, that property could only keep going up in value?

There had indeed been cheap oil for much of the period since the early 1980s. The US index of petrol prices was in money terms 134 in 1990 and more or less the same in 2000 (138).[25] The roaring 1990s, especially house price inflation, which ran two and a half times the increase in per capita income for Americans, was based upon a falling real price of petrol.[26] Such petrol prices remained more or less constant in money terms until 2003 (145).

Indebtedness in the USA in turn fuelled the huge growth in consumption as house prices rose. It became possible to cash in the 'rising values' of property, especially in 2002, 2003 and 2004. That money was used to fund further consumer purchases, especially of goods which were increasingly manufactured within China. This generated a vast US current account deficit.[27] Many Americans nevertheless believed that they really were richer as house prices rose and private debt skyrocketed. Also many people were drawn into purchasing housing through very low rates in the first few years of their mortgage, but where in later years much higher rates were charged ('variable rate mortgages').

Writing about these processes during 2006, Marxist historian Robert Brenner observed how financial speculation was generating a real-estate mania. The total apparent value of residential property in the major developed economies had risen by more than US$30 trillion between 2000 and 2005. This staggering increase was equivalent to 100 per cent of those countries' combined GDPs at the time.[28]

This was only possible through indebtedness built upon indebtedness, which was developing a 'vicious circle of vicious circles'. Such intersecting bubbles of asset price rises seem not to be understood by anyone; nor could they be 'governed'. Even George Soros, one of the financial 'masters of this universe', reports that no one understood this global system and its systemic risks that they themselves were creating![29]

Bubbles burst, and they burst most dramatically and painfully as they fill with more and more hot air. The bursting of this monetary bubble, first in the USA from 2005 onwards and then worldwide, had dramatic consequences for the real economy. This is where oil is central. Throughout the twentieth century soaring oil prices almost always helped to generate economic crises. All major economic crises bar one have had rising oil prices at their core. James Murray and former UK government chief scientist David King maintain that the crash of 2007–08 was not just a credit crunch but an 'oil-price crunch', as well as triggering the long recession that is still ongoing.[30] For societies that are so oil-dependent these increases were particularly significant.

In the middle years of the 2000s shortages of oil led to a rapid rise in petrol prices worldwide and especially in the USA. The USA imports two-thirds of its oil and possesses only a tiny 3 per cent of global oil reserves.[31] The USA is twice as dependent upon imported oil as it was in the early 1970s. Global oil prices rose dramatically. There was a fivefold increase in 'real' oil prices between 2002 and 2008.[32] Over a longer period the price of a barrel of oil increased fourteenfold between 1990 and 2007, partly because it proved impossible to raise the world output of oil beyond around 80–85 million barrels a day. As a result, Mazen Labban maintains, 'the oil crisis arrives as a financial crisis'.[33]

Moreover, hurricanes Katrina and Rita hit the Louisiana coastline during 2005. They helped to burst the oil bubble. These extreme weather events destroyed billions of dollars' worth of gas and oil infrastructures through their flooding of the Mississippi

Delta. Other refineries around the world were working to full capacity and were unable to raise production when these Mississippi refineries shut down. Rita led to the capsizing of a production platform. Such extreme weather events intersected with the crisis of oil supply. This illustrates Thomas Homer-Dixon's argument that 'societies face crisis when they're hit by multiple shocks simultaneously or they're affected by multiple stresses simultaneously.'[34]

These hurricanes were an extreme event that showed the vulnerability of the world's supplies of oil. Without sufficient capacity to replace the Gulf of Mexico supplies, the price of oil skyrocketed. There will be many future occasions when something similar occurs, when floods or hurricanes or blowouts or revolutions reduce supply, dramatically increase prices and devastate patterns of life, including those living in suburbs built upon 'easy oil' and the presumed rising price of property.[35]

These oil shortages were then reflected in the US petrol price dramatically spiking in the 2000s. It reached 302 in 2007 and a peak of 405 in July 2008. By February 2009 the petrol index was still higher at 186 than it had been in 2000.[36] But many living in these new American suburbs completely depended upon cheap petrol. Without it they could have no life. As petrol prices increased, so property owners were forced to reduce their expenditure on housing and other goods and services, including cars. James Hamilton argues that 'the oil price increase was one factor pushing home sales and house prices down' very rapidly.[37] In the heated atmosphere of the bubble, 'gas [i.e. petrol] price increases may have been the trigger that broke the expectations of continued growth.'[38] Suddenly it cost more to fill up an SUV's petrol tank than it cost to buy a week's groceries!

The American housing boom was thus brought to a shuddering halt through the escalating price of petrol in the middle years of the last decade. This increase tipped financially weak households over the brink. They could no longer afford the mortgage payments which they anyway could only just manage to pay given their subprime standing. Suddenly banks and mortgage companies found they had held large amounts of toxic debt; and astonishingly they had no idea how much and how many special packages of debt contained debt that was toxic. The financial models used by these masters of the universe both relied on data going back only a few years and presumed that property values would only go up.[39]

Millions of Americans suddenly could not pay their mortgages and defaulted. They received foreclosure notices and tens of billions in real-estate assets were written off as losses by banks. Suddenly housing prices were doing the unthinkable and falling. Ten thousand homeowners lost their home to foreclosures every day. Many suburbs collapsed with much property for sale, financial institutions around the world were left holding huge amounts of bad debt (albeit rated AAA by the major ratings agencies), some banks went to the wall or were 'nationalized', and there was a global recession on an unprecedented scale, which continued into 2012. There was a vicious circle. Foreclosures helped accelerate the fall of property values, generating further foreclosures. The losses they created brought the financial system to collapse in the fall of 2008. The steep recession that followed led to greater homeowner foreclosures, as homeowners who lost their jobs also often lost their homes.

There was a geographical distribution to these patterns. House price falls were most marked in suburbs rather than in metropolitan cores, and they were especially steep in those distant 'oil-dependent' suburbs. House prices fell most sharply in suburbs where there were no alternatives to the car and hence had the highest dependence upon the price *and* availability of petrol for almost all aspects of people's lives. Households were spending up to 30 per cent of their income on travel.

Because of these increases in the cost of petrol the value of housing in commuter belts dropped very steeply. Many such suburbs turned into 'ghostburbs', full of foreclosures, for-sale signs and empty houses. This meant that 'households are being made to rethink another cherished American institution – the white picket-fenced suburban dream home'.[40]

This reduced US consumer spending more generally, similar to what happened in 1990–91 during the first Gulf War. This reduction led to multiple defaults as banks realized that they held huge amounts of toxic debt. There was an escalating collapse of especially American investment banks and then of banks around the world which had 'invested' in American mortgages. This house of financial cards came tumbling down, beginning in these oil-dependent suburbs full of American households who had been sold 'subprime' mortgages through a vast 'scam' according to Nobel prizewinning economist Stiglitz.[41]

This collapse would have many consequences, including reductions in the distances Americans now drive. This was the first downward shift of US mileage for thirty years or so.[42] Such reductions were reflected in declining car sales, with at least 150,000 fewer people being employed in the US motor industry. Global oil production fell by 2 million barrels per day in 2009, or 2.6 per cent, the largest decline since 1982.[43] Chapter 11 especially examines whether this mileage slowdown marks the beginning of the end for 'oil addiction' as it collapsed first in these American 'subprime', oil-dependent suburbs.

Conclusion

In the final years of the last century, neoliberalism ratcheted up the global scale of travel within the global North. Oil was crucial in this. This travel of people and goods is essential to various social practices that depend upon and reinforce a high-carbon society. Much of this high-carbon production and consumption was based on indebtedness and on the greatly increasing significance of 'finance' within modern economies. Money was increasingly borrowed from the rest of the world, especially China, so as to fuel a carbon extravaganza for the global rich.

But this extravaganza came to a shuddering halt when oil prices increased in the early years of this century. Suburban houses could not be sold, especially where they were in far-flung oil-dependent locations. Financial products and institutions were found to be worthless. Easy money, easy credit and easy oil had gone together. And when oil prices hit the roof in these US suburbs, then easy money and credit came to an abrupt halt and the presumed upward shift in property prices was shown to be a false dream. The financial house of cards had been built upon cheap oil. When the oil got prohibitively expensive the house of cards collapsed to the ground. Timothy Mitchell observes how the 'shortage of oil from 2005 to 2008 ... caused a six-fold increase in its price. ... The surge in oil prices triggered the global financial crisis of 2008–9.'[44]

CHAPTER 2

THE CENTURY OF OIL

In this chapter I go back in time and elaborate how this world of oil, cars and suburbs came to be so important in the first place. How and why did this one energy resource make the twentieth century? Why was it that oil dependence arose in the early years of the last century with such profound consequences? How was oil crucial to the USA becoming the dominant economy, society and military power?

This is moreover not just a matter of 'technologies' but one involving changing relations between human beings and the natural world in which they live, work and socialize.

Humans and nature

This issue can be approached through Karl Marx's thinking on the relations between humans and nature. He argues that workers act upon nature and in so doing change that nature. But in changing nature they also change themselves. For him there is a socio-natural *metabolism* which is central to historical processes of change and development.[1] Humans are part of the natural world but in working on nature they also transform themselves and that world. In these metabolic relations, new socio-natural forms are produced. I noted in the Introduction the concept of the anthropocene, which involves a transformed relationship between humans and nature developing in the West from the eighteenth century onwards.

So while nature has appeared increasingly separate from society, especially during the growth of industrialization in the nineteenth century, there is a metabolic relationship between the two. Especially significant are new kinds of circulation, of people, objects and energy and sets of resources. Marx thought that the circulation of commodities through new coal-powered transport and communications represented a huge upward shift in capitalist industrialization. Production involved the speeding up of the conditions of exchange through the mechanized movements of goods and people. This was especially important as objects were produced in one or more places (the new factories) but then consumed in other places often far away. Coal and iron ore became utterly central resources.

Marx was living and writing in the years around the middle of the nineteenth century (1818–1883). At this time there was increasing 'mastery' of the physical world brought about by new systems of coal power and movement. Unlike water and wind power, coal was a concentrated and mobile source of energy.[2] At the same time, according to Marx, new uses of nature led to capitalism's increasing 'rift' with nature, not only robbing workers but also robbing the soil. Marx writes how capitalist production undermines the original sources of all wealth: 'the soil and the worker'.[3]

What was especially significant here was the *cluster* of new systems that were mostly initiated in Britain within a short two to three year period around 1840. Such new systems are best described as 'socio-technical'. Such systems should be analysed as the combination of technologies with social ideas and ways of organizing. Systems are both technical and social. The term 'system' does not refer just to the technical as such.

Around 1840 these new socio-technical systems included the first railway system (and the first national railway timetable, Bradshaw's), the first national post system (based on rail), the first commercial electrical telegram, the first scheduled ocean steamship service (Cunard), photography (Daguerre, Fox Talbot) and its later use within guide books and advertising, the first inclusive or 'package' tour (organized by Thomas Cook), the early department stores, and the first system for circulating water separately from sewage. Thomas Cook declared: 'To remain stationary in these times of change, when all the world is on the move, would be a crime. Hurrah for the Trip – the cheap, cheap Trip.'[14]

New 'resources' became significant. Humans developed novel ways of using the 'natural' world. Although we often think of resources as natural, they are also in part social. Especially significant in the modern world are those resources which make movement possible. A new human 'mastery' of nature was achieved through novel systems of movement over, under and across nature, especially powered by steam engines. These first systems used the resources of coal and iron ore, which led to the manufacture of new mobile machines.

These in turn transformed human beings, who were often now 'on the move', and people's lives were increasingly intertwined with 'mobile machines'. Later on, Virginia Woolf, after buying her new car in 1927, described this intertwining: 'Yes, the motor car is turning out to be the joy of our lives, an additional life, free and mobile and airy. ... Soon we shall look back at our pre-motor days as we do now at our days in the caves.'[5] Lives and machines were now intertwined.

The origins of oil civilization

This book is mainly about the new 'resource' of oil and how it made possible such new intertwinings of lives and machines (as expressed by Virginia Woolf). We have seen how oil was not seen as a major resource in 'nature' until the twentieth century. The earliest extraction of oil occurred in Russia, beginning in what is now Azerbaijan in 1848, where there were two pipelines. By 1884 nearly two hundred small refineries operated in Baku. In 1878 the first oil tanker was launched on the Caspian Sea. The first ever oil refineries were built in Poland between 1854 and 1856. These were all on a small scale as demand for oil products was limited, with it being used in asphalt, machine oil, lubrication and lamps. By 1900 Russia produced half of the world's oil and dominated international markets. But this was soon to change.

The first US oil well was established in 1859, in Titusville, Pennsylvania (the same year that Marx published the first volume of *Capital*). As noted, oil was mainly thought of as a lighting fuel. It was seen as similar to whale oil. But the overfishing of whales led to rising prices. Research was undertaken to see whether the new oily substance coming out of the ground might be used for lamps. Refining the oil from the first oil well produced kerosene used for domestic lighting. From 1859 onwards, there were increasing discoveries of oil, although what we call diesel and petrol were seen for decades as relatively useless by-products of this oil.

In 1901 a new oil well commenced extraction in Spindletop.[6] It involved an astonishing gush of oil – it was the first 'gusher' and produced one-fifth of US oil. It established the era of cheap plentiful oil, with hundreds of oil wells soon located in the same area of Texas. During the first quarter of the twentieth century the USA overtook Russia as the world's largest oil producer, and the rest we might say is history. Oil civilization was established and formed the modern mobile American way of life. The histories of oil and the USA were fatefully intertwined from 1901 onwards.[7]

In that story a central role was played by John D. Rockefeller and his Standard Oil Company, formed in 1870. Rockefeller pursued ruthless policies, especially fixing prices and undercutting competitors. In 1911 the Sherman Antitrust Act was used to force through the forcible break-up of Standard Oil into various smaller companies, including the household names of Exxon, Chevron, Texaco and Conoco.

A new metabolic relationship between humans and nature was thus established in the couple of decades after 1900. This involved novel kinds of movement involving machines more powerful than anything seen before, except for railway engines. Especially significant were horseless carriages.[8] New innovative automobile designs were developed, especially in France and Germany, and they used various types of power – steam, gas, electricity and the potentially dangerous petroleum-based internal combustion engine.

How did the petroleum-based internal combustion engine become the engine of choice? The answer lies in part in public races held for these emerging 'speed machines'. Developers in Europe demonstrated that the internal combustion engine car driven by petrol was more reliable since these vehicles finished such races. In the USA there were also high-publicity races, the first being the Chicago Times-Herald race in 1895. Only two cars crossed the finishing line, both powered by petrol (the battery-driven car could not cope with the snowy conditions!).

By 1904–05 US car production began to overtake that in Europe, reaching 44,000 vehicles a year by 1907.[9] Cheap American oil was improving the viability of petrol-driven horseless carriages. Proponents of internal combustion engines indeed claimed that 'their dirty, noisy, smoky machines were simply the latest obnoxious manifestation of progress … modern machines … were progressively more intrusive, noisome, filthy, and fouling'.[10] Modernity, as with the railroad and now the car, should thus be noisy.

The early 1900s, then, saw a shift in horseless carriage production from Europe to the USA. The petrol system was established and 'locked' in, with the first Model T Ford appearing as early as 1908, more or less simultaneous with the Futurist thinker Filippo Marinetti's proclamation of the new 'beauty of speed'. US car registrations in the first decade jumped dramatically. The development of petrol-fuelled internal combustion engines is a story of how the USA came to exert industrial dominance over Europe and the world during the early years of the twentieth century through locking-in petrol-based vehicles.

However, the most impressive horseless carriage during this period was actually battery-powered. In 1899 a new land-speed record was set on the outskirts of Paris by a bullet-shaped electric roadster called *La Jamais Contente*. This was the first car to break the mile-per-minute record, reaching an astonishing 65.8 mph. Even by 1900, 28 per cent of the cars produced in the USA were battery-driven, including many manufactured in Henry Ford's factories.[11]

However, as the USA became the world's leading oil producer in the first half of the twentieth century, petrol was consolidated as the fuel for the powering of cars and diesel for the fuelling of trucks. Cars were increasingly manufactured under Fordist conditions of production. The Great War of 1914–18 sounded the death knell of battery-driven vehicles, which could not be recharged on the battlefield. The internal combustion engine was crucial to mechanizing warfare, where speed, durability and power upon the battlefield were essential.

US vehicle production, derived from various relatively small causes, involved petrol/diesel engine domination developing over the last century. This laid down a path-dependent pattern. The history of change in major technologies shows that it is not the best system that wins out but often the one that gets there first (such as the QWERTY layout of the typewriter keyboard rather than one in alphabetical order). Many writers argue that it was cheap American oil that ensured that battery-driven cars did not dominate in the early years of the twentieth century, even though experts considered them technologically superior to the internal combustion engine. The demise of battery-driven cars in this period was significant for the twentieth century. By 1930 three-quarters of the world's cars and 90 per cent of the world's oil were produced in the USA.

By then the oil industry had consolidated into the Seven Sisters, five American companies along with Royal Dutch Shell and British Petroleum. This group of companies conspired to fix prices and supplies from different regions through the Achnacarry Agreement of 1928. This agreement, contrary to US legislation at the time, was the 'greatest cartel the world has ever known'. It was only exposed much later in 1952.[12]

It is also interesting to note how during the Second World War some American oil companies (Exxon, Texaco) continued selling oil to Germany and its allies. Journalist Andy Stern describes the 'cosy relationship between Big Oil and Hitler's Germany'. In the end though the defeat of the Axis powers stemmed from their lack of easy oil and the failure to convert coal to oil on any significant scale, although huge resources were put into this research project.[13]

The Fordist production and consumption system was thus established in the earlier years of the last century.[14] The economic gains accrued from the assembly line meant mass production, with low prices and little choice. And this helped to develop an automobile consumer class in a marketplace previously reserved for mostly young wealthy men using their cars as 'speed machines'. Now the automobile became a commodity for the middle classes and especially for many families living in new American suburbs. These new consumer cars were driven by their owners and not by professional drivers as was more common in Europe. And, having begun in the USA, this pattern then spread back to Western Europe and then on to the rest of the world.

In the early years of the last century cheap oil also transformed shipping. There was a significant switch of shipping from coal to diesel-based engines. The coal-based *Titanic* on its tragic maiden voyage in 1912 needed 150 stokers to move vast amounts of low-density coal into the ship's engines. But the new steamships powered by higher density oil-fired turbines required much less manual labour and fuel. Winston Churchill replaced slow coal-fired ships of the British Navy with oil-powered ships before and during the First World War. There were huge savings in labour and fuel costs and also of time.

By the second half of the twentieth century almost all ships were oil-powered. Also much of the world's oil is transported in vast tankers, especially moving from the Middle East to North America and Europe but increasingly also to Japan and China. Transporting oil regularly and reliably across oceans, with huge oil tankers passing through some very narrow and potentially dangerous straits, is now central to the supply of energy in the contemporary global economy and society.[15]

Oil also powered aircraft, following the Wright brothers' first airflight at Kill Devil Hills, North Carolina, in 1903.[16] This aircraft was powered by a four-cylinder petrol-based engine. According to Le Corbusier aircraft were the greatest sign of progress seen during the twentieth century, although at first the airfields did not reflect this modernity.[17] Flying machines also transformed warfare as the new realm of airpower developed, including the innovation of aircraft able to bomb from the air. The first international scheduled passenger services took place in 1919 from Hounslow in west London, close to where Heathrow Airport is located.

But there was nothing inevitable about the development of passenger air travel. As late as 1918 the *Manchester Guardian* stated that aviation was a 'passing fad that would never catch on'. Crucial to developing extensive air travel was a new kind of modern discourse. This discourse, with many key texts and iconic images, has been described as 'airmindedness'.[18] Such a notion shows that there is nothing 'natural' about new kinds of mobility. They almost always involve enthusiasts, interests, media, technologies, advertisements and corporations promoting the new mobility and making it seem natural to take, as in this case, flights up in the sky.

The most significant technological transformation was the development of jet engines after the Second World War. These enabled planes to fly with less vibration, at higher altitudes, at faster speeds and for much longer distances. In 1952 the first commercial jet flights were initiated using kerosene, the oil originally refined for lighting. Over the past fifty years air travel has shown the highest growth rates of any mode of transport.[19] In some societies air has become the major basis not only for international travel and global lines of flight, but also for domestic travel. For example, it is calculated that at any time there are around 300,000 people in the air above the USA. There is a moving ultra-high carbon city in the sky.[20]

The use of oil for transportation energy (rather than for lighting) was thus central to the twentieth century. The increasingly mobile twentieth century depended upon cheap and plentiful 'mobile' oil. Modern life involves the regular and predictable long-distance movement of people (commuters, holidaymakers, families and friendship groups) and objects (including water and food). In the early years of the last century coal and steam came to be replaced by oil and diesel. Cars, trucks, ships and aircraft all became oil-based.

This oil dependence especially moved upwards through new forms of warfare in the First World War. Lord Curzon, the British foreign secretary, stated that the allies 'floated to victory on a wave of oil'.[21] The mobility, density and flexibilities of oil made it the most valuable of energies in the deadly, moving and dangerous theatres of war. It is interesting to reflect how modern warfare might have been so different and possibly less deadly if oil had never seeped out of the ground in Azerbaijan and Pennsylvania in the later years of the nineteenth century!

There was a further major shift towards oil during the inter-war period in the USA. A cluster of powerful high carbon systems came to be unleashed. Four clustered systems had major consequences for the contours of the last century.[22] First, systems of electric power generation and national electricity grids meant that most homes were lit, heated and populated with electricity-based consumer goods and that Fordist factories were powered up. Such power generation involved a mix of coal, oil and gas. Increases in the generation and consumption of energy led to the USA being the most high-powered society in history with staggering increases in energy compared with previous epochs. The average US household of 1970 commanded more energy than a small town had used during the eighteenth century. The use of electrical energy in the USA increased eightyfold between 1912 and 1970.[23]

Second, the car system spread. Cars made of steel and powered by petrol are the exemplary manufactured objects produced by leading business sectors and iconic firms within twentieth-century capitalism (Mercedes, BMW, Jaguar, Rolls-Royce, Toyota, Peugeot–Citroen, Ford, General Motors, Volkswagen). They are the major item of consumption after housing and until recently more popular with each new generation of young adults. Cars provide status to their owners through speed, security, safety, sexual success, career achievement, freedom, family and mas-culinity. Various 'automotive emotions' are built into owning and possessing a car.[24] This developed into a dominant culture generating new notions of an *Autopia*. Cars are literary and visual icons much explored through film and artistic images.[25]

Cars also provide a sanctuary, a zone of protection between oneself and that dangerous world of other cars, and between places of departure and arrival. The driver is car-cooned in an iron cage away from many risks, strapped into a comfortable if constraining armchair and surrounded by micro-electronic informational sources, controls and sources of pleasure. Eyes have to be constantly on the lookout for danger, hands and feet are ready for the next manoeuvre, the body is gripped into a fixed position, lights and noises may indicate that the car driver needs to make instantaneous adjustments, and so on. The other traffic constrains how each car is to be driven, its speed, its direction, its lane discipline and so on. The car-coon can of course turn into a death trap at moments of crash and major accidents.[26]

Third, suburbs are built distant from places of work and city centres. They are increasingly commuted to by car. Global architect Richard Rogers writes: 'it is the car which has played the critical role in undermining the cohesive social structure of the city ... they have eroded the quality of public spaces and have encouraged suburban sprawl ... the car has made viable the whole concept of dividing everyday activities into compartments, segregating offices, shops and homes.'[27] Suburban houses are filled with household goods including radio, television and many kitchen goods. These goods are powered by electricity and produced in new Fordist-type factories.

Fourth, many specialized leisure sites, supermarkets, fast-food outlets, national parks, sports stadiums, theme parks develop. American society, with its suburbs, urban strips and mobile motel culture, is founded on car-based living. At first these were modest

commercial strips containing supermarkets, other shops and fast
food (the first McDonalds was established in 1952). Most neces-
sitated travel from home and neighbourhood, especially by car.
But the scale and distances began to grow in the post-war period
with mega-malls, distant national parks, huge sports stadiums,
casinos and destination theme parks all developing. Increasingly,
as in the case of the pleasure capital of Las Vegas, these are visited
by air. Such places of leisure and pleasure involve the long-distance
movement of many objects and foodstuffs on trucks, ships and
aircraft.

Thus there are four systems: electricity, individual motor
vehicles, suburbs and places of leisure. They involve production, movement and consumption; and each provides important
preconditions for the others. They form a cluster, and typically
it is clusters of innovation that are significant in periods of major
technological and social change.

These systems developed on a mass scale within the USA
before and after the Second World War. The American Century
involved developing the preconditions for these systems. They
resulted in the USA becoming 'the world's largest consumer
of energy'.[28] Cultural historian David Nye summarizes these
interlocking systems as being a 'high-energy regime [which]
touched every aspect of daily life. It promised a future of miracle
fabrics, inexpensive food, larger suburban houses, faster travel,
cheaper fuels, climate control, and limitless growth'.[29] It also led
to American economic, cultural and military power.

The 'American Century' was not possible without oil.[30] The
USA provides large subsidies to oil companies, with major tax
breaks at almost every stage of oil exploration and extraction.
Capital expenses, including the costs of oilfield leases and drilling

FIGURE 2.1   Sources of global carbon emissions, 1800–2010
(billion tonnes carbon/year)[31]

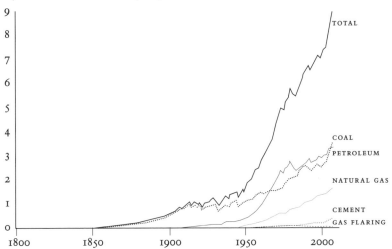

equipment, are taxed at 9 per cent, much lower than the taxes placed on almost all other industries. Later chapters explore the power of carbon capital, which has been central to stabilizing oil within the American way of life and politics.

There was thus an upward shift in the metabolic relations between humans and nature, especially as paler versions of this cluster spread over the twentieth century to western Europe and then to much of the world. Such systems moved across the world through American firms, the US military, and many American cultural practices that represented these energy-hungry products as the latest fashion. Through these systems, as well as military power and many international advisers and organizations such as the IMF and the World Bank, 'the USA shapes the world'.[32]

These systems thus came to construct the high carbon legacy of the twentieth century. This pattern lies behind and explains

Figure 2.1, which shows the growth in carbon emissions over the past two centuries and the relative contributions of coal, oil and gas. This figure demonstrates that although certain trends were in hand by 1950, the rate of increase since then of carbon emissions has been on a vast and seemingly inexorable scale.

It would be impossible for the rest of the world to share this American Dream. Even the relatively prosperous EU consumes energy and resources at half the American rate. American production and consumption got there first and generates CO_2 on a much greater scale than comparable societies.

Although this mobile American twentieth century created a model of unlimited growth available to all, that promise turned out to be a chimera. The Dream is brought about by finite amounts of fossil fuels and especially oil. And oil is not just a means of movement but central to almost all industries and agriculture. David Strahan notes some of the products made from oil: anti-freeze, asphalt, baths, bedding, cameras, carpets, catheters, CDs/DVDs, computers, detergents, fertilizers, fleeces, food colouring, footballs, furniture, golf balls, hoses, nappies, oxygen tents, packaging, paints, pesticides, pipes, plastic bags, plastic cups, plastic bottles, raincoats, seals, shower curtains, surfboards, sweaters, telephones, tights, trainers, televisions, tyres, wellingtons, window frames and X-rays.[33]

Oil is also central to the so-called Green Revolution in world agriculture developing from the 1960s. This turned agriculture into an 'industry' with, in the USA, four hundred gallons of oil used each year to feed each American.[34] There was something like a fiftyfold increase in energy flow into agriculture, with in some cases large increases in output, as people came to 'eat fossil fuels'. Such fuels are used for fertilizers, operating farm machinery, transporting inputs and outputs, irrigating land, feedstuffs, crop drying and pesticides. However, this carbon-based revolution has not solved the world's food supply but has increased unequal access. There are now a billion or so starving people, another billion are obese, there is land and water degradation on a vast scale, crops are increasingly lost to pests despite a huge rise in pesticides, and there are astronomic increases in food miles.[35]

From around 1970 the expropriation of oil went into overdrive. An exceptional new burst of carbon-based developments occurred, in production, consumption, property development and speculation. The USA began importing oil on a major scale as the influence of the Seven Sisters 'Western' oil companies began to decline, from being responsible for 60 per cent of global oil production in 1960 to less than 15 per cent by 2005.

Instead the OPEC countries and state companies became central to global oil production.[36] OPEC had been established in 1960, formed of twelve countries and their national oil companies. Significant price increases orchestrated by OPEC occurred in the early 1970s (after the Yom Kippur War), 1979 and 1991 (the first Gulf War). By 2005 the four largest national oil companies – Saudi Aramco, National Iranian Oil Company, Iraq National Oil Company and Kuwait Petroleum Company – accounted for one-half of the world's official oil reserves. Saudi Aramco is the world's largest oil-producing company. Currently the largest 'Western' company is Exxon, which is globally only twelfth in the world, with about 1 per cent of the world's oil reserves.[37]

With US oil production peaking in 1970 the country's foreign policy became increasingly preoccupied with gaining access to non-US sources of oil (and gas), including especially those produced by these and other national oil companies. The USA became entwined with Middle Eastern oil interests, with major political and military consequences. US foreign policy has been organized around dealing with the aftermath of the peaking of oil discovery during the 1960s. The twentieth-century oiling of American society, and indeed of all other societies, is under a huge challenge, with, according to Michael Ruppert's movie and book, a strong possibility of its collapse.[38]

Conclusion

I have shown how oil is a magical substance resulting from dead matter laid down over hundreds of millions of years – dead matter that has been so crucial to twentieth-century life! Indeed during the last century in the rich north of the world, oil almost on its own is able to move, make and feed the population, and it does so with increasing levels of productivity. Oil is treated as almost costless because for much of the last century it had been 'ready to burn'. Oil is still cheaper than purchasing the same quantity of bottled water. It is said to be the cheapest liquid in the world.[39] It has been underpriced by many times compared with its 'real' productivity.

In the last century oil was dead matter with no one able to represent it and speak up for its especially long-term interests. Dead matter had no voice in what sociologist of science Bruno Latour calls the 'parliament of things'.[40] No one spoke for the rights and responsibilities of oil, so it got exploited as though it was just laid out waiting to be expropriated for the modern world as fast and as furiously as possible. How to ensure that oil should have a 'voice' is a question encountered at various points below.

CHAPTER 3

CONSUMING MILES

Consuming from afar

This chapter examines how the use of oil grew rapidly in the final quarter of the last century, at the same time as the supply of easy oil began to decline and was increasingly produced by forces less and less 'Western'. Oil use became ratcheted up in the final quarter of the last century. There had been initiatives in the early 1970s to wean the planet off oil but these were reversed as neoliberal carbon excess dominated from the late 1970s onwards.

The use of oil grew greatly, following the 1960s' discovery of various super-giant oil (and gas) fields. Oil was increasingly used to fuel high-carbon living across North America and western Europe despite some modest economies in the use of that oil through greater fuel efficiency. Any efficiency gains from improved efficiency were lost, though, through a 'rebound' (or Jevons) effect which led to greater overall use of oil as its cost declined. This is a major problem and means that fuel efficiency often does not result in actual reductions in overall fossil fuel use.[1]

Moreover, the oil-based economy and culture spread to much of the rest of the world, including the former Soviet Union. The countries of the USSR had experienced low levels of consumer choice and 'consumerism' until the implosion of the Soviet Union in 1991. Extensive increases in the oil-based movements of people and objects occurred around the world. Also oil-based consuming lives grew greatly within China.

Crucial here is a widespread 'consumerism'. What becomes central to people is not only what happens in the worlds of work, neighbourhood or education. Rather, the forming of social identities through purchasing, using and displaying an increasingly wide range of consumer goods and consumer services becomes of major significance. Many goods and services relate to new 'needs' and are stimulated through media images, worldwide advertising and global brands.

While various writers connect oil with consumerism, they do so in a rather general way. This chapter tries to detail these links and especially to demonstrate the upward shift in the connections between consumerism and oil dependence within the recent neoliberal period. Overall almost all aspects of contemporary consumption entail the extensive long-distance travel of objects and of people. Consuming very many miles is central to contemporary consumerism.

First, there are 'food miles'. There has been a striking de-seasonization of foodstuffs, at least in parts of the world where more or less any item is 'ready to hand'. A Swedish study found that the food miles involved in a typical breakfast (apple, bread, butter, cheese, coffee, cream, orange juice, sugar) are equal to the circumference of the earth.[2] There has also been, as noted, a spectacular increase in energy deployed in agricultural production following the so-called Green Revolution (which was not 'green' at all).[3]

Second, there are 'container miles'. Over the past forty years there have been large increases in the miles travelled by goods and components, mainly on huge container ships (carrying up to 15,000 containers). These boxes, which are easy to load on and off ships, trains and trucks, have almost eliminated the cost of transporting many goods, redrawn the world's economic geography and ensured that most objects are available anywhere to those who can afford them.[4] Almost all goods in the world are shipped in this intermodal system of containerization, including objects and people smuggled across borders.

Third, there are 'friendship and family miles'. These are the many miles that have to be travelled by car, rail and air around key events in order to sustain friendships, romances and family relations. These relations are often managed over substantial distances and stem from people migrating to or being educated within, or having holidays in, countries often distant from the neighbourhoods where they are brought up.[5]

Finally, there are 'colleague miles'. Many workplaces and professions have been restructured. Miles are built into how people live 'mobile lives' spread out around the world, involving extensive communications and travel in order that people do their work, and maintain and extend their professional standing.[6] Such colleague miles are plentiful within the worlds of business, professions, academia, government, NGOs, trade unions, and even climate-change policymaking.[7]

Steffan Mau observes how these 'miles' involve many 'life-worlds beyond the nation-state'.[8] Such lifeworlds include asylum and refugee seeking; business and professional lives; the discovery or 'overseas experience' of students, au pairs and other young people; medical treatment in spas, hospitals, dentists, opticians and so on; military power, of armies, tanks, helicopters, aircraft, rockets, spyplanes and satellites; post-employment transnational retirement lifestyles; 'trailing travel' of children, partners, other relatives and domestic servants; migration and travel across the key nodes of diasporas; service work around the world and especially within global cities; tourist visiting of places and events; and the keeping up with friends and relatives through intermittent travel and communications.

Adrian Favell in *Eurostars and Eurocities* describes the nature of these mileages across contemporary Europe. He shows the importance of a 'denationalized freedom', how many people 'can now build lives – careers, networks, relationships, families – beyond the nation-state containers that once defined personal identity'.[9] And in these decisions 'romance and relationships', as well as careers, are central to moving and staying. These decisions are significant for people being able to 'spiral up' across Europe.

Such 'lifeworlds' involve much national and international travel and hence presuppose oil. Without oil or some substitute none of these lifeworlds beyond neighbourhood and national territories would have become so significant. In order to illustrate the scale and impact of oil-based consumerism, I turn to one of the most extraordinary places in the neoliberal world order. Dubai demonstrates how various mileages increasingly intersect within some spectacular manufactured environments.

Dubai

This is the story of what had been up to around 1960 one of the poorest places on earth. Dubai was a series of small mud villages located by the sea and sitting on the edge of a vast inhospitable desert. Dubai only became independent in 1971 as part of the United Arab Emirates but has since grown to become the world's largest building site in the 2000s and the eighth most visited city in the world. It is a major hub, 'where global flows of capital, people, culture, and information land and intersect'.[10] The exceptional story of the rise of this City of Gold located in the most desolate corner of a desolate land illustrates many of the extraordinary interconnections of oil and consumption.

Pumping oil in this British protectorate commenced in 1966 during the peak of global oil discovery. But unlike much of the surrounding area the oil did not last for long. It peaked in 1991 and Dubai is now a small oil producer. But Dubai nevertheless took advantage of all the oil being found elsewhere in that period and constructed a vast visitor, real estate, transport and consumption-based oil-dependent economy.

Rather than producing oil, Dubai consumes oil.[11] This oil is used to build islands, hotels and exceptional attractions; to transport in and out, especially via its modern airport (the eighth largest in the world) and leading airline (Emirates), very large numbers of visitors, conference delegates, construction workers and sex workers; to import, especially via the world's largest man-made harbour, vast quantities of food and goods sold in the shopping malls; to become a centre for transportation, with one of the ten largest container ports; to generate the highest water consumption rate in the world through many carbon-based desalination plants; and to use much energy to provide thermal monotony in pretty well all built environments through climate control operating in the desert where average temperatures are 40°C.

Dubai rapidly became a key global site for holidays and leisure, meetings and conferences held in excessive contemporary hotels, shopping complexes and visitor attractions. Dubai is a place of and for consuming to excess with limited constraints. And this is principally male consumption – women only make up a quarter of the Dubai population. During the 2000s it was perhaps the number one site for ostentatious consuming, shopping, eating, drinking, gambling and prostitution (with thousands of victims of human trafficking). Guilt is not to consume beyond the limit in what is strangely an Islamic country. There are over seventy shopping malls, although the population is only around 2 million. As befits this paradise of consumption, Dubai's official national holiday is the celebrated Shopping Festival, a month-long extravaganza.

Developments in Dubai include two palm islands extending the coastline by 120 kilometres; a string of new islands shaped like the countries of the world; a domed ski resort and many major sports venues; the world's tallest building, the Burj Khalifa at 818 metres; the world's largest hotel, the Asia-Asia with 6,500 rooms; the world's first 7 star hotel, the Burj Al Arab with 100 mile views, and the world's biggest party at the opening of the Atlantis hotel complex.[12] Dubai's annual rate of growth was 18 per cent in the early 2000s.

Dubai strives for visual and environmental excess, to create countless enticing 'playscapes'.[13] There are many places for play: the Hanging Gardens of Babylon, the Taj Mahal, the Pyramids and a snow mountain. These copies of the 'real' are in a way more perfect than the original. They are what the Italian cultural critic Umberto Eco once termed the 'hyper-real'.[14]

Locals boast that Dubai is a place for 'supreme lifestyles', or what we might call 'supreme mileage'. This iconic place of excess became the exemplary site for the consumption of objects and services, but also from 2002 for real estate even if one was not 'local'. This generated a gold rush as Dubai became the fastest growing city in the world, with vast speculative building of houses and apartments.[15] For example, the Jumeirah Beach Residence is the largest single-phase residential development anywhere in the world, containing forty towers and accommodating about 15,000 people.

Dubai's development has only been possible because migrant contract labourers travel from Pakistan and India. They are typically bound to a single employer. Up to 90 per cent of labourers working in Dubai are imported, with their passports removed upon entry and forced to live in distant labour camps.[16] The best known of these is Sonapur, lying in a far corner of Dubai next to the refuse area and very overcrowded with major sewerage problems. There are also many industrial accidents on Dubai's building sites, with, it seems, hundreds of workers dying each year, as well as very high death rates on Dubai's roads.

Dubai shows 'accumulation through dispossession', as neo-liberalism was described in the previous chapter. Overall Dubai has been characterized as an oasis of free enterprise without income taxes, trade unions, corporation taxes, planning laws, opposition parties or elections. Many of the major companies that have made Dubai are in fact state-owned, the state and private sector being virtually indistinguishable.

Consuming cheap oil is absolutely essential to the Dubai miracle. Cheap oil enables people to get to Dubai, to power the sites of consumption excess, to ship and fly in the objects for the shopping malls, to theme and then re-theme such environments, and to move people around in order to do sufficient consuming.

The per capital energy consumption in Dubai is the second highest in the world (Qatar is number one).

Jim Krane summarized the overall paradox of Dubai: 'It's the earth's most barren landscape, a land with nothing in the way of historic sights, and big spending visitors fly half way around the world to see it.'[17] How did Dubai and other oil-dependent consumption centres develop and be so 'successful', at least up to 2008?

From neighbourhood lives

Central to contemporary consumption is a general shift from 'neighbourhood lives' to lives that are 'lived beyond the neighbourhood'. Once lives are lived beyond the neighbourhood then this presupposes much movement, of objects and of people. And once there is such movement then there is a huge need for oil.

In the former pattern the scale of most work and leisure practices is a few miles. Most consumption, family and friendship patterns are 'localized' within neighbourhoods. There is a dominance of slow modes of mobility, especially walking and cycling. These are what cultural analyst Richard Hoggart in his classic study of neighbourhood lives *The Uses of Literacy* terms literal 'small worlds'. He describes how life centred on groups of known streets, on their complex and active group life.[18] The disciplining of young people (particularly men) took place within these neighbourhoods. Consumption involved conforming to the norms present and reinforced within each such neighbourhood. There was little separation of production and consumption.[19]

Many agricultural communities and industrial-urban communities are organized through such strong neighbourhood lives, with slow modes of travel, relatively limited consumption of goods made elsewhere, and an overall low carbon consumption pattern. Even when working-class holidays developed in Europe at the end of the nineteenth century these were often neighbourhood-based, involving groups of employees or neighbours journeying away together with much mutual regulation and use of collective forms of travel.[20] Excess was regulated through the presence of family and one's neighbourhood. These were low-carbon holidays and generally low-carbon forms of small-scale life.

Twentieth-century consumerism in the rich north increasingly involves patterns of life moving 'beyond the neighbourhood'. The systems that link production and consumption became more extended in time and space, especially because of the way 'electricity and the automobile transformed society'.[21] Consuming goods and services took place over much greater distances.[22] Goods were produced by others at a distance within large energy-intensive factories and offices. And large shops and places of leisure developed, which then need to be travelled to and stocked with items purchased from around the world. During the last century, global economic output grew eighteenfold while global population merely trebled.[23]

Modern lives involve much movement beyond the neighbourhood. As Amory Lovins and colleagues point out, almost all jobs in the USA ultimately depend upon mobility.[24] Caren Kaplan's account of her early life in post-war America captures this. Because her family was scattered across the USA and various other continents, travel was 'unavoidable, indisputable, and always necessary for family, love and friendship as well as work'.[25] Indeed she was 'born into a *culture* that took the national benefits of travel for granted' as well as presuming that 'US citizens [could] travel anywhere they pleased'.[26] Implicit here is the idea that people are entitled to travel and indeed should travel; that it is an essential part of life and a fundamental human right. Travel for North Americans is a primary activity of existence and not a sign of distinct progress.

People thus shift from neighbourhood-based lives to more varied forms of social practice, often distant from their neighbourhood and involving multiple movement to keep up with the lives of others. So everyone demands a more expensive bundle of goods and services so as to participate as full members of a society that is increasingly on the move. This locks most people into such a society, with purchasing, using and displaying goods that have extensively travelled, and consuming services often from beyond one's neighbourhood.

The spreading of consumer goods and services from outside one's neighbourhood is thus ratcheted up. Most people's social practices come to be organized in this fashion. It is increasingly necessary to move about and to acquire consumer goods and services produced 'elsewhere'. This is partly because many of one's workmates, friends and family also live 'beyond the neighbourhood'. They all depend upon buildings, heating, lighting and objects that come from distant places. This involves much energy to move people and objects about on this increasingly vast scale.

However, these lived experiences may turn out not to be 'better' or 'happier' lives. This contradiction of contemporary capitalism is shown in economist Fred Hirsch's classic analysis of the self-defeating nature of leapfrogging in positional competition between consumers. Such leapfrogging, as for example in trying to get a nice suburban house with a rural view, can leave everyone no better off and total energy use much higher as a result of what is self-defeating competition.[27]

Moreover, when people mainly experienced neighbourhood lives, they tended to compare themselves with other people who were also living locally within the same neighbourhood. Sociologist Barry Schwartz points out the contrast between neighbourhood lives and those beyond the neighbourhood where comparison and dissatisfaction appear to be more extensive. With neighbourhood lives,

> We looked around at our neighbours and family members.
> We did not have access to information about people outside
> our immediate social circle. But with the explosion of
> telecommunications [and long-distance travel – JU] … almost
> everyone has access to information about almost everyone else
> … This essentially universal and unrealistically high standard
> of comparison decreases the satisfaction of those who are in the
> middle or below.[28]

These comparisons produced through advertisements and media representations of the lives of others beyond the neighbourhood engender further frustration and dissatisfaction. There is less sense of place and much more sense of the lives and experiences of others, especially as represented through television and other media.[29] Schwartz says that people experience regret about the consumer choices they made as well as disappointment with what they did not consume.

Moreover, what is crucial is that such disappointment generates further consumption as more movement, adverts and media images impress in upon the self and generate further possibilities. Global advertising expenditures total $550 billion (in 2011).[30] These adverts present further enticing opportunities for different goods and services often only available in other locations that are then travelled to. The more television is watched, the more consuming takes place of goods shipped in from elsewhere and of services that involve travelling somewhere else.[31]

Thus in this neoliberal period, according to an influential American adviser/consultant insider, the principal value is 'to inspire us all to consume, consume, consume. Every opportunity is taken to convince us that purchasing things is our civic duty, that pillaging the earth is good for the economy.'[32] This became especially marked during what the economist Joseph Stiglitz terms the 'roaring [nineteen] nineties'.[33] The proliferation of choice involved multiple mobilities, the making available of an astonishing array of food, products, places, services, friends, family and gambling. High-carbon systems ensured plentiful and increasing choice.

People thus get 'locked' into escalating consumer purchases and experiences. Especially significant are global brands. Some suggest that people increasingly come to live 'branded lives' rather than lives lived and experienced through older social identities and, especially, those locally based. Consumerism is based upon lives experienced 'beyond the neighbourhood' and partly generated within 'brand factories', according to radical author Naomi Klein.[34]

But such brands and choices often involve products that no one knew that they had needed in recent previous periods. With lives being lived beyond the neighbourhood, huge new consumer industries develop to meet these unknown 'needs'. Some contemporary examples include the $60 billion bottled water industry, the $120 billion fast food industry, the $42 billion pet food industry, and the \$40 billion cosmetic surgery industry.[35] These are all hugely wasteful energy-intensive industries.

Obsolescence is built into both products and places (and people!), in terms of technology and function, design and look. Sociologist Barry Smart describes the many ways in which 'designed obsolescence', or pointless waste, is the principle on which products and places are designed and redesigned.[36] They are meant to waste and to be replaced.

As people in richer societies experience the 'pleasures' of choice, so most are drawn into similar consuming practices, of being 'free to choose'. One element of that apparent choice is the freedom to become 'addicted'. Affluence undermines the regulation that was once found within neighbourhoods. Anthony Giddens argues that 'The other side of that freedom, however, is the risk of addiction. The rise of eating disorders coincided with the advent of supermarket development in the 1960s. Food became available without regard to season and in great variety, even to those with few resources'.[37] Avner Offer demonstrates how the flow of novelty under 'affluence' undermines existing commitments and conventions, producing the 'freedom to be addicted'. This includes 'shopping addiction' itself, which is especially common not in shops but on the web since there is no neighbourhood regulation and moderation of desire.[38] Every new consumer experience is just 'one click' away.

There are many potential addictions lying outside the neighbourhood. As a result many people are emotionally and/or physically dependent upon various products of global capitalism, legal (sugar), illegal (heroin) and semi-legal (tobacco). Sociologist Anthony Elliott also describes the powerful 'addiction to the ethos of instant self-reinvention' through countless new products, including the extensive cosmetic surgery industry.[39]

Almost all these addictions are energy-intensive. In the late twentieth century hyper-high-carbon societies developed. These involved gigantic buildings, the profligate use of energy and water, a kind of luxury or excess fever, huge levels of indebtedness, the vast use of oil to transport people and objects in and out, the planned obsolescence of products, services and places, and multiple addictions generated under the name of 'choice'.[40] Oil man and former US president George W. Bush used the language of addiction to refer to the unsustainable American way of life based on oil and the dependency on consuming.[41]

The State of the World in 2010 notes how

> the world's richest 500 million people (roughly 7 percent of the world's population) are currently responsible for 50 percent of the world's carbon dioxide emissions, while the poorest 3 billion are responsible for just 6 percent ... it is the rich who have the largest homes, drive cars, jet around the world, use large amounts of electricity, eat more meat and processed foods, and buy more stuff.[42]

Eliminate the 500 million richest consumers and this would halve the world's CO_2 emissions!

Finally, a particular set of high-carbon places became especially significant after the Second World War. 'Militarization is the single most ecologically destructive human endeavour.'[43] There is a treadmill of destruction which raises the scale and impact of militarized carbon use. Militaries generate the most hazardous waste and cause the most devastation. They are normally exempt from environmental protection legislation. High-tech weaponry and vehicles consume massive quantities of fossil fuels and emit large quantities of carbon dioxide. The US military uses sixteen barrels of oil per soldier per day compared with just one during the Second World War. There is a vast amount of travel of people and equipment between military bases. The US Department of Defense owns the most extensive transport fleet in the world. The movement of military personnel, planes, satellites and tanks connects together extensive webs of military bases. Huge amounts of land are used for bases and other installations. A US military base commander summarizes this situation: 'We are in the business of protecting the nation, not the environment.'[44]

Places for consuming

Dubai and other extraordinary new places are designed to attract visitors, for people to make and remeet friends and colleagues, to experience new themed spectacles, and to buy to excess. Paradises of seductive attraction are designed, constructed and imagined as places of, and for, the movements of peoples and objects.

This presupposes large numbers of visitors roaming the world and consuming places built for them and their excessive consumption. One important aspect here is the change in the way people experience 'places'. They become less something belonged to and lived within, and more something experienced through being consumed. People are collectors of places which come to be known about, branded, themed and collected. Markers of place in the contemporary world include beaches, clubs, views, walks, mountains, history, surf, the music scene, icebergs, historic remains, sources of good jobs, food, landmark buildings, the gay scene, party atmosphere, universities, conferences and so on.[45]

Examples of newly consumed places range from narco-capitalist *favelas* in Rio or Capetown to the Antarctic, from the Paris tunnel where Princess Diana died to nuclear power stations, from Ground Zero to holidaymaking in the danger zone.[46] As fast as places are so generated and marketed, so they get visited. Places are sets of abstract characteristics described in multiple guides, especially on the Internet, and are much less dwelt within.

Many new or designed places of consumption excess develop. There is in Macao a $25 billion investment to provide leisured gambling for the emerging middle-class Chinese. This includes a vast Fisherman's Wharf of themed reproductions, a Roman Coliseum, buildings from Amsterdam, Lisbon, Cape Town and Miami, as well as an exploding volcano.[47] A further planned paradise is a €17 billion entertainment city, Gran Scala, in the Los Monegros desert in north-east Spain, where water and oil are very scarce.[48] If built, this development would include 32 casinos, 70 hotels, 232 restaurants, 500 stores, a golf course, a race track and a bullring.

Many consuming places lie on or near beaches (and/or deserts). Over the past two centuries the beach went from a place of repulsion and danger to one of attraction and desire; and one increasingly designed and constructed. A beach is the classic place for visitors to display themselves and reveal the approximation of their body to a designed tanned ideal. For the affluent classes of Europe and North America, the beach is that place of paradise and excess, the other to factories, work and domestic life. This thin line between the sea and the land becomes the space of and for a life of leisure. In Dubai massive construction projects enlarged the scale of the beach through the building of artificial islands in the sea.

In the Caribbean all-inclusive resorts are common.[49] They carve out spaces for less controlled consumption largely cut off from the surrounding territory and local people (apart from those providing these excess services). Gated and often fortified, they secure excessive consumption of goods and services away from the prying eyes of locals and those back home. Mimi Sheller describes how the neoliberal Caribbean is restructured for the super-rich, yacht-owning, aeromobile global elite.[50] On occasion whole islands provide secure sites for excess consumption for the private jet set, those who accumulate planes, houses and servants as others accumulate cars.[51]

Very similar to islands are huge cruise ships organized around consuming to excess. Royal Caribbean Cruise Lines recently launched the largest ever cruise ship. It contains 1,815 guest staterooms, the first ever surf park at sea, cantilevered whirlpools extending twelve feet beyond the sides of the ship, a water-park complete with interactive sculpture fountains, geysers and a waterfall, a rock-climbing wall and the Royal Promenade with various shops and cafés, all located in the middle of the ocean.[52]

A further extreme version even of this is the recently launched *The World*, a residential cruise liner that roams the world's oceans on a semi-permanent basis. It is a fortress world always moving beyond people's neighbourhood. *The World* is detached from national jurisdictions, tax regimes, moral commitment to nation, local people, and most limits on consumption. But at the same time it is connected to modern informational networks.

The World is designed for 'High Net Worth Individuals'. Its development reflects how wealth produces novel ultra-high-carbon infrastructures of luxury and security. *The World* 'could perhaps be best compared to a luxury private island, a kind of free-floating, certainly isolated, but territorial property. Islands play an important role in fantasies of escape and control for celebrities and the super-affluent.'[53] Seven further 'ships' similar to *The World* are now planned, places if anything to avoid most of the world!

These dreamworlds for the super-rich provide models of mobile lives for others to emulate. Through multiple media and global travel these generate desires for similar experiences of consumption, exclusion and security away from much of the world's population. These dreamworlds are part of a 'splintering urbanism', which excludes most people and reduces the availability of public space and access for people who live locally.[54]

Such places, whether stationary or on the move, establish models for subsequent mass market copies. Other developers produce mass versions of these worlds, including themed restaurants, downmarket resorts, suburban shopping malls and even vehicles named *Enclave* or *Territory*![55] So what gets imagined and constructed for elites then moves on to other more popular sites; or the same development goes downmarket. Consuming to excess spreads out, enveloping ever more in its tender embrace.

More consumers

The growth of this mobile consumerism also increases because of population growth. The world's population is growing by about 900 million per decade. This is equivalent to a new London every month. In 2011 the world's population was 7 billion. The total is expected to reach between 7.8 and 10.8 billion by 2050, depending on assumptions as to future fertility, diseases and gender relations.[56] The impact of a child varies enormously, with a newborn American generating future carbon emissions 130 times that of a child born in Bangladesh.[57]

By 2007 the world had become more urban than rural.[58] Contemporary cities are the largest structures ever created. There are various mega-cities, with around 33 million people in the Greater Tokyo Area, 24 million in the Seoul area, 23 million in Mexico City, 22 million in Delhi. Future increases will be particularly marked in developing regions which already possess huge populations. These include many cities in China, India and parts of Africa and Latin America.

Rising urban populations add to the global consumption of energy and raw materials, as well as to reduced environmental carrying capacity, leading to further resource depletion. Today's cities consume three-quarters of the world's energy and account for at least three-quarters of global pollution.[59] Thus while cities were once viewed as the cradle of civilization, they now generate social inequalities, environmental pollution, vast energy use, 'global slums', and much death and injury to citizens caused by cars and trucks.[60] Global slums are places of dwelling for at least 1 billion people worldwide.

Especially important has been the decentralization of cities, spreading out faster than they have grown in population, with rapid development of suburban areas and in 'edge cities'. This decentralization created both a growing demand for fast travel to maintain work, family and friendships and an urban pattern much less easily served by public transport.[61] As cities spread out, so their residents become more car- and truck-dependent in order that they and the objects they consume can move increasingly long distances.

Thus there is a global shift towards what Ian Roberts terms the 'motorization of movement'. This generates both global warming through greenhouse gas (GHG) emissions produced by burning oil, and global fatness through the worldwide growth of obesity, partly caused by inadequate exercise.[62] I noted that there are now over 1 billion obese people in the world, more or less equal to the numbers underfed and undernourished.[63] Roberts shows that obesity is not produced by people eating on average much more. It is that they are getting much less exercise because oil-based fast movement replaces walking and cycling, while simultaneously walking and cycling are less feasible and more dangerous, so creating a vicious circle of oil and fat.

Conclusion

This chapter shows the importance of miles – the miles travelled by objects and people and their coming together within some exceptional places in the new world order. There has been a remarkable upward movement in the scale and impact of carbon economy and excess. One consequence is that more than half of the world's population lives less than one hour from a major city. Only 10 per cent of the world's land area is classified as remote or more than forty-eight hours from a large city. The world is thus highly connected through communications and mobilities – and even the most remote of regions are tied to relatively adjacent cities.[64]

A further set of impacts is upon all beach locations which depend upon transporting in visitors but which could be washed away by rising sea levels and flooding through changing temperatures. This nearly occurred in 2005 in New Orleans, a place partially built below sea level and hence threatened by extreme weather events. Hurricane Katrina shows what can happen to those living in a major rich city when severe weather washes away the resources of those forced to live by the sea. Television pictures showed how populations are 'disposable', with bloated corpses of many black poor people displayed on the billion or so screens around the world. Katrina demonstrated the vulnerability of oil supply to flooding, and how reduced supply has led to increased prices in recent years, events contributing to the global economic collapse of 2007–08 (see Chapter 1).

But perhaps the biggest gamble is Dubai. We have seen how over a million men and women from across Asia turned Dubai from a sleepy village in the desert into a shimmering Arabian Las Vegas. But if sea levels rise, then all those newly constructed palm islands may sink back into the sea.

Indeed, Dubai's astonishing growth has already gone into reverse. Dubai did not actually make anything much. The money for all that building was borrowed. Expats are now fleeing and leaving their cars, bought on credit, at the airport; thousands of construction workers have been laid off, with half the construction projects on hold or cancelled; there is a predicted 60 per cent fall in property values; *The World* island development is allegedly slipping back into the sea; major companies like Dubai World have defaulted on their huge debts; the population is shrinking, perhaps by up to 17 per cent; and Dubai has had to be bailed out by a $10 billion loan from Abu Dhabi. As journalist Paul Lewis pronounced: 'Too high, too fast: the party's over for Dubai.'[65]

Is this rise and fall of Dubai a forerunner of the future? Is Dubai the leading example of twentieth-century hubris, which will begin to disappear once the oil runs down and sea levels rise? The possible rise and fall of Dubai may thus index a more general peaking of oil-dependent consuming, tourism, property and finance.

CHAPTER 4

CARBON CAPITAL

Energy inequalities

The twentieth-century growth in energy production and consumption generated much inequality both within and especially across different societies, with the USA appropriating an astonishing share of the world's resources.[1] Such energy excess gave rise to companies and individuals who disproportionately benefited from oil-based carbonism through deploying resources thousands of times greater than those enjoyed by most organizations and citizens around the world. Powerful social and political 'interests' organized to sustain these unequal resource relations and especially carbon-based systems and lives.

This chapter is about these carbon interests and their dominant role in determining the trajectories of twentieth-century societies. Former oil consultant (and solar enthusiast) Jeremy Leggett maintains that the oil industry in particular is 'without doubt the most powerful interest group on the planet'.[2] Many oil companies are bigger and more powerful than governments. The power of these companies, what I call 'carbon capital', is not just economic but also political, cultural and military.[3] Carbon capital consists of a complex of oil and gas exploration, producing and refining companies; vehicle, plane and ship manufacturers; media, advertising and cultural corporations; and many think-tanks and consultants. Such carbon capital has been enormously effective in wielding power, especially in the USA but also within Britain, the Russian Federation, parts of Africa and Latin America, and most Middle Eastern countries.

This chapter documents the power of this carbon capital. As the world's most powerful 'interest', carbon capital made the twentieth century's global economy, politics and culture.

I turn first to consider how carbon capital came to be assembled together over the first two-thirds of the last century. I then examine how it was significantly challenged by the growth of environmentalism during the 1960s and early 1970s; and then how carbon interests combated and increasingly reversed strong anti-carbon thinking and practice. The chapter finishes with some observations about recent carbon politics in the 2000s and how 'energy wars' are likely in future decades.

Establishing carbon capitalism

J.G. Ballard wrote at the end of the last century: 'If I were asked to condense the whole of the present century into one mental picture I would pick a familiar everyday sight: a man in a motor car, driving along a concrete highway to some unknown destination.'[4] How was it that this practice of driving, especially by men, became so taken for granted, so familiar, so possible on a global scale?

We saw in Chapter 2 that the innovations of Rockefeller and Ford brought together cheap oil and cheap petrol-driven cars. These cars were produced under conditions of Fordism, a system satirized by Charlie Chaplin in *Modern Times*. They were responsible for the 'takeover' of the globe by humans moving around the world in these individual machines and drawing down the earth's finite resources at a rapid rate. This produced what some commentators saw as 'Autopia', and others critiqued as 'Autogeddon'.[5]

But however it is assessed, this car system growth resulted in part from various companies conspiring to undermine alternatives. In the USA between 1927 and 1955, General Motors, Mack Manufacturing (trucks), Standard Oil (now Exxon), Philips Petroleum, Firestone Tire & Rubber, and Greyhound Lines, came together to share information, investments and 'activities'. Their objective was to eliminate streetcars (what are called trams in Europe). These companies established various front companies, one of which was National City Lines (NCL). During especially the 1930s, NCL together with various subsidiaries bought up many electrified streetcar lines. They then tore them up. At least forty-five cities lost their streetcars. The strategy was to shift to motorized petroleum-based transport. Local citizens were left without alternatives to oil-based cars and buses. This carbon conspiracy was in strict violation of US anti-trust laws. It was only discovered in 1955, whereupon the companies were found guilty of violating the Sherman Anti-Trust Act but then subjected to tiny fines.[6]

The president of the car manufacturer Studebaker Corporation adopted the same attitude as these conspirators when he expressed outrage that some people who could own a car actually did not. He exclaimed in 1939: 'Cities must be remade. The greatest automobile market today, the greatest untapped field of potential customers, is the large number of city people who refuse to own cars.'[7] But soon the car did become *the* method of movement within city centres and between cities and their distant suburbs. The car's unrelenting expansion of, and domination over, other systems of movement came to be viewed as natural and inevitable. Nothing was to stand in the way of the car's modernizing path within the trajectory of American modernity. The US auto industry ensured that petrol was cheap, which in turn meant that this non-renewable resource of oil was used up too quickly.

At first cars, buses and trucks did not have many roads to travel along even in the USA. Extensive paved roads funded by local or state taxpayers only appeared from 1932, with federally funded interstate highways developing after 1956 (costing $25 billion in 1950s prices). Road building in interwar Germany was especially significant, with the National Socialist Party developing the innovation of roads built only for cars and excluding pedestrians and cyclists.[8] Later motorways were provided for cars and trucks in many societies, with states funding them out of general taxation. These were newly designed roads for fast traffic, separated from other systems of movement which had fewer thoroughfares to travel along.[9] There was thus a kind of literal takeover of the environment by this new machine, beginning in Germany and the USA.

Carbon capital was thus able to get widely accepted the notion that roads are good for business; they are natural and necessary to a modern economy and society. The car and oil lobby created the idea that roads were 'needed' and that taxation should be used to pay for them. Over the twentieth century cities and suburbs became monopolized by cars, which took over most road space and city environments.

Public policy was often based upon the 'predict and provide' model. This involved a number of stages. An apparently independent report would be commissioned and this would predict that there would be a certain growth in 'demand' for road space in that area; it was therefore concluded that the state should build such a road to reduce future congestion; the rate of traffic growth would then turn out to be what had been predicted; the new road would thus fill up; and a further report would make the case that more roads should be built because of the high levels of congestion. In almost all cases traffic expands to fill the road space available. For most of the twentieth century it was thought that states should provide this road space if 'demanded' by road users. But of course most road users would 'demand' such roads since they had few plausible alternatives to that of driving to carry out their lives.

Combating environmentalism

However, carbon politics shifted during the 1960s. The publication of Rachel Carson's book *Silent Spring* in 1962 is thought to be the founding moment in modern environmentalism. Her sustained attack on the use of the chemical DDT was part of a progressive turn in various 'Western' societies and politics during the 1960s and up to the mid-1970s. This turn increasingly saw carbon as a crucial part of the growing environmental problem. Publicity around Carson's book (sales of over half a million and on bestseller lists for thirty-one weeks) initiated many new kinds of environmental argument and practice.

Indeed the 1960s more generally involved much protest: against the US war in Vietnam, nuclear weapons and energy, environmental damage and, to some extent, 'Western consumerism' (even if much 1960s' protest involved 'alternative' consumer products). There were campaigns for black civil rights in the USA, for civil rights in Northern Ireland, for women's and gay rights, for student and trade union rights (especially in Paris in May 1968), for consumer rights, and for the protection of various kinds of endangered species. The Cultural Revolution in China began in 1965. Over thirty countries gained independence from colonial rule. Various communes developed espousing anti-consumerist or alternative lifestyles. Many NGOs developed in this period, including Greenpeace, which was established in 1970.

In December 1968, as Apollo 8 completed the first manned circuit around the far side of the moon, astronaut William Anders photographed the distant Earth. This picture of the blue Earth became perhaps the most iconic image of the second half of the twentieth century. A few weeks after the flight, the Apollo 8 commander received a telegram that said 'You saved 1968'. This image of the fragile and vulnerable blue Earth played a key role in inspiring the first Earth Day, held in 1970, with over a million people demonstrating in New York.[10] The photos helped scientists and the general public to imagine the *whole* climate system and how this could be assembled from data collected from around the world. Environmental writer Eugene Linden summarizes how the image of the Earth from space revealed 'a system in which everything, from earth's position in its orbit around the sun to what's growing on the ground, influences climate'.[11]

This was in turn connected with the concept of the Earth as a 'spaceship', developed first by the futurist Richard Buckminster

Fuller. The economist Kenneth Boulding described how 'Earth has become a space ship, not only in our imagination but also in the hard realities of the social, biological, and physical system in which man is enmeshed'.[12] This echoed President John F. Kennedy's pronouncement, made shortly before his assassination in 1963, that 'the supreme reality of our time is our indivisibility and our common vulnerability on this planet.'[13] In the 1960s, British NASA scientist James Lovelock proposed and developed the concept of Gaia, of the Earth as a self-regulating system made up of the totality of organisms, surface rocks, oceans and atmosphere.[14] More generally, cultural images critiquing carbon capitalism were key to the cultural politics of this period.[15] Many writers developed environmental critiques of contemporary capitalism during this era of 'anti-carbonism', including the iconic *The Limits to Growth* in 1972 and *Small is Beautiful* in 1973.[16]

So during the 1960s and early 1970s there were developed images of the vulnerable Earth, new 'environmental' texts, data indexing processes of environmental decline, concepts emphasizing the systemic nature of the environment, and much organized cultural and scientific resistance to corporations and the state. These generated a more participatory politics attacking the 'pollution' of the fragile Earth system caused by chemical, nuclear, fossil fuel and excessive industrial development. Corporations, especially in coal and oil, were targeted as responsible for many 'environmental' problems, especially when these were revealed by massive oil spills and evidence of the depleting of the limited resources of 'one Earth'. US president Richard Nixon increasingly talked of the 'energy crisis'. Many Western states developed new regulations to constrain environmentally damaging corporate activities. The US Environmental Protection Agency was established in 1970, while DDT was banned in 1972. Much changed in this time.[17]

However, the interests of carbon capital soon began to fight back. Carson was personally attacked by the chemical industry for being hysterical and an extremist, before she tragically died in 1964. Car and oil companies vigorously resisted efforts by campaigners to reduce lead in petrol and to improve car safety following Ralph Nader's extensive campaigning to reduce air-quality-related emissions.[18] During the 1970s the American conservative movement came to organize against 1960s radicalization. The mobilization of American conservatism was fivefold: against new regulations on business; against 1960s welfare state programmes; against abortion and other rights; in favour of road-building programmes; and in favour of free-market economics rather than democratic or participatory politics to manage the conservation of mineral rights.[19]

American conservatism in particular argued against the need for environmental regulation. The capitalist class came to express its class interests in opposing most environmental regulation, as well as other regulations such as that banning tobacco advertising. When oil prices increased in the early 1970s due to an oil embargo against the USA, a time that saw fights at service stations to gain access to petrol, US president Nixon did not change the overall direction of policy even though the world economy was suffering its greatest crisis since the 1930s. This was a key moment since US oil output peaked in 1970. The high-carbon economy and society could have shifted onto a different low-carbon track at that moment. A little later President Jimmy Carter in 1977 referred to this energy crisis as the moral equivalent of a war and developed a ten-point plan to change the direction of carbon capitalism and to cut US oil imports by one-half by 1985.

However, this failed, with Carter being replaced by Ronald Reagan as president in 1980. Oil imports in fact doubled over the next twenty years.[20] Vast tracts of land were opened up for commercial energy exploitation, while the restrictions designed to minimize acid rain were reduced. Subsidies for conservation were eliminated, and symbolically the solar panels fixed by President Jimmy Carter to the White House roof were removed by Reagan when he became president in 1980.[21]

Corporations did, however, find that the ways they engaged with the state no longer worked so well. They became more politically active, building coalitions and putting aside rivalries with each other. They deployed some of the strategies that environmental activists had previously used against them, including grassroots organizing and coalition-building, commissioning research reports, telephone and letter-writing campaigns, testifying at hearings and using the media. Corporations mobilized large financial resources and professional advice, putting much money into advertising and sponsorship. Corporations thus developed during the 1980s a 'counter-activism' against environmental activism and brought about a virtual moratorium on new environmental legislation, as well as reversing other US environmental regulations.[22]

However, debate did shift again by the end of the 1980s as new public concern about *global* environmental issues developed. Amidst public protest and organization, regulatory agencies got tougher, and new laws and global accords were enacted. Even Margaret Thatcher, one of the high priests of neoliberalism, famously spoke up for the environment in a much-reported speech in 1988. She noted the exceptional dangers of acid deposition, ozone depletion and global warming resulting from a global heat trap. Along with much scientific thinking at the time, she argued to the UK's Royal Society that, with 'all these enormous changes (population, agricultural, use of fossil fuels) concentrated into such a short period of time, we have unwittingly begun a massive experiment with the system of this planet itself'.[23] The First Assessment Report of the Intergovernmental Panel on Climate Change was published in 1990 and the Rio Earth Summit, with around 170 governments and 20,000 people attending, was held in 1992.

However, these shifts in science, policy and organization in turn induced new waves of oppositional corporate activity. Corporations took advantage of novel public relations techniques and consultancies, as well as information technology, for raising money, building coalitions, organizing public opinion and lobbying politicians. Media analyst Sharon Beder describes how the emerging practices of public relations were extensively used by corporations to deal with environmental issues.[24] Public relations firms developed expertise in 'greenwashing' their corporate clients.

Many corporations found ways to counter environmentalism and new environmental regulations, but often not through directly challenging the arguments being presented. It became unwise to attack environmental protection directly.[25] Rather, what came to be attacked was the underlying 'science'. Corporations hired specialist public relations firms to initiate front groups and create the impression that there was extensive grassroots support for corporate causes. This is sometimes characterized as 'astroturfing'. This denotes political, advertising, or public relations campaigns formally planned by an organization, but disguised to look as though they involve spontaneous, popular grassroots behaviour.

They can be bankrolled by major corporations or super-rich individuals such as the Koch brothers, who head a hugely rich private oil-based company.

The use of front groups meant that corporations often participated in public debates and government hearings by hiding behind public concerns. In campaigns designed to alter public opinion, front groups choose names so as to mask their real interests.[26] ExxonMobil initiated forty-three different front organizations to create the illusion of widespread doubt about whether global warming was really occurring. This doubt was powerfully engineered, even though only a relatively small number of scientists, often physicists from the Cold War era, dispute the general idea that the extensive burning of fossil fuels is forcing climate change.[27]

Public relations and powerful media empires such as Rupert Murdoch's News Corporation are also involved in gathering information on environmentalists and sympathetic journalists, who are then branded as extremists and subjected to dirty tricks campaigns. Such firms also help their corporate clients to convince key politicians that there is widespread public support for their activities or their demands for less environmental regulation.[28]

My focus here is on the USA because, as noted, the 'oil party' began there and established such enormously strong tentacles. The USA provides a model for modern mobile economic and social development. It also possesses the world's most powerful military machine, one which depends upon oil and has been central to sustaining oil supplies through its activities. Richard Heinberg argued that 'the US would become increasingly dependent on imported oil and would no longer be in a position unilaterally to stabilize world petroleum prices'.[29] From 1970 it seems the US military was well aware that American oil supply was a major problem. Interestingly the 1975 Sydney Pollack movie *Three Days of the Condor* is based on a CIA oilfields plan. The story line is that in the event of major oil shortages, Americans expect the government to use all possible means to obtain sufficient oil to sustain the non-negotiable American way of life.[30]

Thus a more integrated 'carbon complex' in the USA has shaped the world to its developing interests from 1970 onwards. This was especially enhanced during the 1990s when the USA discovered that, although it seemed to have 'won' the Cold War, it could not guarantee a new American twenty-first century because of insufficient energy. The USA deployed many tactics to keep acquiring the 'foreign oil' so essential to the high-carbon American way of life.

First, the USA imposed the doctrine of 'free trade' whenever it suited its interests. If significant resources are found, then the USA typically insists that they should be available to the highest bidder and paid for in American dollars. The rules of the World Bank, the IMF and the World Trade Organization all state that whoever has the money, and especially the dollars, to buy particular products has a legal right to buy them, especially energy resources. The world is one's oyster, one might say, possessing the world's richest economy and being able to print dollars in order to buy the oysters.[31]

Second, the USA used these and other bodies to promote and help fund various exploration and pipeline developments in poorer parts of the world. Huge amounts of 'aid' were channelled to such countries by international bodies. The energy resources opened up were then linked especially to US companies so the oil was channelled back to the USA. A special role in this was played by the US energy trading company Enron, which struck deals in half a dozen countries, so giving it preferred access to emerging energy resources. Enron was George W. Bush's largest campaign funder and grew to become the USA's seventh largest company. As well as paying almost no taxes, it turned out to be a vast fraudulent conspiracy and collapsed with huge debts in 2001.[32]

Third, the USA developed a significant number of client states, especially in the Persian Gulf where 61 per cent of the world's known oil reserves (and 40 per cent of gas reserves) are located. In 1980 President Carter declared that any attack on the Persian Gulf region would be regarded as an attack upon the USA. This Carter Doctrine has been repeated by all subsequent presidents, so much so that some observers have described the oil reserves in the Gulf as being 'an American lake'.[33] In the Bush administration of 2000–2008 almost all leading cabinet members were oil multimillionaires![34]

In particular the USA forged an almost symbiotic relationship with Saudi Arabia, which possesses over one-fifth of the world's known oil reserves. Saudi Arabian leaders enjoyed close relations with the Bush family and more generally with many US corporations. Saudi Arabia's domestic politics are some of the most unequal, authoritarian and patriarchal in the world and yet the USA rarely seeks to modify or critique the Saudi regime. Many human rights abuses which in other societies provide the USA with a pretext for invasion are ignored. It is also surprising that no investigation seems to have occurred regarding the involvement of Saudi Arabia in the events of 11 September 2001, even though fifteen of the alleged bombers possessed Saudi passports. Moreover, the only US flights apparently allowed in the aftermath of 9/11 were those enabling the bin Laden family and other influential Saudis to leave the USA in a great hurry.[35]

Fourth, the CIA engages in covert regime destabilization. It notably funded radical Islamists so as to destabilize the USSR during the 1980s. However, these groups then turned their attention to and generated various attacks on the USA, including the 11 September destruction of the Twin Towers of the World Trade Center. Some argue that there are such anomalies in the published account of the events of 11 September that this one-off and astonishingly mediatized event must have been known about or even assisted by parts of the US administration in the two to three years beforehand. It seems scarcely credible that this attack could have been entirely engineered from the caves of Afghanistan.

Certainly leading US politicians had identified the 'need' within the USA for a major external threat following the ending of the 'war on the Soviet empire' after victory in 1991. Such an external threat would make legitimate the invasion of oil-rich Middle Eastern countries and develop a 'global war on terror' that would justify draconian changes in the security of populations worldwide. The palpable weakness of the 'weapons of mass destruction' argument for invading Iraq certainly adds fuel to 'conspiracy theories' here. It is also suggested that the USA and its oil-desperate allies needed the figure of bin Laden and this explains why he remained uncaptured for a decade, even though he was living in a big house in the middle of a town housing the Pakistan military!

Michael Ruppert goes so far as to claim that bin Laden was a 'CIA asset' who could not be brought to justice after 2001 because of the secrets he would reveal; and of course such secrets disappeared with his assassination by US forces operating in Pakistan in 2011.[36] No reason is convincing as to why he could not have been simply arrested and brought to trial in Pakistan or the USA after capture.

Whether or not this conspiracy theory is correct, there is no doubt that 9/11 was helpful to carbon capital. Its occurrence provided the pretext for invading both Afghanistan and Iraq – the latter possessing 11 per cent of known global oil reserves. When all else fails the USA uses military might to get its oil. The secretary of energy under President Clinton, Bill Richardson, stated this very clearly back in 1999:

> Oil has literally made foreign and security policy for decades. Just since the turn of this century, it has provoked the division of the Middle East after World War I; aroused Germany and Japan to extend their tentacles beyond their borders; the Arab Oil Embargo; Iran versus Iraq; the Gulf War. This is all clear.[37]

And this has become even clearer since the end of the last century. In less than a decade there have been oil-related wars in Afghanistan, Iraq and Libya. Historian William Engdahl concludes that 'US foreign and military policy was now about controlling every major existing and potential oil source and transport route on earth … Washington appeared to be waging … resource wars', acting as a global oil policeman.[38] Wherever significant oil and gas fields, pipelines or refineries are found, then there are US military bases, of which there are around 820 in at least 135 countries. There are ten major US military bases in the Gulf region alone.[39]

The noughties

Simultaneous with the 'war on terror' has been a war on global climate change. This came to develop as *the* environmental issue

during the early 2000s, marginalizing other issues, including
nuclear risks, ozone depletion and the loss of biodiversity. Climate
change became central to environmental politics and indeed to
many events that are increasingly part of the global calendar.
By 2007, the science showing the role of human behaviour in
changing climates was reported by the Intergovernmental Panel
on Climate Change (IPCC) as 'unequivocal'.[40]

This climate science orthodoxy was circulated and celebrated
around the world through key bodies such as the IPCC, which,
together with Al Gore, won the Nobel Peace Prize in 2007. This
orthodoxy was found in the more than 47,000 peer-reviewed
journal articles on climate change that had appeared by 2010,
compared with just two published before 1970![41] There were also
powerful indicators of carbon-induced change. These included
images of the rapidly reducing scale of the huge carbon sink of
the Amazon rainforest and the retreating ice fields upon which
Arctic polar bears increasingly struggle to survive.[42] Particular
years, such as 1998 and 2010, were taken to show that climates
are unambiguously changing. In 2010 there were record high temperatures in Iraq, Kuwait, Canada, Pakistan, Russia and the USA,
as well as exceptional flooding in Australia, China and Pakistan.[43]
Leading climate scientist James Hansen demonstrates the increased
frequency and scale of storms because of the greater power they
possess as temperatures rise and ice sheets disintegrate.[44]

These climate change analyses dominated worldwide agendas
and interconnect with how future supplies of energy, food and
water are increasingly insecure. In less than a decade climate
change science redrew the contours of politics and global debates
relating to future conditions of life. Apart from nuclear science
in the post-war period, climate science is the most political area

of science. The biosphere is in effect a laboratory in which a unique 'global experiment' has been taking place since the widespread burning of fossil fuels commenced in the late eighteenth century.

There are many different carbon-based politics with groups and networks seeking in various ways to ameliorate, modify or challenge carbon-induced climate change. One variant is the promotion of free-market techniques for dealing with climate change, such as tradable property and pollution rights, tax incentives, pricing mechanisms and various voluntary agreements. This development of carbon markets has recently been described as involving 'climate capitalism'.[45]

Another variant is the mainstreaming of carbon politics into popular culture. Here CO_2 has developed as an external enemy for households. They are encouraged to assess all their actions through their CO_2 consequences. This can be seen in the UK government's website Act on CO_2. Visitors to the website are encouraged to 'Try the ACT ON CO_2 calculator and find out how you can help tackle climate change.'[46]

More overt conflicts include direct action, marches, demonstrations, camps, underground protests, petitions, political parties, pressure groups, international NGOs, global summits and so on. There are many movements here, including direct protest such as climate camps. Much of this climate change environmentalism seeks to develop alternative imaginaries to that of global 'overconsumption'.[47]

Politics here involves developing models, demonstrating these through actions, and building alternative material futures (see Chapter 11). For example, the Transition Towns movement promotes local solutions to global issues of peak oil and climate change, through developing local Energy Descent Actions Plans (EDAPs).[48] The first of these was in Kinsale, a West Cork town of about 7,000 people, in 2005. The resulting report was

> the first attempt at setting out how Kinsale … could make the transition from a high energy consumption town to a low energy one … This report, prepared by permaculture students from Kinsale Further Education College. … looks at most aspects of life in Kinsale, including food, energy, tourism, education and health.[49]

This is now a widespread phenomenon with over a thousand Transition Towns, projects and initiatives around the world.[50]

Related analyses involve studies of the entire life cycle of products such as a car. These analyses examine the extraction of raw materials, vehicle production, operation and maintenance, as well as the maintaining of the road infrastructure, hospital costs, the emotional costs of many deaths and injuries and so on. The typical car requires 680 kg of steel, 230 kg of iron, 90 kg of plastics, 45 kg of rubber and 45 kg of aluminium. Between 8,000 and 28,000 kilowatt hours of energy are needed to produce a single motor vehicle. This analysis thus shows the huge carbon costs involved in replacing the world's current fleet of 'steel-and-petroleum' cars with, for example, a billion electric vehicles.[51]

However, combating this fossil fuel dependence faces intense, organized and covert opposition from carbon capital. Many books were published in the 2000s which dispute climate change orthodoxy.[52] There are powerful interconnected think-tanks, especially within the USA, combating climate-change science and promoting high-carbon 'business as usual'. These include the American Enterprise Institute, Americans for Prosperity, Cato Institute, Competitive Enterprise Institute, Energy for America, Global Climate Coalition, Heartland Institute, Marshall Institute, the Nongovernmental

International Panel on Climate Change (NIPCC), Science and Environmental Policy Project, Science and Public Policy Institute, The Heritage Foundation and World Climate Council.[53] Many are 'front' organizations intended to 'greenwash' issues.

These think-tanks cast doubt on the sciences of climate change and exploit the very nature of science, which should involve dispute, controversy and uncertainty. Climate sceptic think-tanks emphasize the uncertainty in IPCC reports, partly through denying the relevance or robustness of peer review as a system. They 'manufacture uncertainty' about climate science and of the likelihood of oil supplies actually peaking. They typically insist on the notion of balance, that there must be one climate sceptic for every climate change advocate at events where climate change is debated, especially those covered by the media. Overall US media place greater emphasis upon the uncertain nature of future climate than does reporting within Europe.

One leading example of 'fossil fuel money' is Senator James Inhofe. He stated that climates are not changing and that 'catastrophic global warming is a hoax', a conspiracy.[54] Inhofe is said to receive much of his income from the oil and gas industry; he regularly votes to increase offshore oil drilling and drilling in the Arctic National Wildlife Refuge, and denies funding to low-income energy assistance and environmental stewardship.[55] Almost all candidates for the Republican nomination to the 2012 US presidential election were climate change sceptics. Republicans have attacked more or less all Green agendas, especially seeking to bar the Environmental Protection Agency from using air pollution laws to reduce carbon dioxide emissions.[56]

There are thus powerful 'merchants of doubt' as well as much popular support for continued carbon dependence, what might be called 'carbon populism'. There has been a 'pro-car backlash' during the last decade or so. For example, the USA has the Coalition for Vehicle Choice, the UK the Association of British Drivers, and Australia the National Motorists Association of Australia. There is also extensive media and popular support for the 'carbon' car. Some 350 million people worldwide are regular viewers of the BBC programme *Top Gear*, which articulates a popular carbon enthusiasm especially among younger male viewers.[57] This 'popular carbonism' is seen in the extensive protests in many societies against fuel tax and fuel price rises.[58]

I noted above that the USA provides large subsidies to oil companies, with major tax breaks at virtually every stage of oil exploration and extraction. Capital expenses are taxed at lower rates than are paid by other industries. In most societies, even where tax rates are higher, as in most European countries, the car user does not pay the full cost of driving since many environmental and public health costs of car use, emission and accidents are not included in the taxes levied on fuel and vehicles.

Interlocking carbon interests operate globally, which prevents their power being wrested away. An immensely powerful politics of carbon capitalism has held the world in its grip since Spindletop. The Worldwide Fund for Nature (WWF) notes that 'nine of the ten largest corporations on Earth are either oil companies or automotive manufacturers'.[59] Nevertheless, carbon capital has undergone three significant shifts in recent years.

First, from 1970 onwards there has been a major decline in the importance of the large Western oil companies (ExxonMobil, Chevron, BP, Shell, Total) and a rise in the significance of 'national oil companies' based within producing countries. Especially significant from 1970 were the OPEC countries; easily the world's biggest oil company is Saudi Aramco. These national companies now control four-fifths of world oil reserves.

Second, the importance of these OPEC countries has itself declined recently. 'New' producers in Russia, Kazakhstan, Mexico, Brazil, Nigeria and China are becoming central to the emerging global economy and various new 'oiligarchs' have emerged. Many strategic alliances are developing between these companies and Western oil corporations, which often possess superior technical capacity to extract oil in dangerous and difficult environments, notwithstanding BP's recent major oil spill in the Gulf of Mexico.

Third, these new kids on the block sell oil products to many different countries. The USA in particular and the 'West' in general no longer have a monopoly on future oil (or gas) supplies. And given the peaking of oil, as examined in the next chapter, accessing sufficient oil is of major geopolitical significance and likely to determine the shape, scale and character of future economies and societies. China, as we will see in Chapter 6, is already developing major diplomatic initiatives to ensure future oil supplies from the Caspian Sea basin, the Persian Gulf, Nigeria, Russia, Venezuela and so on. It is calculated that the increase in energy demand in China up to 2030 is equivalent to all the energy currently used in Europe![60] Given the locked-in high-carbon legacy generated in the last century, oil is just not any commodity. Energy resources are the future, we might conclude.

Conclusion

This chapter has documented the power of carbon capital. It is not an unchanging 'interest'. It has used different strategies and tactics over the past half century or so. It has also encountered significant forces that have disputed its power to determine how societies are organized and operate. The most significant contestation was in the late 1960s and early 1970s when a different path might have been taken. A fourfold oil price increase followed the 1973 war between Egypt and Israel. There could have been a major shift to a low-carbon path, especially given the significance of global environmentalism at the time, a movement originating in the USA in the 1960s. The USA led the world at the time with its anti-carbon thinking and policy, with not paving all paradises with yet more parking lots. This was a potential turning or tipping point which did not last. Those parking lots quickly came to account for a quarter to half of all space in many major cities. As US oil production peaked, so US foreign policy ruthlessly pursued 'foreign oil', of which there was plenty being brought on stream, and indeed to pave most paradises with parking lots.

Now even 'oil insiders' are spilling the beans as to the limited prospects of future oil supplies and of the dire effects of oil upon global temperatures. John Hofmeister, former president of Shell, says of the USA: 'we will begin an era of energy suffering it has never known. As a nation, we will enter the energy abyss. … we will feel like we are living in a third-world nation.'[61] Oil is not any old energy source. It is the only one that so far is able move people and objects on the scale that the twentieth century brought into being, and has locked the world into social practices that will not continue if there really is an apocalyptic 'energy abyss'.

CHAPTER 5

PEAKING

Previous chapters have shown how oil is central to modern mobile civilization. But oil is now a huge problem, perhaps the biggest problem the world faces. This is for three reasons. First, its widespread and growing use, alongside gas and coal, generates greenhouse gas emissions and hence changes climates in apparently irreversible and seriously deleterious ways. These emissions will reduce living standards and demobilize existing patterns of economic and social life.

Second, the supply of oil is non-renewable and finite. Many argue, as we will see in this chapter, that we have reached a peak in the global supply of oil. Declining supplies and rising prices of oil affect more or less all manufactured goods, foodstuffs and the movement of people and objects.

Third, in the case of many of the uses of this oil to which the world is 'addicted', to use George W. Bush's term, there is no plan B: nothing can replace oil on a global scale within the foreseeable future. Oil and energy shortages, combined with changing climates caused by too many GHG emissions generated by fossil fuel use, represent an astonishing 'double whammy'. There is no escape on offer. The last century has done for this century, especially as it wasted the one opportunity to take a different path that became briefly available during the 1970s.

Peak oil thesis

We saw how the peaking of oil occurred in the USA in 1970. In the 1960s the 'problem' of oil for the USA was that there was too much and the price was deemed too low. Now the problem is very different. The USA imports 75 per cent of its oil and possesses only 3 per cent of the world's reserves.[1] Evidence suggests that the US oil industry and the federal state have been aware of this peak oil problem for the last forty years although this was mostly hidden from public debate.[2] The peaking of oil also recently occurred in China.[3]

Overall the peak oil thesis states that extracting oil reserves has a beginning, a middle and an end. At some point the oil reaches maximum output, this peak occurring when approximately half the potential oil has been extracted. After this peak, oil becomes more difficult and expensive to extract as each oilfield passes the midpoint of its life. Oil production typically follows a bell-shaped curve following Hubbert's peak model, which intriguingly was developed at a time when US oil was still plentiful.[4]

This thesis of peak oil does not mean that oil suddenly runs out but rather that it becomes increasingly difficult and expensive to extract as oil companies move down the slope after the peak. Once in the dregs then prices will rise in the form of sharp spikes. After the point of peak oil, extraction within each field becomes

FIGURE 5.1   The discovery and consumption of oil, 1900–2030
(billion barrels/year)[5]

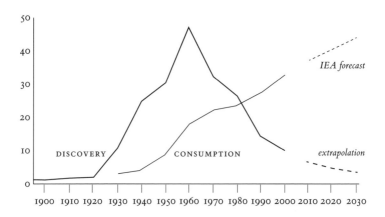

less profitable and more energy has to be expended to draw out
the same or diminishing amounts of oil.

The problem here is that the world's largest oilfields were
discovered over half a century ago, the peak year of discovery
being 1965. There have been no discoveries of really vast oil
resources since the 1970s. At least four barrels of oil are now
consumed for every new one discovered, with some suggesting
that this ratio will soon rise to 10:1.[6] Figure 5.1 shows that the
period of peak discovery was in the 1960s when there was a huge
gap between the scale of new fields being discovered and relatively
limited consumption of oil.[7] This explains why oil was so cheap
and why it was so difficult at the time to set a route to a post-oil
future. There seemed to be sufficient new oil being discovered
around the world. Why change path when the road to heaven
was paved with black gold?

Some commentators suggest that global peak oil occurred in the late 1990s; others estimate that it peaked in 2004 or 2005.[8] The generally optimistic International Energy Agency (IEA) long maintained that the global peaking of oil would not occur until at least 2020.[9] But by 2011 its chief economist, Fatih Birol, stated that the IEA now considers that crude oil production peaked back in 2006. There is reasonable agreement that there remains around 2 trillion barrels of conventional oil; and that the world's total oil production during the last century was about half of this, 1 trillion barrels.[10]

Birol argues that the existing fields are declining so rapidly that in order to stay where the world is, in terms of extraction rates, over the next twenty-five years, it is necessary to develop four new Saudi Arabias.[11] Somewhat similar calculations by Lloyds of London suggest that maintaining current extraction levels of oil production require a new Saudi Arabia coming on stream every three years.[12] The annual depletion of current oilfields is resulting in a loss of 4 million barrels per day, consumption which has to be replaced by similar-sized new fields in order just to stand still.[13]

Even the UK government is becoming alarmed about the viability of future oil supplies. Previously it ridiculed as alarmist any talk of peak oil. It seems now to have changed its position but without acknowledging this or revealing the new evidence it has available.[14] Figure 5.2 shows the dramatic rise and fall of oil derived from the North Sea. It shows how supply peaked around 2000, and has steeply declined since then.

Those oilfields that are discovered first and most easily tend to be those that are initially exploited. After the 'easy oil' has gone, the world is left with more difficult and costly fields to exploit.

FIGURE 5.2   North sea oil production, 1965–2010
(million barrels/day)[15]

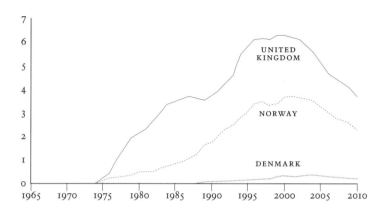

While the early fields had a return on energy invested (EROEI)
ratio of fifty or more, current fields are well below twenty.
Proportionately more energy has to be expended in order to get
the same energy extracted. It is thought that even now a barrel of
Saudi oil costs $2–3 to produce while a barrel of tar sands oil costs
more like $60.[16] Nevertheless oil extraction still has much better
EROEIs than all other energy sources apart from the sun.

One reason why there is such uncertainty about the moment of
peaking is that there is little independent scientifically established
evidence as to the size and ease of extraction of the world's
oilfields. The IEA depends upon the owners of the fields for
estimates of reserves. Oil interests, both corporations and states,
consistently exaggerate their estimates of these reserves, thereby
distorting official figures. Shell was notably exposed in 2004 for
overstating its reserves by 24 per cent.[17] This is common practice,

designed to keep up the share price of oil corporations. With the now much more important state companies, the larger the declared reserves the greater will be their extraction quota allowed by OPEC. In each case there are incentives to overestimate the size of reserves and hence the scale of global oil reserves.

In terms of conventional oil, significant increases in oil extraction would have to be met from the Middle East. However, few Middle Eastern countries possess more production capacity compared with 1990. Currently 60 per cent of the world's recoverable oil reserves lie in a small area about the size of Kansas located in parts of Iraq, Qatar, western Iran and eastern Saudi Arabia.[18]

Although Saudi Arabia holds 22 per cent of recorded global oil reserves, commentators both doubt whether it can significantly increase its production and question what its real level of reserves really are. Indeed Saudi oil reserves are a state secret. Half of its capacity comes from one oil field, Ghawar, measuring 280 by 30 kilometres. This is the world's largest oil field. The future of Ghawar is in a way the future of mobile modernity. No new field anything like the size of Ghawar has been discovered since it was first identified in 1948.

Moreover, information from US sources recently released on WikiLeaks states that Saudi oil reserves are 40 per cent lower than official estimates; that Saudi Arabia does not have sufficient reserves to drive down prices; and that this oil will be increasingly used to fuel and air-condition the homes and cars of the rapidly growing Saudi population and not Americans![19] Also Ghawar only maintains its level of output through raising the water flow that forces oil out of an oilfield that is past its prime, which makes it increasingly waterlogged. No other giant new fields have been discovered in the same area. After analysing many technical reports, the late oil consultant Matthew Simmons suggested that Saudi oil extraction may have peaked. Saudi Arabia is 'nearing or at its peak output and cannot materially grow its oil production'.[20] Ghawar is owned by the world's largest oil company, Saudi Aramco. It was once American-owned, only being fully nationalized in 1980, which means that there is some evidence outside Saudi Arabia as to the size and likely scale of the future development of the field.

Tough oil

There are some unconventional sources of oil, sources in part made possible by new technologies. These dregs of oil are very difficult and costly to exploit and yet they need to come on stream on a vast scale in order to compensate for the decline in easy oil.

The first is the deepwater extraction of oil, especially in the Gulf of Mexico, Alaska, Nigeria, Brazil and ultimately the Arctic. These deepwater wells are made possible by significant increases in the depth at which drilling can now take place, from around 1,000 feet to around 7–8,000 feet. Off Brazil billions of barrels have been recently 'discovered'. But their development involves exploiting the so-called sub-salt fields that are more than two hundred miles off the coast of southern Brazil, located in waters more than 5 miles deep. This pushes at or even beyond the margins of when drilling and extraction can be safe. Such deepwater exploration and drilling presuppose exceptional technological and human coordination between the companies involved. They often operate with conflicting cultures in such a risky and price-sensitive enterprise.

The spectre of the explosion on BP's Deepwater Horizon rig on 20 April 2010 in the Gulf of Mexico animates much resistance and opposition to such exploration and shows the risks of companies that draw upon conflicting organizational cultures.[21] The Deepwater Horizon was a vast semi-submersible oil rig floating on the surface. It exploded forty years to the day after the first Earth Day in 1970. The rig was drilling for oil off Louisiana, where the offshore oil industry was really invented. There had been a significant drive in the USA towards much more aggressive leasing of offshore lands, beginning with the first Reagan government in 1980. Three-quarters of the 3,500 offshore production facilities in the Gulf are located off Louisiana.

This rig was drilling in water 1 mile deep, with the 'oil reservoir' being another 2.5 miles below the seabed. Such reservoirs contain not only rock but also water, oil and gas. The gas produces the danger of a blowout. The cement for the blowout preventer had been put in place by Halliburton, part of the system of fragmented authority that BP established. The rig was owned by Transocean, which had set previous records for offshore drilling but was subject to less regulation and lower staffing levels, being registered in the Marshall Islands. Also, BP was well known for its draconian cost-saving shortcuts. It was often referred to as the 'renegade refiner', although overall the Gulf saw an astonishing 12,087 oil-related safety incidents over the previous five years. The major companies involved in this accident – BP, Halliburton and Transocean – were collectively responsible for an explosion that killed eleven workers and produced the world's largest marine oil spill, with almost 5 million barrels of crude oil deposited in the Gulf during 2010.

Following this explosion there was a six-month moratorium on new deepwater drilling, but it has since resumed. Nevertheless the extracting of oil and gas in deepwater environments is now less likely to be permitted, especially in the USA, and when it does occur it will tend to be more expensive.

It is hard to imagine what similar disasters will occur if oil extraction develops in the Arctic. Such oil extraction will take at least a decade or so to come online since there is no relevant infrastructure, its development rests on temperatures rising further to melt more ice, the drilling period will only last for a few months of the year, there is much contestation over the ownership of the area, likely fields are widely dispersed, total oil is thought to be limited in scale, and all potential oil requires deepwater extraction in extraordinarily challenging conditions.[22] If extracting does occur the resulting oil will have a much lower EROIE, and there will be a great danger of spills and explosions, without the knowledge as to how such spillages would be cleared up. By 2015 some estimate that these deepwater projects in the Gulf of Mexico, the Arctic and off Brazil will have to make up almost one-third of new oil capacity. If these sources of oil fail to deliver this new supply, this will further compound the likely global shortfall.[23]

A further source of tough oil is tar sands, or what the oil industry renamed as 'oil sands'! This has only developed on a large scale since 1999 when Shell started the Athabasca oil sands project in Alberta, Canada. Other big deposits are in Venezuela and Siberia. Tar sands are deposits of sand and clay that are saturated with bitumen. The bitumen is solid, or semi-solid; getting it to flow requires injecting up to 1,000°F of heat into the reservoir. The resulting 'oil' has then to be converted into crude oil, which in turn is refined into normal oil products. This heavy oil is not nearly as valuable as 'light crude' oil. Two tons of tar sands produces just one barrel of oil.

Extracting tar sands oil is subject to many technological difficulties, much political contestation and huge economic uncertainty
because of the long-term nature of required investment.[24] And
even if Canadian tar sands were as productive as their advocates
argue, extraction would generate at best 4.7 million barrels of
oil per day by 2035.[25] The biggest problem with extracting this
oil is that it generates at least three times the GHG emissions
as normal oil extraction. It also uses huge amounts of energy,
especially natural gas, as well as water. The natural gas now used
in Alberta tar sands extraction is equivalent to that needed to heat
half the homes in Canada. Some speculate that such gas will be
increasingly used in a liquefied form in transportation and hence
will be much more expensive if used in tar sands extraction.

Another source of oil is shale oil, which is found especially in
Colorado in the USA. This too is a misleading term.[26] There is no
oil in shale but rather the solid inorganic material called kerogen.
After an extensive recovery process one ton of shale oil can produce
the petrol needed to fuel one car for a fortnight. This recovery
involves mining, transportation, accessing vast amounts of water,
heating to 900°F, adding hydrogen, and disposing of the waste.
Not surprisingly, no company has yet managed to develop a viable
long-term oil shale industry because the energy return is so low,
although rapidly rising oil prices may alter this in the future.

Thus the opportunities for very significantly increasing oil
extraction are limited. And yet the demand for oil could in
theory rise 50 per cent from the current 80–85 million barrels
a day.[27] Fatih Birol from the IEA has stated that oil supply will
need to rise to 120 million barrels a day by 2030, so ensuring the
continued expansion of modern mobile society around the globe
and especially within much of China and India.[28]

But future decades will surely be characterized by shortages and rising prices, with large levels of demand that are not met. This is especially so since the downward slope after peak for each field is steeper than the slope leading up to the peak and generally seems to take the society involved by surprise. There is no possibility of oil extraction increasing by 50 per cent over current levels by 2030 to maintain 'business as usual' for current and developing systems of global production and consumption.[29] The easiest sources of oil are exploited first.

At the current rate of extraction and use there are forty-two years of oil left.[30] Due to growing population and the proportion of the world's population who are new 'consumers' of oil, there are already large reductions in oil available *per person* across the world. BP calculates that world oil production per capita actually peaked over thirty years ago in 1979.[31]

Rising populations in cities in particular add to the global consumption of energy, as well as reduced environmental carrying capacity, which leads to further resource depletion. I noted how today's cities consume at least three-quarters of the world's energy and account for three-quarters of global pollution.[32] Generally speaking, cities have been decentralizing. They have spread out faster than they have grown in population, with a rapid growth in suburban areas and the rise of 'edge cities' in the outer suburbs. This decentralization created a growing need for travel and an urban pattern not easily served by sustainable modes of public transport.[33]

There is thus not enough oil. And if there is insufficient oil, then economies cannot grow because of how they are locked into oil. Peak oil analyst Richard Heinberg argues that 'industrial civilization is based on the consumption of energy resources that are inherently limited in quantity, and that are about to become scarce ... in the end, it may be impossible for even a single nation to sustain industrialism as we have known it during the twentieth century.'[34] Hence the 'petroleum interval' in human history will turn out to be a brief (the twentieth) century or so. Energy is thus increasingly expensive and there will be frequent shortages, and these will get worse if the world's population continues to soar and per capita supplies dwindle much further.

Because of the rush for oil, major states and corporations will try to secure available supplies and distribution channels using legal and illegal means. The cheap energy interval of easy oil in the twentieth century is winding down as we move to 'tough oil', with huge increases needed in resources and energy so as to extract, refine and transport those remaining dregs.

Political peaking

But there is a further problem here. Some commentators now emphasize less the technological peaking of oil and the literal peak so far examined. Rather, what may be more important is what we can call the political peaking. This political peaking occurs sooner than the technological peaking due to the array of powerful social and political processes occurring within oil-producing societies. These processes reduce the effective discovery, production and refining of oil to below what is technologically optimal. There are three important points here.

First, oil reserves are concentrated among relatively few countries. Amory Lovins et al. summarize how 'oil supplies are becoming more concentrated and less secure'.[35] Unlike coal, let alone wood, water or sun, oil energy derives from few societies. There is a dependence on them to ensure continued supplies. Thus these oil producers can hold oil-consuming countries to ransom. Since 1970 there have been various occasions when oil-extracting countries allowed prices to rise and indeed showed no interest in ensuring a smooth upward supply of oil to keep prices stable. Moreover, getting the oil from where it is produced or refined to where it is actually used often involves journeys of thousands of miles, by pipeline or by tankers. And tankers have to pass through some very dangerous narrow straits.[36] These all reduce the EROIE.

Second, many countries where oil is produced experience what Dan Sperling and Deborah Gordon refer to as 'terrorism, wars, supplier countries underinvesting, holding back, and even collapsing'.[37] Some of these societies are the very worst places for producing the resource upon which modernity depends. Many oil-producing states are governed by authoritarian regimes. Some are highly corrupt with oil revenues going to fund family fortunes located in overseas tax havens. Much oil revenue passes 'offshore'; indeed $11.5 trillion of the world's wealth is estimated to be held in offshore secrecy jurisdictions.[38] Also one outcome of the 'Arab Spring' uprisings in 2011 is that more Middle Eastern oil will be consumed by the rapidly growing populations of those countries rather than exported to the 'West', as happened in the past for semi-colonial reasons.[39]

Also, oil-extracting societies often generate internal protest and sometimes terrorism through their authoritarian and corrupt practices. At the same time oil pipelines and refineries are often visible entities that are difficult to police. Terrorist attacks are relatively easy. Some such societies are also places of intense political opposition to further carbon emissions and the expansion of oil extraction. There may be oil, but in some contexts it will not be exploitable at the rate and in the form that the continued mobilization of the world appears to demand. Both terrorism and political opposition increase the costs of potential oil extraction.

Third, earlier chapters noted that oil is subject to speculation in financial markets through new financial instruments. This speculation destabilizes oil supply and price and hence further reduces energy security, according to Lloyd's of London.[40] Oil prices reflect financial flows as much as they do real flows. Oil may be traded several times before it comes to market in futures, swaps and options, indeed in some cases before it comes out of the ground. There are thus two parallel systems, of real exploration and financial speculation. The issue of peak oil and the likely price of oil, like much else in the world, is bound up with the ways that so many relationships involve financial speculation.[41] The power of finance is dominant and this makes it unlikely that benign energy futures will be realized.

Thus a political peaking of oil extraction almost certainly occurred before the technological peaking of conventional oil, which seems to have happened around 2006.

Climate change and multiple crises[42]

On top of all that we can anticipate increasing problems of climate change. Over the next few decades changing climates will engender extra energy requirements to deal with increasingly extreme weather. Such events may include droughts, heatwaves, floods, rising sea levels and storm surges, food and water shortages, more desertification, fires and so on. Many such events were experienced during 2010 and 2011, even in resource-rich societies such as Australia and the USA. These weather patterns necessitate extra energy resources to provide heating, shelter, food and lighting for often large and desperate dispossessed populations. The insurer Swiss Re estimates that losses from these weather events have risen fivefold since the 1980s. Oxfam reports that, while earthquake numbers have remained relatively stable, there has been an almost threefold increase in flooding and storm events. As environmental journalist John Vidal writes: 'Warning: extreme weather ahead.'[43]

At the same time, these extreme weather events make obtaining 'tough oil' increasingly difficult and costly.[44] Thus the warming of the waters of the Gulf of Mexico generating more powerful hurricanes makes deepwater extraction in the area much riskier. Also, in this century the move to tough oil will increase the resulting GHG emissions from oil extraction, which will add to likely climate change and the scale of extreme weather events.

Moreover, states and corporations are often 'vulnerable' and unable to cope with fast-moving and unpredicted disasters. These disasters include potential oil shortages, droughts, heatwaves, flooding, desertification, mobile diseases and the forced movement of up to 150 million environmental refugees predicted by 2050.[45] There are many instances where 'states', relief organizations and companies cannot deal with complex and unpredicted disasters, which necessitate improvising new kinds of unexpected mobilities and systems.

Two recent examples show this: New Orleans in the USA in September 2005 and the nuclear disaster in Fukushima in Japan caused by the massive tsunami on 11 March 2011. These events demonstrate how most organizations cannot deal effectively with failures in institutions and process that impact upon each other. Urbanist Mike Davis concludes more generally how by 2030 'the convergent effects of climate change, peak oil, peak water, and an additional 1.5 billion people on the planet will produce negative synergies probably beyond our imagination.'[46]

Especially significant are negative synergies occurring within the belt around the centre of the earth between the two tropics. The recent book *Tropic of Chaos* powerfully examines the resulting consequences of anthropogenic climate change and especially extreme weather events already occurring within this huge area. There are many 'damaged societies' lying between the tropics. Shortages of water and food, rising sea levels, poverty, lack of access to energy, refugees, extreme weather and regime failure all 'compound and amplify each other' through what is termed 'catastrophic convergence'. Up to 2.7 billion people are thought likely to experience violent conflicts as climate change interacts with these other system problems.[47]

Moreover, women within such societies will be especially affected by such 'catastrophic convergence'.[48] If there is mitigation funding it mostly supports large-scale clean technology projects rather than the smaller-scale projects benefiting poorer people and especially women farmers. There is a danger of developing 'masculinist', 'green monumentalism' such as high-speed train lines or huge geo-engineering projects, which in their construction and operation will generate very high levels of GHG emissions. And yet it is local knowledge and technologies that are of greater importance, and they are more likely to be developed by and relevant to women's interests.

Conclusion

Peak oil author James Kunstler writes about these multiple vulner-abilities: 'At peak and just beyond, there is massive potential for system failures of all kinds, social, economic, and political. Peak is quite literally a tipping point. Beyond peak, things unravel ... all bets are off about civilization's future.'[49] There will be large reductions in all oil-dependent industries – that is, in almost all manufacturing, services, agriculture and transportation.[50] System effects flow from the peaking of cheap oil. Once we are on the downward slope, then oil extraction gets tough. This is especially so in the face of changing climates particularly impacting in the tropics.

There will be a more general 'peaking' here, not only of oil, gas and water but also of American power, of European welfare states and of 'Western life', and even of global population levels. Significant oil price increases have almost always generated worldwide recessions. They also involve colossal redistributions in income, away from those economies where oil is consumed to those where it is extracted, and within those towards the interests controlling the oil resources.

In the rest of this book peak oil is partly examined not as a specific issue of a particular energy source but as a more general characteristic of the early twenty-first century. Much may peak, including the wealth and power of the oil-poor West (includ-ing Japan).[51] And the notion of 'peak' is being taken up as an idea which may help to shift thinking and practice towards a post-carbon economy and society. Media and policy attention is now increasingly directed to the issue of peaking. It is coming out of the closet; and it is one important way in which NGOs, policymakers and activists can achieve some traction in at least thinking about how to move beyond fossil fuel economies and societies.

CHAPTER 6

THE CHINESE CENTURY?

Oiling Chinese development

Previous chapters have examined how the twentieth century was largely dependent upon the energy resource of oil and its widespread use, beginning in the USA. This oil helped to make possible a mobile modern world and globalization, as oil and its friends moved around the world. This oil made the American century and led some 1990s American commentators to believe that a new American twenty-first century was on the cards.

In 1997 a campaign called the Project for the New American Century (PNAC) was established, which lasted until 2006. PNAC included key figures in the Bush administration from 2000, including Cheney, Wolfowitz, Rumsfeld and Rove. It fed policy into that administration, especially in its early years. Its goal was to ensure that the twenty-first century, like the twentieth-century, would be based upon American pre-eminence. It was especially concerned with how the USA would access sufficient oil and related resources and to prevent other powers from challenging such enduring American hegemony. The publications of PNAC developed and justified the notion of the pre-emptive war – which then occurred in Iraq in 2003.[1]

It is now impossible, though, to imagine a new American century emerging, following the economic collapse of 2008, the rise and rise of China, and the diminishing supplies of American oil. Previous chapters showed how oil is a distinct non-renewable resource whose availability in the USA peaked as early as 1970. Since then it has peaked in most countries worldwide and at a global level from around 2006. According to Ian Morris's encyclopaedic text on world history, the 'West' still rules but it will do so only for a limited period, which is coming to an end. There is taking place what Martin Jacques terms a general 'changing of the guard'.[2]

A new American century would have to be based upon a new resource 'after oil'. The USA could not expect to build a new century based upon diminishing supplies of oil derived from other countries. Some other way of energizing society would need to be found. There is a crisis of the dominant or hegemonic power of the USA. This crisis involves sharply increased competition, social conflict and systematic chaos, with existing political structures unable to address the problems they face.[3] Indeed the limits on oil supply threaten the capacity of the US military to act, a consideration now animating many American defence analysts.[4] There is increasingly a multipolar world.

The last chapter also demonstrated how oil issues are now centrally significant within many 'developing societies'. These societies are growing rapidly in scale and in their energy use (which is generally less 'efficient' than in developed economies). The general peaking of oil is particularly significant because of oil's increasing use within 'Chindia' (China, India) and the BRICs (Brazil, Russia, India, China, South Africa). So not only are we down to the oil dregs but there are many conflicts around who gets to drink those dregs, with some very thirsty new mouths to satisfy. The early years of the new century see not so much a new American century but one of various 'rising (or resurgent) powers' and of scarce and bitterly contested energy resources within this multipolar world.

I consider here China, the world's most populous society with over 1.3 billion people.[5] Its economic growth and development of urban, mobile living is dwarfing developments occurring in the rest of the world. Up to the point of eighteenth-century industrialization of the West, beginning in England, China and India were the world's largest economies, generating one-third of world GDP. Before coal power burst upon and transformed European and North American economies, these two Asian socie-ties were the centre of world economic power.[6] They were both larger than 'Europe' in the mid-eighteenth century. China was the home of much technological advance and invention, as described in Joseph Needham's extensive research on Chinese science and technology. These advances included cast iron, the ploughshare, stirrups, gunpowder, the printing press, paper money and the magnetic compass. China reasonably thought itself as being at the centre of civilization, stretching back at least two millennia.[7]

But both India and China went into relative decline from the eighteenth century onwards. This occurred as first coal power and then oil became central to energizing societies. But only by the early decades of the twentieth century did the USA actually account for a greater share of world GDP than that of China and India. This US share itself peaked in the 1960s. The growth of

China's share recommenced around 1980. China now accounts for the same share of world GDP that it generated around 1820. Hence China, along with India, is a 'resurgent power' within this new century. China is now the world's second economy with its consumption of oil skyrocketing.[8] This resurgence of China occurred following the process of post-Maoist marketization, starting around 1978. Thus the new century is much more likely to be Chinese than American, as Martin Jacques argues in detail in *When China Rules the World*.[9]

I first describe China's recent transformation into a more mobilized society, as its citizens, especially those living in cities, increasingly developed 'consuming and mobile lives'. In 1949 China's GDP had been less than 3 per cent of that of the USA. But after the death of Mao in September 1976 and the victory of the 'reformer' Deng Xiaoping, a spectacular increase in Chinese economic and social development occurred from 1978 onwards. Deng argued in favour of the 'four modernizations' and that the main objective of the Communist Party should be economic growth and not social revolution. To 'get rich is no sin', Deng proclaimed, directly contradicting the Maoist position that had been expressed, in particular, during the period of the Cultural Revolution, 1965–69.[10]

1978 is arguably one of the most significant turning points in world history. Thereafter firms and agricultural units in China were increasingly allowed to make their own investment decisions, reward workers with material incentives, generate new products and services, attract foreign investment and collaborations, and develop novel products for export. By 2011 the Chinese economy was valued at $6.9 trillion. Within probably ten years the Chinese economy, with typically 7–10 per cent annual growth rates, will be larger than the American economy, especially if the latter contracts significantly following the crash of 2007–08 onwards (the 2011 US economy is valued at $15 trillion).[11]

Also over the past couple of decades China had the fastest rates of growth of scientific research, albeit beginning from an almost zero base as late as the 1970s.[12] This astonishing rate of development within an enormously populous society led to many changes in how China is 'energized'. In 1973, the USA was by far the largest consumer of energy in the world, devouring over 30 per cent of the total.[13] But now China is the world's leading energy user, consuming 20 per cent of global energy, more than twice its proportion even as late as 2000. This is the fastest rate of increase of energy use ever recorded by a major power, with the exception of Victorian Britain.

So far it has been mainly coal that has powered China's economy, accounting for 71 per cent of its energy. China is the largest producer and consumer of coal and steel in the world. It is the workshop of the world. In 2009 it replaced the USA as the largest car market. Moreover the trend of rising energy consumption has only recently begun; future energy consumption per person will skyrocket. China has started importing coal partly so that its factories can continue to make goods for the rest of the world. Some of the GHG emissions generated by the rest of the world are thus in effect 'exported' to China, which is now the world's largest GHG emitter.

But as Chinese society becomes a more mobilized society, so oil will become a very significant energy source. As noted, coal compared with oil is less energy-dense; it is mostly unsuitable for transportation, and is not much used as a manufacturing or agricultural raw material. It is calculated that China requires three times the oil and coal energy to manufacture the same item as is now needed within the USA or Europe.[14]

So starting from a low base there will be a huge increase in oil use in China. China is now the world's second largest consumer of oil. As recently as 1990, China used only 2 million barrels of oil each day. The figure is now 7 million and will at least double by 2030. That extra consumption will add 10 per cent to the world's consumption of oil (if it is available) and will generate many further oil price spikes. China's biggest oil company is PetroChina, which is the world's most valuable company by market value (September 2010). It was the first company in the world to reach a market value of US$1 trillion.

From 1999 to 2004 China's oil imports doubled, increasing over 11 per cent in a single year, 2003. This growth in Chinese demand partly explains why oil and petrol prices in the USA and world-wide rose so dramatically in the middle years of the last decade. This helped to generate the economic and financial collapse in the 'West' beginning in 2007–08, as shown in Chapter 1.

China currently consumes one litre of oil a day per person, compared with eleven litres a day in the USA. The Chinese figure will rise dramatically. If China's oil use were to reach the US level, total world consumption of oil would double. But this is impossible, as shown in the analysis of peak oil in the previous chapter. We already noted estimates that suggest at the current rate of growth China could in a few decades consume all available world exports. This assumes no growth in demand elsewhere in the world and no fall in global production.[15] Who gets the remaining dregs of oil is thus the number one question. There are many Chinese initiatives to secure its future oil supplies.

China is obtaining oil assets from around the world. It lent $10 billion to the Brazilian company Petrobras to fund its new offshore exploration and development. In return, China will receive long-term oil deliveries from Petrobras of 160,000 barrels per day. China lent money to Russian oil companies Rosneft ($15 billion) and Transneft ($10 billion) in return for oil supplies and a new pipeline spur to China. This locks up 15 million tons of oil every year for the next twenty years. China and Venezuela have signed agreements and invested in a $12 billion fund to finance and develop oil projects, infrastructure and agriculture. The ambition is to boost Venezuelan oil exports to China to 1 million barrels per day by 2015.

In each case Chinese president Hu Jintao met the respective leader of the other power, so emphasizing the strategic significance of the proposed deal.[16] Since 2002 he has played a major role in securing future energy supplies for China, especially oil. This is utterly important business, in which central leadership is thought essential. These supplies are not left to the market. On current estimates China will consume 15 million barrels per day by 2030, with domestic production providing at most only 4 million of this total. The rest has to be imported.

China is thus pursuing a threefold strategy to secure that extra 11 million barrels per day. First, it diversified its sources of oil (and gas) to a much wider range of countries. Controversially this includes Sudan, where China allegedly sold arms to those who have been responsible for genocide in Darfur. Nigeria and Equatorial Guinea are two further African countries now with a strong Chinese presence. Chinese oil company CNOOC has even been trying to buy American oil interests; in 2010 it acquired a 33 per cent stake in a south Texan shale oil and gas field. China obtains at least 13 per cent of its oil from Iran, and a memorandum of understanding was signed between the Chinese company Sinotec and Iran to co-develop the very large Yadavaran Field.[17]

Second, China is developing connections with countries where it is possible to send oil by pipeline rather than by tanker, which is how most oil arrives in East Asia. Such pipeline deliveries would make it less likely that China could be blockaded. For example, it built the 1,384-mile-long pipeline from Kazakhstan's Caspian shore to Xinjiang in China. It is jointly owned by the China National Petroleum Corporation (CNPC) and the Kazakh oil company KazMunayGas.

Third, China relies on three major state-controlled companies to procure these foreign energy supplies. This often involves links with other national oil companies such as Saudi Aramco or Gazprom rather than Western oil companies.[18] Unlike the USA or Western Europe, which leaves oil security to the operations of corporations and the market, Chinese energy development is far more 'statist'. Overall its planned scale of future oil consumption has many other leaders worried, including those in India and Japan, as well as in the 'West'. It should be noted, though, that most countries seeking to secure oil engage in illegal and unethical behaviour. Oil brings out the worst in policymakers and powerful corporations. Peter Maass refers to how the world down to its dregs enters 'the violent twilight of oil'.

The following sections outline some determinants of this growing use of oil within recent Chinese development. How was it that increasing amounts of oil were needed in China? Apart from the use of oil in manufacturing products for the rest of the world, what else happened in China that made oil so necessary?

Chinese urbanization

Until the 1970s China was a fairly poor if relatively egalitarian country, albeit with high death rates from starvation, especially during the Great Leap Forward of 1958–60. A third of Chinese people could not read or write. Around 80 per cent lived in the countryside, most journeys were made on foot and by bike, there were few street signs, lights or advertising, and there was little use of electricity apart from domestic lighting and for power used in factories. Trains were coal-powered and there was limited air travel. Few foreign visitors went to China, most travelling on organized 'friendship tours'. There was very limited foreign travel for the Chinese with only party cadres and sports stars allowed to make overseas journeys.

All enterprises were state or collectively owned, with Revolutionary Committees in charge. There was little development of market mechanisms, with much provision of basic services according to presumed need. Apart from Communist Party cadres, there were few people with ostentatious wealth, and there was an attempted levelling of incomes and status especially since the Cultural Revolution beginning in September 1965.[19] As late as 1976 most men wore 'Mao jackets'.

There was even some de-urbanization between the 1950s and the 1970s, partly under the leadership's anti-urbanization policies. A household registration system (*hukou*) was designed to keep the population in its place by restricting access to most services, including food, to the place in which a person was registered.[20] The main social divide was between those living in rural and those living in urban areas, with rural residents prevented from migrating to the more prosperous cities. There were some huge migrations nevertheless, such as the forced relocation of more than 17 million youth from the cities *to the countryside* during the Cultural Revolution.[21] Car production effectively ceased during the Cultural Revolution. There were cities, but the heartland of China was the countryside and its peasantry. This peasantry had been the crucible of the Chinese Revolution that finally succeeded in taking power in 1949. Uniquely Mao sought industrialization without urbanization.

Many old neighbourhoods or *hutongs* in Chinese cities were models of low-carbon living with a hugely dense population and much intermingling of housing and commerce, rather like Jane Jacobs's account of Greenwich Village in the 1950s. But major steps towards a more mobile society were initiated with the post-Maoist reforms in the late 1970s. Some involved facilitating internal migration for people to work on huge construction projects such as the centrally organized building of dams and other hydroelectric projects. Other internal migrations resulted from the development of Special Economic Zones, of skilled workers, construction workers and unemployed agricultural labour able to work in factories, and of those seeking work in western border areas. Many old high-density neighbourhoods were simply demolished on the grounds of economic catch-up and progress.[22]

These processes set up new inequalities. Those without rights of residence in growing cities developed into a reserve army of the poor and dispossessed, often working in sweatshops, even in so-called high-tech industry (with, for example, many resulting suicides among those making iPhones in Foxconn's plants in China[23]). There is a clear divide between those who are legally resident within a city and those who are migrants from other parts of China, who possess few rights. For the rich and educated there is now said to be a 'national mobility' pattern in China.[24] Significantly the private ownership of cars was only allowed after 1984, but the striking growth of private car ownership is used to justify much rebuilding of city centre areas, with many old neighbourhoods being demolished.

Shanghai is notable here. Four thousand skyscrapers were built in this one city, with another one thousand planned, pretty well all with air conditioning and some designed by prize-winning celebrity architects.[25] It is said that the carbon footprint of each person in Shanghai is greater than in the UK. This is a place of ultra-rapid conspicuous consumption, mirroring the West and its worst follies.[26]

Other 'Chinese' cities are being developed for leisure visits by the new rich and the middle classes, including Hong Kong and Macao. There is now an 'Individual Visitation Scheme', at first available only to residents of various large cities, which facilitates much tourist travel.[27] Hong Kong and Macao are located in the Pearl River Delta, the astonishing transformation of which 'starchitect' Rem Koolhaas describes as the 'relentless pursuit of development at a scale and velocity previously unseen in the world'.[28]

Macao is becoming the world centre of casino gambling or 'gambling tourism', following the break-up of the gambling monopoly on the tiny island. By 2007 this island of fewer than half a million people was annually attracting 27 million tourists, more than half from mainland China. Macao is a place of peda-gogy, teaching the newly prosperous Chinese how to behave as tourists and especially as purchasers and users of both goods and, especially, services such as those of a café culture. Macao is described as a kind of laboratory of consumption, as the Chinese learn to be individualized consumers of goods and services that on an extraordinary scale are being generated from within China itself. Macao is perhaps the extreme illustration in modern China of Deng's maxim of 'one country, two systems'.[29]

Moreover, Deng Xiaoping pronounced in 1977 that 'foreign connections' were a 'good thing', rather than part of a 'bourgeois lifestyle' as Mao maintained. Through the liberalization of travel, China is becoming one of the world's leading countries for tourism. Those Chinese who can afford to do so, and are from the right cities, are able to travel to most countries in the world. Tourist travel is increasingly a lifestyle feature for higher income city populations. The exceptional numbers of Chinese visitors are leading some countries outside China to adapt their 'sights' to be more pleasing to the Chinese eye, such as replacing Hindu with Buddhist gods in Bali. It is also said that social advancement in China now requires a family's son or daughter to acquire a degree from an overseas university.

China is thus at the centre of oil-based tourist, student, business and family travel, especially for those living in major cities. It is also thought that in a decade China will be the world's leading tourist destination for visitors from the rest of the world.[30] China could be both the workshop of the world *and* the centre of world travel and tourism, if cheap oil lasts.

The most striking urban project in the world is China's plan to build over the next twenty years 400 new cities, each housing up to half a million people.[31] It is planned that the populations of cities in China will increase by 326 million people over the next two decades, a number greater than the current population of the USA![32] This will involve the most extensive migration ever to occur in human history. Scores of millions of Chinese will move from rural areas to these newly constructed urban centres so as to work in the new factories producing goods for the world.[33] Since urban dwellers are much more carbon-hungry this will increase carbon consumption and GHG emissions, as those emissions and uses of energy are exported from the once rich North. These new cities will be mostly car-based rather than follow the old neighbourhood model. The proposed car-free eco-city of Dongtan near Shanghai famously failed to get beyond the design phase and a single wind farm.[34] Also much long-distance travel will be generated as the new city dwellers go back once a year to keep up family and friendships back home – where home is often thousands of miles away.

Cars in China

I have noted how the Chinese car industry is recent. There had been an exceptional urban transport system up to the 1970s based upon cycling. Many factories produced a million or so bikes a year and roadside repair workshops kept those bikes on the road. It was one of the most egalitarian of travel systems and ensured reasonable levels of fitness and health. As late as 1978 there were in China only fifty-six relatively small car manufacturing plants, producing 150,000 cars a year. These cars were mainly for the use of Party and state officials.[35] But this, like much else, was to change with the 1978 reforms.

If there were no cars in the world, no one would know that they needed one. But it is estimated that the 85 per cent of the world's population not now owning a car would acquire one if they could. Given rapid urbanization and industrialization, particularly in China and India, potential growth in car and truck use could be astronomic. If 'Western' levels of private car use were to develop in China, this would transform domestic infrastructures, air quality, road safety, energy supplies and future climate.[36]

Car registrations have been growing in China by 10–20 per cent per annum since the 1980s. Some cities have banned bicycles from the busiest urban roads, such as Shanghai where bicycles are no longer allowed on over fifty major roads, including where the city's new financial and industrial centres are located. There has been lavish support for the Chinese car industry, which is seen as central to the Chinese miracle, one of the four pillar industries. Roads have been built at a frenetic pace. This is all part of the programme of national 'catch-up', which is for the Chinese state non-negotiable. Almost all the leading car companies are joint ventures between state-owned Chinese companies and overseas companies.

The International Monetary Fund (IMF) estimates that the number of cars in China will increase from 21 million in 2005 to 573 million in 2050. After personal incomes rise above $5,000 per annum, car ownership in all societies seems to rise dramatically. This growth in China is part of an almost sixfold projected global increase in car ownership over this period, according to the IMF.[37] These projections are based upon a presumption of 'oil business as usual'.

This shift from a cycling society to a car society, at least for urban dwellers, is the fastest ever automobilizing of a major society. China's growth, fuelled by a rapidly developing indigenous car industry, is dwarfing developments taking place elsewhere. This growth in car-based mobility in China has many consequences: for the cities, which are being redesigned, often by celebrity architects, around the car system and its smooth operation; for atmospheric pollution, which makes some cities intolerably unhealthy for those walking or cycling; for health and safety, with car death and injury rates among the highest in the world; for obesity, with Chinese men acquiring a car being twice as likely to be obese as previously;[38] for the global environment, where automobility growth is one of the fastest growing sources of GHG emissions; and for the rapidly rising consumption of oil and the need to secure the complex routes by which oil is actually got to China day in, day out.

However, recently the petrol-driven car has not had it all its own way. A decree in 2006 led to the reinstatement of the bike lanes previously removed. The relevant minister was determined that China should once again be the Kingdom of Bicycles.[39] Also China introduced mandated emissions standards that for new cars are tougher than in many countries in the rich North and it phased out leaded petrol in a brief two-year period. There is also much experimentation with the development of electric bikes, of which there are now over 100 million in contemporary China, and which could be a very significant disruptive innovation relevant to cities throughout the developing world. There are many other experiments in developing alternatives to the car, although there is a huge issue in turning one or more of these into something more than just a niche.[40]

Supertankers

Although it has been noted how China is developing oil pipelines, most of the country's oil arrives in many of the world's 5,500 oil tankers. The moving of oil in slow supertankers from very distant producers is key to contemporary energy. China has barely a fortnight's strategic reserve of oil and hence it must ensure that the tankers keep on arriving. These tankers themselves require much oil and they generate very large and unregulated GHG emissions so as to move the oil that arrives each year. China is at once seeking to be the world's largest shipbuilder by 2015 and is building many new tankers.[41]

Roughly 80 per cent of this slow-moving oil passes through the South China Sea. As the tankers go east, so they meet vast container ships going west. The latter are laden with goods made in East Asia and destined for the rest of the world, following what might be called the Walmart model based upon novel supply change management.[42]

China would cease to be the cheap labour workshop of the world if oil arriving in these supertankers were to cease for even a few days. Globalization is now focused much more upon the South China Sea than on North Atlantic airspace. Globalization has returned 'home' to the 'east'. With shipping the centrally important means of movement, its smooth passage is absolutely vital.[43]

There are many ways in which this smooth passage of oil can be threatened, especially in the East Asian context (quite apart from diminishing global supplies). These include piracy, with hundreds of attacks a year; the payment of ransom money; the recruitment of criminal crews; poorly regulated ships flying flags of convenience; a total lack of unionization and worker protection; many oil leaks and ships likely to break up due to poor construction.

Thus the oil dregs are moved around the globe in conditions which are themselves at the bottom of the barrel in terms of transparency, safety, rights, decency and security. Shipping typically involves a race to the bottom in terms of regulations and rights, with sometimes the race coming to be literally to the bottom.

China's emissions

Until recently China's GHG emissions were of little significance to the country's policymakers, who strongly believed in the doctrine of economic catch-up – that nothing should interfere with it becoming a prosperous modern, mobile urban society. At the COP15 Summit in Copenhagen in 2009, China and the world's second biggest emitter, the USA, both refused to sign up to binding GHG emissions-reduction targets. Together they effectively prevented agreement on enforceable carbon reductions, which might have slowed the cumulative build-up of GHG emissions in the atmosphere. By 2030 it is estimated that the USA and China will together generate 45 per cent of global carbon emissions.[44]

However, China's hostility to reducing its GHG emissions is weakening. US journalist and academic Thomas Friedman writes how in various ways over the past decade 'Red China decided to become Green China'.[45] First, it is increasingly clear that China will directly suffer from the effects of global warming and other environmental damage. In 2010 China experienced extreme weather events as increased global temperatures worked their way into localized weather patterns.[46] If changed climates are permanent, then droughts, floods, tropical storms, falling water tables, and the melting of Himalayan glaciers will be common in China. These developments will engender further policy change. Securing future food and water supplies will turn out to be as important as economic growth. Much of China's limited water supply is already so polluted that it is unusable for most purposes; this is partly because the massive dams and hydroelectric schemes have mostly turned into large-scale environmental disasters.[47]

Already 18 per cent of Chinese land is desert, with the Chinese dust bowl in the north being the largest ever conversion of productive land into sand. This sand forms into violent dust storms that batter the capital Beijing and much of East Asia. Meanwhile, the Chinese population mostly lives in coastal or low-lying areas which are threatened by future flooding.[48] China will produce many 'climate change refugees' as well as suffer continued loss of income through pollution and ecological damage, calculated at between 7 and 20 per cent per annum.[49] There have been many protests about environmental damage in China related to issues of pollution, air quality and related corruption.[50]

Second, oil and gas supplies are increasingly constrained. Thus China would benefit from very significant reductions in the energy cost of its manufacturing and service industries. Unlike the rise of the USA in the early years of the previous century, China does not enjoy a monopoly of an abundant energy resource. Enabling even some proportion of its colossal rural population to escape from poverty entails both finding and saving exceptional amounts of energy. But China's effort to use supposedly renewable hydroelectric power has been mostly a disaster and has not provided the hoped-for green solution to the energy crisis.[51] It needs a robust alternative.

Third, there may be huge market opportunities in developing new green products and services. This century one country will almost certainly become *the* centre of low-carbon innovation. There is growing support in China for it to be that country. This is reflected in the latest Five Year Plan. It would enable China to move away from its current role as the world's low-cost manufacturer. This would also be consistent with the rising rankings of Chinese universities and their development of low-carbon innovation centres. Particularly in solar, windpower, battery technology, high-speed rail and electric cycles, China is a developing world centre.

Through its massive market China can obtain substantial economies of scale in developing and producing products such as high-speed trains, which are often publicized as icons of the low-carbon future.[52] However, one of China's high-speed trains suffered a major crash in Wenzhou in Zhejiang Province in July 2011; several carriages derailed and Chinese media confirmed forty deaths. This accident and the lack of accountability of the railway officials caused a public uproar and heightened concerns regarding the safety of China's high-speed rail system. These concerns will have a serious impact on China's ambition to export high-speed train technology to other countries. It has also led to a reduction in the speed of its trains and in the system's scale of development, which until then had been staggering. It was thought that by 2012 there would be as many miles of high-speed trains in China as in the rest of the world, even though the first high-speed Chinese train only started running in 2007.[53] There is also evidence that high-speed trains have, on account of their huge building and usage patterns, much higher GHG emissions than conventional trains.[54]

Conclusion

Future Chinese development will see much low-carbon innovation and development combined with high levels of energy exploitation and use. It is estimated that China's energy consumption could increase 6.6 times by 2050 (and India's 4.3 times). By 2050 84 per cent of world energy would be appropriated by China and India combined. But it is surely inconceivable that the rest of the world would share the remaining 16 per cent, although by then the world will be very much less 'Western' than now.[55] So who gets the world's energy is absolutely crucial. Oil supplies also very much affect which countries appropriate what are likely to be declining global food supplies.

Although climate change, decreasing exports and dwindling food resources will affect China's ability to grow, the availability and affordability of oil will impact first. Global oil supplies are likely to start running short. Although China may be in better shape to weather the initial stages of a price spike than the average American consumer, it is impossible for China to continue to grow its economy at 10 per cent per annum without large increases in the supply of oil. China's progress in becoming the world's dominant economy and society will involve huge resource contests with existing and newly rising powers. Unlike the USA in the first part of the last century, China is confronted in the early years of this century with multiple problems: increasingly widespread effects of GHG emissions upon agriculture and livelihoods; falling supplies of oil both at home and worldwide; and rising competition for remaining energy supplies. There will be no smooth path to a Chinese century and it may be that these circumstances will make China a dominant force in a multipolar world for only a brief period before some other global future begins to unfold.

Eighteenth-century India and China were the two largest economies at the time, accounting for one-third of the world economy. It could be that the domination by the West since then until the early twenty-first century was a kind of aberration, uniquely made possible by the extravagant exploitation of non-renewable fossil fuels. In particular there was an 'oil civilization' during the last century. We can anticipate that in some way the twenty-first century will re-establish the ordering of the world, in which Western powers are not central and no longer able to monopolize energy resources and especially oil. China is pursuing oil in many different countries, so generating massive resource competition. And as China comes to 'rule the world' in the decades to come, it is hard to imagine that it will share out the oil dregs in some equitable fashion. Following the examples of Britain and the USA, it will seek to appropriate a share sufficient to keep growing a modern mobile China, as its population and economy power upwards, accounting for maybe a fifth of the world's supply of people and goods. That will require much oil. Andy Stern maintains that the 'second half of the Oil Age will be even bloodier and more violent than the first', and that is saying something indeed.[56]

CHAPTER 7

THE CURSE OF OIL

There will be blood

It seems that oil is a blessing and a curse. This substance is both magical and the stuff of nightmares. The prophetic title of the 2007 oil movie is *There Will Be Blood*.[1] And blood there has been in plenty, with murders, spillages, hostages and pipeline explosions in the Niger Delta; rig explosions, deaths and vast oil leaks in the Gulf of Mexico; tanker fires and huge leaks off Alaska; pipeline explosions and deaths in Mexico resulting from drug-related thieving; vast high-tech oil wars across the Middle East and North Africa; and explosions on drilling rigs in the North Sea with deaths and injuries.

This chapter considers a few of these places blessed *and* cursed with oil. They generate some astonishing visions of a new world order, with shimmering palaces in the desert, as well as visions of hell on earth, as environments, peoples and lives are ravaged and destroyed. Ivan Illich, the radical 1960s' critic, once said that 'only a ceiling on energy use can lead to social relations that are characterized by high levels of equity'.[2] And oil normally provides no such ceiling, no equity.

We have seen how oil is concentrated within a relatively small number of places around the world. Where it is found it is like gold and promises so much, glistening as it spews from land or sea. And for some those promises are realized. There is unbelievable wealth. Oil is better in many ways than gold itself. It is so astonishingly valuable given how the modern world is built around its availability and uses. Oil (along with gas) is highly concentrated; lives and environments are changed forever by its discovery and exploitation. Being so concentrated, oil makes income and wealth intensely unequal.

This pattern interestingly contrasts with coal. As a resource base of very many societies coal is widely distributed and generally requires large numbers of workers to mine it. Sometimes those workers are organized into trade unions to ensure protection of their rights and bring about some redistribution of income. Mining for coal also generates solidarity between workers and their families. They often see themselves as part of what sociologists call an 'occupational community', as described in the classic study of a former Yorkshire mining community *Coal is Our Life*.[3] This leads to mass demands for democracy; for a coal-based 'carbon democracy' according to Timothy Mitchell.[4]

Oil-producing societies and sites are not like this, with little chance of solidarity developing between oil workers, some of whom may well be 'foreigners'. Oil generates a quite different politics and one often pursued, such as by Margaret Thatcher in Britain in the 1980s, to undermine the organizing power of coal miners and their unions. Coal miners provided much industrial leadership in the nineteenth and first half of the twentieth century.

Mitchell describes it as a 'machine for democracy'.[5] But oil was to undermine that machine.

Places of oil production are centres of affluence, generating huge flows of income and wealth within and between societies. It is thought that $7 trillion in profits have been transferred from oil-consuming to oil-producing societies over the past thirty years. In 2008, OPEC's oil revenues exceeded $1.25 trillion in that one year.[6] These exceptional flows of income and wealth transform domestic and foreign-policy relations and produce new and distorted alliances and connections. Until oil is actually extracted there are huge costs and no income. The oil companies seek to ensure a favourable image so that they can keep exploring for oil. There is the most immense gap between failure and success. The oil industry has the characteristics of gold prospecting and then of a gold rush, or of 'blood diamonds' and their role in engendering African warlordism. Most oil drilling is a failure since no oil spurts to the surface.

Within these societies oil mostly generates inequalities, autocratic government, militarization, corruption, instability and intermittent protest and resistance. The higher the price of oil the more likely it is that the society will be autocratically governed and the local population suffer many deprivations, including oil itself. Accidents, oil spills, explosions, deaths, corruption and a lack of regulation are commonplace. Sometimes these conditions go on to generate terrorism and war. Low-carbon innovators Amory Lovins and colleagues point out how 'Countries often become unstable once they discover oil.'[7] Overall an exceptional infusion of oil wealth undermines many existing social institutions within a country. If a society is not already democratic with a diverse and pluralistic set of institutions, then the exploitation of oil will often damage any movement towards 'democratization'. Oil and democracy are not great bedfellows, we might say. There exists what Terry Lynn Karl terms the 'paradox of plenty'.[8]

Oil is thus no simple solution to a society's problems but generates many troubles. It is a curse, but one which few if any societies or corporations or states can resist. In this chapter I first detail some consequences of oil exploration in places without much democratic and institutional support. Second, I briefly contrast the experiences of these societies with that of Norway, a country which developed a 'social democratic' treatment of its North Sea oil. In conclusion, it is shown why the discovery of oil has such varied consequences within different societies. Is it possible to institute democratic control of oil or is it always going to generate exceptional inequality, injustice and inhumanity? Can oil energize societies in ways more equal, just and humane? Subsequent chapters examine how societies might be organized in the future when oil no longer functions as such a significant energizer.

Oil and 'troubled waters'

Extracting oil is particularly troublesome if found within a 'newly created society' without well-established democratic and institutional supports. Part of oil's curse is that it is often expropriated in societies where democratic practices and processes are limited or non-existent. This is most obvious in the Middle East, which accounts for 55 per cent of proven oil reserves and 30 per cent of production.[9] Not one of the societies is yet a parliamentary democracy and only Iran regularly conducts elections where power changes hands.

Moreover, many of the borders of these Middle Eastern countries are relatively arbitrary twentieth-century 'constructs' resulting from European colonial rule and its aftermath. The extraction of oil occurred relatively recently and almost always well after the companies had discovered likely oilfields. The extraction of oil was often slowed down by the companies and colonial powers, which acted together so as to sustain the world price of oil.[10]

Oil did, though, in the end transform what were overwhelmingly poor countries in the desert into centres of immense wealth and privilege, glinting away in the unrelenting sun. Saudi Arabia had been one of the very poorest of countries, even into the 1950s, largely illiterate, preindustrial, puritanical, and with a population of less than a quarter of its current size. Thanks in part to British and American funding and weapons this was to change dramatically.

The Saudi monarch was once known for piety and thriftiness, with Ibn Saud living in a modest palace made of mud bricks. But after his death in 1953 his many heirs became notorious for ostentatious wealth, generated both from direct payments funded by oil revenues and through corruption and bribery. The oil royalty in Saudi Arabia is paid direct to a single household, the descendants of Ibn Saud, from whom the country astonishingly got its name. Maass writes how the term '"Saudi prince" became a synonym for fantastic riches'.[11] And there are many princes and princesses dipping their hands into the oil wealth, as well as into other monies generated from related infrastructural projects. There is enormous inequality and deep resentment.[12]

Oil extraction requires relatively little labour. The owners of land, as peasants, do not usually control the oil that lies beneath. There is normally no democratic or union power to effect redistribution of income or ensure effective welfare, as was the case with coal-based societies. Mostly these authoritarian states can extract vast amounts of money from selling oil without taxing the population. A brutal security apparatus generally keeps the population in line.[13]

Nevertheless, there have been protests in Saudi Arabia against the House of Saud. These have targeted its westernization, its petro-decadence, and its connections with various 'infidels' such as American troops. To show they were real Muslims the House of Saud supported fundamentalist movements across the Middle East, including al-Qaeda in its early years. Osama bin Laden was one of fifty-four children of Mohammed bin Laden, said to be the wealthiest non-royal in Saudi Arabia during the 1960s. The bin Laden group employs around 36,000 people. Osama bin Laden himself was outraged by the corruption of Islamic values brought about by oil and he vehemently opposed the 'infidel' American military with bases located within Saudi Arabia.[14]

Saudi oil money initially funded bin Laden in his struggle to rid Afghanistan of Soviet troops. But such money also provided the wealth, excess and connections to US power that bin Laden wholly opposed. This in the end apparently resulted in the 11 September bombings of the Twin Towers and the Pentagon in the USA. Without the curse of oil within Saudi Arabia, there would probably have been no consumption and military excesses on the part of the Saudi royal family, no al-Qaeda orchestrating bombings over two decades, no 9/11 and probably no 'war on terror'. This is a huge catalogue of disasters to be laid in part at the door of oil.

Women are particularly discriminated against within these oil societies, this being clearest in Saudi Arabia. Here women are banned from many activities and forced to work within proscribed places. Women are treated as legal minors, with male guardians determining whether they work, study, marry, travel or undergo certain medical procedures. The Saudi government has not fulfilled its 2009 pledge to the UN Human Rights Council to dismantle this system of 'male guardianship'.[15]

Women are even banned from driving cars and hence using that Saudi oil. In 1990 forty-seven women defiantly drove around Riyadh. They were characterized as 'immoral', with male members of their families being denigrated for not controlling 'their' women. In 2011 Saudi activists campaigned for months through social networking sites, developing the 'Women2Drive' initiative. Driving is treated as a moral crime, although curiously women are able to fly planes – but female pilots cannot drive to the airport. The 17 June campaign, as a manifestation of the Arab Spring, led many women to take to the roads and defiantly drive through Saudi cities.[16] These women saw overcoming the driving ban as part of a broader campaign for women's rights within Saudi Arabia.

This is one element of broader political campaigning that draws upon huge levels of dissatisfaction in Saudi Arabia, where 30 per cent of Saudi men are jobless. Most of the better jobs and many others are held by foreigners, with two-thirds of all Saudi jobs.[17] Even the world's largest oil company Saudi Aramco only employs 50,000 workers and that includes many 'foreigners'.

So the oil wealth does not percolate down to the population and especially not to the 75 per cent of the Saudi population under thirty (total population is around 25 million). Ironically, the most frequent cause of death of this young population is road fatalities caused by very dangerous driving. As throughout much of the

Middle East, death and injury rates on the roads are extremely high.[18] Oil kills in this way as well.

To combat the bad publicity, various oil museums celebrate the initial discovery of oil, the technical achievements of local engineering and the benign role that oil plays in 'modernizing' Saudi society. The Aramco Exhibit, near Saudi Aramco's Dhahran headquarters, is one such high-tech museum that tells the story of the Saudi petroleum industry.[19] And yet it is said to be more or less empty of visitors. Some Saudi citizens regard oil as a terrible curse. As one of Peter Maass's informants states, 'I do not believe that in this region there is a nation that received all this wealth and squandered and looted it the way it has been in Saudi Arabia'.[20] This is probably accurate, although a fair number of other countries in the Middle East and worldwide have also squandered and looted oil, burning it up in an orgy of emissions and excess.

Various societies have sought to emulate Middle Eastern countries by also becoming energy giants. The most striking recent example is the Russian Federation. Oil was discovered in Siberia in the 1950s – some was used by the USSR, some was given to various allies including Cuba, and some was sold on the open market. Around 80 per cent of the USSR's hard currency came from these energy sales. Analysts consider that this oil kept the Soviet Union going as long as it did; without it the Soviet Union would have imploded earlier.

Significantly lower oil prices were engineered in the 1980s through an agreement between US President Reagan and Saudi King Fahd so as to sustain a high level of oil supplies. This reduction in oil prices undermined the Soviet economy, which lost around $20 billion over this decade.[21]

After the collapse of the Soviet Union in the early 1990s, Russia turned into a country of shrinking incomes and reduced life expectancy, as well as escalating crime and corruption. Much Russian industry was privatized during Yeltsin's presidency but often with state assets underpriced, as oil was at the time relatively cheap. But this began to change as rising oil (and gas) prices developed after 2000. Russian oil production increased year on year and by 2010 Russia was producing 12.9 per cent of the world's oil. With Saudi production flatlining since 2003, Russia became the world's largest oil producer by 2010.[22] Three of the world's fifteen largest oil and gas companies are Russian, and now almost household names, namely Gazprom, Rosneft and Lukoil.

Russia thus became an energy superpower, with rising incomes and wealth, especially for the new oil (and gas) super-rich. Peter Maass describes the effects of 'hundreds of billions of dollars in oil revenues flowing into the wallets of an elite that had already run out of sensible ways to spend its wealth. America's gilded age had nothing on this' (nor in a way on recent Middle Eastern equivalents).[23]

Roman Abramovich symbolizes this new Russian age. In 1995, in the frenzy of post-Soviet privatization, he bought a half-share in Sibneft for $100 million, and ten years later sold most of it to Gazprom for seventy-five times as much. Abramovich has admitted making various bribes for political favours and has also been accused of theft. With a fortune estimated at one time of over $13 billion, Abramovich is the world's 53rd richest person. With a personal bodyguard of forty, he owns Chelsea Football Club, a London house worth £150 million, the world's largest privately owned yacht (in 2009), a Boeing 767, three helicopters and many bullet-proof cars.[24]

The privatization of energy resources during the Yeltsin regime has been reversed over the past decade. Much of the oil and gas industry is now state-owned and central to Putin's national state policy. The attempt by opposition leader Mikhail Khodorkovsky to sell the Yukos Oil Company to Exxon was unsuccessful and he faces long-term imprisonment on what many assert is a set of invented charges.[25] Yukos assets are now owned by the state. And when Putin passed on the office of president of the Russian Federation, his successor was Dmitry Medvedev, the former board chairman of Gazprom, the state-owned oil and gas company. Peter Maass refers to the immensely powerful 'merging of oil power and state power' within contemporary Russia, somewhat similar to Saudi Arabia.

Finally, there is the Niger Delta, what some describe as *the* contemporary hell on earth. This area in Nigeria is a major source of oil for the USA and Europe. It has been termed the 'next Gulf'.[26] Nigeria was established as a country by the British in 1914 and only British companies (especially Shell) were allowed to prospect there for oil. Significant reserves of oil were first discovered in 1956. This oil was used to fuel the cars newly travelling along Britain's motorways and the first transatlantic flights from London to New York. These both commenced in 1958, in the same year that the basic licence for oil exploration was signed by Shell, which pays $2 a barrel regardless of the world oil price.

Although Nigeria became independent in 1963 Shell never lost this key position within the country. Half of Nigeria's oil is produced by Shell from around a thousand oil wells. Rowell, Marriott and Stockman show how 'Nigeria has helped fuel Shell's global empire, run predominantly from the Shell Centre in London. During the decades, as military dictators came and went, Shell stayed put in Nigeria ... In this country of change, Shell stayed solid as a rock ... Shell and the Nigerian government became intertwined.'[27]

Nigeria is the world's twelfth largest producer of petroleum, accounting for 40 per cent of Nigeria's GDP. Initially it seemed that Nigeria would develop a sustainable oil-led industrialization. It even has good oil, light and sweet, and it is located not so far from what have been its major markets of North America and western Europe. Nigerian oil reserves are now larger than those of the USA and Mexico combined. It was possible that Nigeria could avoid the 'paradox of plenty', but it did not.[28]

The central city of the Delta is Port Harcourt, which one might expect would gleam with ostentatious wealth, like Qatar or Dubai. But instead Port Harcourt rots and looks more like a large poor shanty town. Wherever the oil money goes, it does not provide ostentatious city development in Nigeria, let alone decent incomes for the people.

In the Niger Delta oil fouls almost everything, with Shell apparently adopting lower standards than would be acceptable in Europe or North America.[29] Oil spills from pipelines; it poisons soil and water; it stains people's hands through extensive corruption of politicians, generals and Western companies; it corrupts young people, who fire guns, steal oil from pipelines (called 'bunkering') and take foreigners hostage; the air is contaminated by gas flaring; and it fosters a deficit of democracy. Beyond Port Harcourt lies the labyrinth of creeks, rivers and pipelines that stretch across the Delta. This is one of the world's largest wetlands, with high levels of biodiversity. It used to be the bread basket of Nigeria. But decades of oil spills, acid rain from gas flares, and the stripping away of mangroves for pipelines have killed off both land and fish. Nigeria has gone from being self-sufficient in food to importing much more than it produces. Oil killed off agriculture as many Nigerians flocked to the cities.[30]

For all the oil wealth in the Delta there is little electricity, no clean water, limited medicine, few schools and even little petrol for the population of 12–27 million who live in the Delta (estimates vary). In terms of its 'human development index' ranking, Nigeria rates below all other major oil nations from Libya to Indonesia. It lies 142nd out of the 169 countries with comparable data.[31] Nigeria's annual per capita income is less than that of Senegal, which mainly exports fish and nuts. The World Bank categorizes Nigeria as a fragile state, beset by high risk of armed conflict, epidemic disease and poor governance. Many college graduates are unemployed, corruption is widespread, there are many private warlords, and the Niger Delta is one of the poorest areas in the world. It has certainly not avoided the paradox of plenty.

There has been much resistance to the role of Shell and the Nigerian government.[32] In 1967 the area known as Biafra, which contains much of the Niger Delta, declared that it was seceding from Nigeria. The Nigerian government declared war on Biafra so as to prevent the secession of this oil-rich area. Some of Shell's installations came under fire from the Biafrans and Shell did its best to support the Nigerian government's reaction but without appearing to do so. A staggering 1 million people died in the Biafran War and related famine. In 1970 Biafra was reintegrated back into Nigeria and Shell re-expanded its oil activities.

At the height of the Biafran War, Ken Saro-Wiwa wrote his first pamphlet seeking to rally the Ogoni people against Shell and its oil operations. For the next couple of decades Saro-Wiwa and others orchestrated opposition to Shell and the effects of the oil industry on the land and peoples of the Ogoni tribe that live in part of the Niger Delta.

However, it transpired that there were extensive links between Shell and the Nigerian military and probable complicity in bringing about the deaths of various environmental campaigners. In 1995 Ken Saro-Wiwa and eight other Ogoni non-violent activists were executed by the Nigerian authorities. Shell did not prevent these executions, vehemently defending its actions despite worldwide condemnation. Shell paid a large sum to the Saro-Wiwa family to settle a lawsuit without admitting any liability. There are enduring protests against Shell and the Nigerian state involving many NGO activists and grassroots organizations, as well as continuing 'petro-violence' involving gangland fights orchestrated by various warlords.[33]

Helon Habila's recent novel *Oil on Water* evokes the death, despair and degradation of life, where everything is reduced to or covered in or contaminated literally or metaphorically by oil.[34] Isaac Asume Osuoka, director of Social Action, Nigeria, believes that the treatment of the people of the Delta stems from their economic irrelevance both to the state and to the oil corporations, both of which have blood on their hands. He bleakly asserts: 'With all the oil money coming in, the state doesn't need taxes from people. Rather than being a resource for the state, the people are impediments ... Nigeria was a much better place without oil.'[35]

Oil from Nigeria and other parts of Africa is now central to the emerging world economy, with more oil now imported by the USA from Africa than from the Middle East. And yet maybe one-third of these huge oil revenues disappear offshore, and did so even in the 1990s.[36] The slowing of growth, the decline of agriculture, the corruption of politics, astonishing inequalities and environmental destruction are all, according to Shaxson, the consequence of how oil 'spreads poison' in a globalizing world.[37]

Norway

By extreme contrast with the societies just examined, Norway has the world's highest human development index ranking (HDI). Between 1980 and 2010 Norway's HDI rose annually from 0.788 to 0.938, giving it the top rank out of 169 countries with comparable data.[38] Saudi Arabia is 55th, Russia 65th and Nigeria 142nd in these HDI rankings.

And yet Norway is a major oil-based economy. On a per capita basis, it is the world's largest producer of oil and gas outside of the Middle East. Oil and gas account for around a quarter of Norway's GDP. Export revenues from oil and gas are 45 per cent of total exports and more than 20 per cent of Norway's GDP. Norway is the ninth largest oil exporter and second largest gas exporter in the world, although oil production beyond its peak has declined by around one-third over the past decade.[39] Almost all of Norway's electricity is generated by hydroelectric power. Norway successfully maintains a social democratic welfare model with universal health care, subsidized higher education and comprehensive social security. *Foreign Policy Magazine* ranks Norway second to last in its listing of 'Failed States Index' for 2011, judging it to be more or less the world's best functioning and stable country.[40] It is tenth best for its perceived lack of corruption.[41] It ranks as the second wealthiest country in the world in terms of monetary value.

Norway is the clearest illustration of how oil and democracy can be effectively combined. This seems to be because it possesses a 'deep democracy' with institutionalized patterns of non-violence resulting from being one of the most equal societies in the world in terms of class and gender divisions.[42] It has somehow been able to sediment non-violence.[43]

It is reasonable to anticipate that Norway will remain among the richest countries in the world, even though its direct income from oil and gas is falling. The government controls its oil and gas resources through state ownership of the major operators (approximately 62 per cent ownership in Statoil in 2007) and the fully state-owned Petoro. The Norwegian government also controls the licensing of exploration and production of the gas and oilfields.

Central to its 'social democratic' treatment of oil is the sovereign wealth fund established in 1995, based on taxes, dividends, sales revenues and licensing fees from oil. This fund was designed to reduce overheating in the economy, to minimize uncertainty from volatile oil prices, to provide a cushion for the ageing population, and to deal with the inevitable decline in North Sea oil and gas revenues. The fund invests in financial markets outside Norway, spending no more than 4 per cent of the fund each year. By 2010, the fund was the largest in Europe, with assets of around $556 billion.

Projections indicate that this Norwegian fund may become the largest single capital fund worldwide. Currently the fund is second only to the Abu Dhabi Investment Authority, while the third is SAMA, based in Saudi Arabia.[44] The investment choices of this Norwegian fund are directed by ethical guidelines. This transparent investment scheme is lauded by some parts of the international community. Other natural resource-based economies, such as Russia, are learning from the Norwegian model and establishing similar funds.

Norway also runs a 9 per cent state budget surplus, being the only Western country to run a surplus as of 2009. Norway is among the countries least affected by the international economic crash from 2007/8 onwards. Neighbouring Sweden is experiencing substantially higher unemployment. In 2009 the GNP of Norway surpassed Sweden's for the first time in history, despite a population only about half that of Sweden. It remains a nation of stowed-away wealth, financial stability, economic power and social equality among Norwegians (but this is not extended to all in-migrants). Norway is also an innovator in green shipping, with one concept ship being powered by wave, wind and solar energy.[45]

Norway is also an interesting model in relation to developments in Scotland, which is moving in a more independent direction. Scottish nationalists believe that 'Scottish' oil and gas has been unfairly appropriated by the rest of the UK since much lies on what is termed the Scottish continental shelf. The more 'statist' Scotland is also developing an impressive array of expertise in tide, wind and wave technologies whereby it will be able to sell renewable electricity to the rest of Europe. Energy is central to an increasingly influential Scottish nationalism that might lead to the break-up of the current UK, in part learning from the Norwegian model.

Democracy and oil

One of the founders of OPEC, Pablo Pérez Alfonso, speaks of oil as a curse, bringing waste, corruption and excessive consumption. With the exception of Norway, Denmark and maybe Canada, power corrupts, and oil power can corrupt absolutely.[46] Peter Maass notes how 'most of the world's oil and gas resides in countries with bribery-prone systems.[47] Or, as former US vice president Dick Cheney inimitably comments: 'The problem is that the good Lord didn't see fit to put oil and gas reserves where there are democratic governments.[48]

Such corrupt and/or authoritarian systems develop for three main reasons. First, oil (and gas) reserves are highly concentrated. Lives and environments are changed forever by the discovery of oil (and gas). Being so concentrated, oil normally makes income and wealth unequal, with gains from oil being astronomic. This untold wealth gives rise to extensive transport infrastructures, services and more general consumerism, but rarely to a robust manufacturing sector or opportunities for productive work for most of the population.[49]

Second, most oil and gas installations are located away from where workers live, often in some exceptionally inhospitable locations. And there are anyway relatively few workers employed on most such sites. A lack of worker solidarity characterizes oil and gas operations, and often much of the workforce is from abroad, with workers' homes many hundreds of miles away. Workers are often flown to installations by helicopter. We have already noted the contrast with the organization of coal mining, with the close proximity of very many miners, their families and trade-union organization.[50]

Third, oil is not produced but extracted. It was 'produced' hundreds of centuries ago. Hence the licence which permits such oil extraction is crucial, and this enables exceptional rents to be earned by its owner. This licence normally involves a complex relationship between the oil company and the owner of the land under which oil reserves appear to be located. Such permission from the host government to allow drilling is crucial, making or breaking companies as huge rents can be earned. This provides much temptation for corrupt relationships to develop between landowners, the oil companies and the state over the granting of these extraction licences.[51] Indeed it would be surprising if relationships in oil and gas were not in part based upon bribery and corruption.

Oil and democracy do not fit comfortably together, although exceptionally there can be a social democratic treatment, as in Norway. Political scientist Michael Ross shows how oil wealth inhibits democracy developing within states that are broadly authoritarian. Oil's anti-democratic effects seem to have grown stronger, except possibly in Latin America. The existence of oil rents is part of what generates various kinds of oil wars. These are referred to by Kaldor, Karl and Said as 'rentier wars'.[52] They involve struggles for control over the exceptional gains once oil begins to flow, involving not only states but also many private groups, which may dismantle the state as they each gain some share of vast oil rents. The 'rentier effect' would seem to explain the links between oil and autocracy. Oil-rich states are able to combine low taxes and high government spending funded out of oil revenues. Such a pattern dampens support for democratic transitions because autocratic governments can devote high government expenditure to buying off the resistance and rebellion of local populations, to their own consumption, to excessive infrastructural projects, and to military and security expenditures. The rulers of 'petro-states' rarely have to justify patterns of expenditure because most income derives not from taxing the population but from owning rights to exploit the oil and hence to earn these 'rents'.[53] Their wealth arrived with the blessing of oil and it can be used to offset some of its curse.

Oil revenues, then, are rather like the ring in Tolkien's *The Lord of the Rings*, a blessing and a curse. Oil first produces dependency, then begins to run out. The ring is being rapidly thrown away. What happens as the ring (of oil) disappears? If the ring of oil does run out, will a local democracy (the Hobbits?) win out, or will new more deadly empires take over instead? How can a peaceful, fair and just powering down be achieved as the ring of oil is set to be thrown away?

PART II

SOCIAL FUTURES

CHAPTER 8

MAGIC BULLET FUTURE

Energy and its futures

Part 1 showed what a big problem energy is. Not only are exist-ing energy resources changing climates but over the next few decades there will not be enough energy of the right sort in the right places at the right price. Supplies will be inadequate to continue to 'energize' worldwide systems of global production and consumption and hence people's lives more generally.

Contemporary societies have come to depend upon energy resources, many of which are limited in scale and are becoming scarcer per person and in absolute terms. The twentieth century was utterly dependent upon the energy resource of oil for rapidly moving objects and people. David Strahan points out that 'the last oil shock is not principally about power generation – replac-ing coal-fired power stations with windmills and so on – but overwhelmingly about transport fuels; oil supplies 95 per cent of all transport energy.'[1]

Given this huge constraint there are a limited number of possible futures for societies looking forward over the next three to four decades. No future is without its downside. In Part II I assess each future and its likelihood of significant societal development.[2]

The first such future considered in this chapter is that a viable, global magic bullet is discovered which offsets the problem of massive oil depletion. Some new 'high-tech system' (hydrogen, solar, windpower or geo-engineering) substitutes for the energy descent of oil and other fossil fuels, without worsening GHG emissions. Fast travel and high-carbon lives continue with the forms, scale and intensity of contemporary globalization further enhanced. Twentieth-century patterns of economy and of 'mobile' social lives spread worldwide.

The second future, as examined in Chapter 9, is also a 'high-tech' future. Here the widespread development in digital worlds substitutes for much physical travel. Co-present conversations are seen as a 'luxury' since they presuppose high energy. Production systems also change through three-dimensional 'printing'. Digital travel significantly replaces the physical transport of people and things. This future is part of a broader shift, with 'digital capital' becoming the dominant fraction of capital.

The third future is a continuing shift from easy oil to a new century of tough oil. Oil dregs require increasingly more resources to extract oil and offset global temperature rises. Such energy resources are fought over by countries and corporations. Resource wars, violence and economic crises are commonplace. Especially significant are the two forces of the USA and China 'fighting' over diminishing oil resources and the related supplies of food and water. Various oil, food and water shortages forcefully 'localize' much economic production and people's social lives. This 'warlord' future is considered in Chapter 10.

The fourth future, explored in Chapter 11, is that there is an organized and planned powering down to low-carbon lives. In this future, societies are planned to cope with reduced energy and yet they sustain some of the pleasures of contemporary wealthy societies. Societies are as 'happy', with long life expectancy, but not as rich. There is a global transition to lower oil and other energy production and consumption systems. States, NGOs and corporations all engineer low-carbon systems resting upon dramatically less energy.

Magic bullet of hydrogen

This future involves the discovery of a magic bullet solution to the problem of energy.[3] A new high-tech system substitutes for the descent of oil and other fossil fuels while not increasing future GHG emissions. Fast travel and high-carbon lives continue, with the forms, scale and intensity of contemporary globalization further enhanced. Twentieth-century patterns of economy and of 'mobile' social lives spread throughout China, India and most of the world. Doomsday futures turn out to be wrong and the problems of energy supply and climate change can, it turns out, be fixed.

This future occurs because a new energy system is innovated and implemented around the world. This enables the multiple mobilities of peoples and objects to be further extended. Movement is even more part of each people's 'persona'. Status is acquired through one's travel and consumption patterns and those of one's children and friends. The average citizen travels for up to four to five hours a day, with regular trips, at least for the middle classes, into inner space, perhaps via Virgin Galactic spaceships.[4] Astonishing new consumer goods and experiences are even more widely available. Such a new energy system and set of economic enterprises enable the mobilities of peoples and objects to become extensive and frequent. This magic bullet would be similar in global scale to the first oil gusher emerging so spectacularly at Spindletop in 1901 and organizing the last century.

What could this high-tech magic bullet be? The only possible candidate here is hydrogen. A decade ago it looked as though hydrogen power would indeed be a magic bullet energy socio-technical system that could come to replace the fossil fuels of oil, gas and coal. Hydrogen makes up 75 per cent of the universe and in theory could provide a virtually unlimited source of energy. It is ubiquitous on earth. Energy expert Jeremy Rifkin described the main features of *The Hydrogen Economy* as an 'energy elixir' producing zero emissions.

Various sustained research programmes in the 1990s began to explore how hydrogen could provide this alternative energy system. In 2001 Shell announced that it was preparing for the end of the hydrocarbon era by developing a new system based upon hydrogen. It was planning a billion-dollar investment in this new energy source.[5] Companies developed large hydrogen research teams (e.g. General Motors) and certain national and municipal governments set about becoming in part hydrogen-based (Chicago, Hawaii). In 1999 Iceland announced to an astonished world that it was to become the first 'hydrogen society'. By 2003 it had established a hydrogen filling station and was running three municipal buses using hydrogen fuel cells.

However, by 2012 there had been little further development of the hydrogen society in Iceland or elsewhere. There is no longer an expectation that a whole new energy system is about to develop on a global scale.[6] One obvious problem with hydrogen is that it has to be produced. It is not a free-floating resource as fossil fuels are – although many of these require huge resources to produce them, as we have seen in the case of tough oil. Hydrogen is an energy carrier that, like electricity, has to be produced, stored and distributed. At least half the hydrogen so far produced has required natural gas – that is, a fossil fuel – for its production. There are non-carbon forms of hydrogen production, but so far these are many times more expensive and rarely used.

The hydrogen fuel cell that would be used in, say, a globally significant car system is basically a box that takes in hydrogen and oxygen and produces electricity and water. Fuel cells convert energy from a chemical reaction and produce electricity, in a similar way to batteries, and promise a clean car future and near-zero road emissions. Unlike batteries, fuel cells are never recharged and produce energy for as long as the fuel is provided.

These cells convert hydrogen into electricity once many production, storage and distribution problems are solved. But this is where the problems arise. The type of fuel cell suited for transport is known as a proton exchange membrane fuel cell, requiring very pure hydrogen. Current models, however, supply the hydrogen from converted natural gas or oil with an energy efficiency of around 35–40 per cent. This is an efficiency level similar to that of the internal combustion engine.

To overcome this, hydrogen need not be converted in the fuel cell but can be delivered, or 'pumped', directly at filling stations. This, though, requires a whole new production and distribution infrastructure around the globe. Also hydrogen is a low-density and volatile fuel which could not use the existing pipeline infrastructure. It is highly corrosive and makes pipelines brittle. Thus a new infrastructure system would have to be established using suitable materials. The pipelines would also need to allow for a high level of leakage and for hydrogen's tendency to evaporate. Another way to transport hydrogen would be in tankers carrying it in liquefied form; however, because such liquefaction of hydrogen occurs at the astonishingly cold temperature of −253c, refrigerating the gas to achieve this extreme cold would be an 'economic nightmare'.[7] On top of this there would be increased haulage traffic.

A further problem with the onboard storage of hydrogen is that it must be stored in cylinders that are much larger than current petrol tanks. At room temperature hydrogen takes up more space than normal petrol fuel. The cylinders would contain a gas that is prone to leaking and they would need to withstand all imaginable high-impact crashes.[8] If it is to be used as a fuel that is stored onboard vehicles, pure hydrogen gas must be pressurized or liquefied so as to provide sufficient driving range.

For all these reasons various reports now estimate that renewable hydrogen will not be available for use in vehicles for at least thirty years, and even then it would be many decades before a whole new socio-technical system was in place around the world.[9] But, as energy writer Richard Heinberg notes, those on the planet need a solution now and not decades hence.[10] Joseph Romm thus concludes that waiting for the technological breakthrough of hydrogen is a distraction delaying action on reducing GHGs and replacing oil.[11] Few analysts now expect hydrogen to provide the magic bullet solution.

Technological fixes

So, all considered, a magic bullet future is unlikely; there is no more than a one in ten chance of it developing. This kind of future is technologically simplistic because it suggests that different technologies are made up of relatively simple elements. But in fact new socio-technical systems comprise many technical, social and organizational elements. A new 'technology' is not just a technology but involves elements that take a long time to be realized and to be assembled together. A new magic bullet technology involving a complex combining of pre-existing elements would take decades, according to complexity analyst Brian Arthur.[12] Also new technologies are often patented in one society, which makes it hard to globalize the innovation in question. David Edgerton describes the powerful forces of 'techno-nationalism' which prevent innovations moving easily across national borders.[13]

Indeed such a novel system would need to be well established and already developing on a significant scale so as to gain global traction within the next couple of decades. The Spindletop moment should have already occurred. Historically new clusters of socio-technical systems take decades to become widespread, as Frank Geels shows in previous 'transitions' in systems.[14] In order to develop a new system to impact within the next two decades this system must be developing now. The US National Intelligence Council summarizes the timescale involved here: 'An energy transition from one type of fuel (fossil fuels) to another (alternative) is an event that historically has only happened once a century at most with momentous consequences.'[15] But there is no such system currently waiting in the wings and ready to spring on stage.

This future scenario is also deterministic in suggesting that the new magic 'technology' will necessarily produce appropriate economic and social change in a low-carbon direction. It suggests that it is the 'technology' that determines outcomes rather than understanding how systems fit into and become part of new or reorganized kinds of economic and social practice. It is an example of what has been termed the 'economics of techno-scientific promise'. This in part involves developing a fiction so as to attract resources and almost, in a self-fulfilling way, engendering a future that then appears to be necessary and inevitable.[16]

This future is also optimistic because it presumes that such a system is developing now, will gain global traction and will not lead to increased use of the cheaper energy source of hydrogen through a rebound or Jevons effect.

Any new technology has to be embedded in society for successful development; this means that however innovative it may not gain sufficient traction and instead remain a 'niche'. The supersonic plane Concorde is an interesting case here. It was technologically very advanced but it did not take off as a widespread system of fast airborne travel. Indeed it was rapidly overtaken and eclipsed by the Boeing 747, partly because the economics stacked in favour of the Boeing, which facilitated mass and not elite air travel.

The history of socio-technical systems shows that the best system is not necessarily the most successful system. This is shown in how VHS rather than Sony's Betamax became the dominant system of video recording during the 1980s and 1990s, although few considered it the better system. So, thinking here of technological fixes will tend to lead to an over-optimism with regard to likely futures. And also it tends to presume unchanging 'demand', while what is striking about new socio-technical systems is that they in part engender wholly new needs and activities, as for example with the development of networked computers, wirelessness and mobile phones.

Conclusion

A magic bullet alternative to oil which could develop beyond the 'niche' phase of development thus seems unlikely at the present time. The only possible energy source that might provide such a solution is hydrogen, but progress in developing this is painfully slow, both technologically and organizationally. With regard to vehicle development, electric vehicles (EVs) are the only possible game in town, but these are not of course a new form of energy and so far depend upon fossil-fuel-generated electricity. EVs are a significant development, as discussed below, but they are not the once-in-a-lifetime new energy system that is at all comparable with the 'discoveries' of coal, gas, oil, electricity or even nuclear energy.

CHAPTER 9

DIGITAL LIVES

Digital worlds

This chapter assesses another high-tech future, this time involving the widespread substitution of the physical travel of people and objects by many forms of digital communication and experience. Such a high-tech digital future has been increasingly possible since around 1990. Before then two kinds of objects provided the background to people's everyday lives. First, there was the 'natural world' of rivers, hills, lakes, soil, storms, crops, snow, earth and so on. This physical world constituted the taken-for-granted background during almost all human history. Second, there was the background made up of the 'artificial' objects of the Industrial Revolution generated from the eighteenth century onwards. These objects include trains, pipes, steam, watches, lights, paper, radio, cars and so on. This background gradually spread around the world, especially during the twentieth century, as high-carbon systems became commonplace.

But from 1990 onwards a third background to life emerges.[1] This is the world of 'virtual' or 'digital' objects. These objects include screens, cables, computer mice, browsers, smartphones, satellites, ringtones, the Kindle, social media, sensors, software, networks, databases and so on. Many digital objects are now in the background of human experience and transform the very nature of what human life is like.

Some commentators claim that this digital background leads from hierarchical to more horizontal ways of organizing social life. It enables the (mostly) seamless jumps from link to link without regard to certain conventional borders of country, language, subject or discipline. The 'digital' is less directly tied to place. Information and communication are everywhere. Sociologist Manuel Castells summarizes how 'What is specific to our world is the extension and augmentation of the body and mind of human subjects in networks of interaction powered by micro-electronics-based, software-operated, communication technologies. These technologies are increasingly diffused throughout the entire realm of human activity by growing miniaturization' (and hence portability).[2] Central to such a background are flickering 'screens' that are carried close to or often now on the body, what elsewhere I term 'miniaturized mobilities'.[3]

Some physical backgrounds are themselves 'smart', so producing a convergence of the real and the digital. Such a smart background senses, adapts to and transforms people's lives more interactively, especially as people move around various environments. Many digital objects are only noticed when they break down, which they intermittently do. In the future they are likely to be in some way merged into a 'sixth sense' through gesture and projected data screened onto people's clothing and surroundings.[4]

These digital objects are developed by large private-sector corporations and small businesses. They depend upon software that makes it certain that actions are unexceptional. The digital background means that the product can be purchased, the meeting will happen, the hire car is ready, the components will arrive at the factory, the message will get through, the money will arrive, the friends can be met, that life can go on.

So could this complex of newish digital objects become life itself, become how most connections worldwide are established and realized? So while people talk of 'mobile lives', is it possible that 'digital lives' develop into life instead, so much so that there is very little need for travel, especially over long distances? And what would such life be like when much business, social and family life is not face to face at all. Could we be said to know others although we have never 'met' them, never shaken their hand or kissed them on the cheek? Or, rather, we have met them, but virtually and this seems to be as good as, or even merely the same as, meeting them face to face. In such a digital future there might be nothing special about 'physical meetings' as such.

In discussing this digital future, there is a danger of over-emphasizing the power and significance of the *new*. It is known that many visions of the future have not unfolded as technology optimists or technology pessimists predicted. There is a strong danger of technology-determinism. There are many 'failed tech-nology futures', and this is why it is necessary to imagine and assess a range of *alternative* scenarios. Few if any 'technologies' emerge and impact upon society in anything like the way tech-nology developers, corporations and policymakers imagine and predict.[5] Matters are much less 'planned' and more socially 'situated'.[6] Things are more contingent.

Sociologist of design Harvey Molotch brings out how material objects derive from diverse roots and routes. Developing new materials is not inevitable. How and why a whole system of production and consumption is established would seem to be a relatively contingent process and a matter of fashion, desire and place. Molotch concludes that 'production success comes from the cultural currents that make up social life in general and from all over the world.'[7]

So when we consider this future of digital lives we should not examine just how the digital world could directly substitute for physical travel. Rather, we need to analyse how the digital world changes the overall 'ecology' of machines and technologies that organize economic and social life. The 'new' technology does not simply replace the 'old'. David Edgerton talks of *The Shock of the Old* as much as of the new.[8] One example is the centrality of the 'old' technology of paper (originally invented in China) within many 'new' digital technologies. So when we imagine here a digital future world, it is not something that would only involve replacing physical movement technologies with the digital.

Rather, multiple digital communications change the ecology of machines and technologies, and within that ecology we should examine to what degree the digital dominates and engenders lives that can be sustained without the large amount of physical movement that previously seemed 'necessary'. Some physical movement of people remains, but may occupy a different place within the changed ecology of movement and communications in this possible future of predominantly digital lives. I turn to characterize this digital world in more depth.

Digitizing manufacturing

First, will digital worlds come to transform the very character of the physical world? Philosophers have typically regarded the physical world as made up of objects, such as tables or chairs. Such objects possess various properties which ensure the enduring object-ness of such things. Many such objects are 'made', but in order to be made materials have to be worked on by humans who directly turn, say, wood or more indirectly turn chemicals into a table or chairs. There is a co-present relationship between humans and the objects being manufactured deploying various designs. These designs are located within each person or in books and drawings or in computer software. The objects once 'made' are then transported elsewhere to be used for eating or sitting upon. Key here is what we might call 'co-present manufacturing', even if most of the using of the objects that are manufactured takes place well away from the site of their production. Indeed there are often large distances travelled by such objects once they are made.

Some possible transformations in manufacturing popularly termed '3D printing' are examined here. Since the development of digital printing technologies it has been common for printing to occur remotely. In fact the 'printer down the corridor' is a familiar feature of many office and factory environments. Now what can be 'printed' is changing. Various machines enable the printing of 3-dimensional shapes and not just 2-dimensional printed text or pictures. So, while we are familiar with printing at a distance, what can now be 'printed' are objects, and they can be printed or manufactured thousands of miles away from where the digital designs are located. The designs are transmitted virtually and then turned into objects through remote 3D 'printing'.

There are various technologies involved here, the main differences being in how the layers of the print are built up as they are laid one on top of the other as they are extruded from a cartridge.[9] As they are laid down, so a 3D object is produced. Each layer is in effect a digital slice generated through a given computer-aided design. After each layer is complete the build tray of the powder that is used in the printer is lowered by a fraction of a millimetre. The next layer is added until the object is fully printed or, we should say, 'manufactured', normally with the addition of a binding agent to the powder, which might be nylon, plastic, carbon, titanium or stainless steel. This process is technically known as 'additive' manufacturing, by contrast with most previous 'subtractive' manufacturing processes that involve cutting, drilling or bashing wood or metal or other materials. Such subtractive processes necessarily generate much 'waste'.

3D printing was initially developed during the 1980s and 1990s to produce prototypes of an object before tooling up a workshop or factory to produce thousands of more copies of the 'real' object. Manufacturing individual prototypes is very expensive, but 3D printing is much cheaper. But as 3D printing developed, so it was realized that a much wider range of shapes and materials could be produced in quantity, and not just the prototypes of real objects. Something like one-fifth of additive manufacturing is now of final products rather than of prototypes, and this figure is rapidly increasing.[10]

The objects now 'printed' in this additive manner include medical implants, car parts, jewellery, football boots designed for individual feet, furniture, lampshades, batteries, parts for aircraft, stainless steel gloves, dental crowns, customized mobile phones, and soon even artificial blood vessels.[11] Researchers are envisaging 'printing' the entire wings of an aircraft, an electric vehicle or even whole buildings, as there is a planned scaling up of such printers. At a recent trade fair in Frankfurt three hundred or so 3D printing companies showed off 'printed' objects, many of which simulated very effective design features drawn from the natural world.[12]

Such a digital manufacturing system has potential cost savings. These savings include customizing objects for particular consumers, printing or manufacturing on demand, being able to make small modifications to products at almost zero cost, saving on raw materials since little gets thrown away, and the local adaptation of design to suit particular environments. There are also significant possibilities of recycling both the unused powder and existing objects so as to save on the raw material costs of many products.[13]

But the biggest potential saving is that objects can be manufactured close to or even by consumers with their own 'printer'. What could proliferate are 3D printing shops on the high street or in shopping centres. There are many possibilities for much greater localization of manufacturing. One particular innovation is that of 'self-replicating printers' based upon open source software. For some products the capacity to scan the object and then make endless copies by or near consumers would produce large cost savings and reduce transport-related emissions and oil use, assuming that roughly the same number of products are being manufactured worldwide.

Some commentators note that these innovations could be game-changing since they involve a completely new 'system', transforming the very notion of 'manufacturing'. For the past two hundred years this has been typically conducted in workshops or factories distant from consumers. But there may be forming a system here where 'manufacturing' is relocalized and undertaken on a small scale. Indeed maybe there is here a 'system innovation' which eliminates the very notion of manufacture as a separate and spatially distinct activity. This could also be linked with the innovation found in the Internet whereby music or films or books are accessed and downloaded. People would similarly not so much buy objects as pay for accessing or gaining a licence to produce or download the design of the objects they want. This downloading and 'manufacturing' would be part of an 'access' economy, rather than an 'ownership' economy, that has mushroomed in other spheres with recent digital developments.[14]

The consequence of potentially vast savings in transportation costs could mean that at some point the low-cost manufacturing centres, as in the Far East, would no longer possess a comparative advantage in manufacturing objects that are then 'containerized' over thousands of miles. Additive manufacturing developing 'outside transportation' could lead to the descent of oil being partially dealt with through eliminating the transportation of many manufactured objects. It could perhaps even eliminate the whole discipline of 'logistics'.[15] Digital objects can travel almost for free, although oil is the basis of many of the powders used in such printing/manufacturing. If this new system went global this could bring the incipient Chinese century discussed in Chapter 6 to a premature ending. It might mean that no single society would be dominant within this emerging system of additive manufacturing.

Such a system innovation could thus be highly significant. Frank Geels describes how all major innovations in science and technology tend to be very wide-ranging and not confined to the merely 'technical'. System innovations, such as the possible transformation of manufacturing discussed here, involve not just changes in technical products, but also 'policy, user practices, infrastructure, industry structures and symbolic meaning etc.'. Geels goes on to argue that such world-changing socio-technical innovations are 'created and maintained by human actors embedded in social groups'.[16]

The question here is whether additive manufacturing is indeed a world-changing innovation that could generate a new long wave of socio-technical change. As analysts of such long waves note, the structure of goods and services, of the dominant technologies, firms and social activities, does dramatically change over a fifty-year period. This can be seen by comparing 1951 with 2001. By 2051 much of what now exists will not be so much replaced as having grown up alongside it a cluster of novel technologies, firms and social activities that are as yet more or less unknown except in the laboratory. Yet some will be core to life in the mid-twenty-first century.[17]

Digitizing social life

By contrast with objects, humans are not yet teleported around the world and reconstituted out of powder, although some of their organs increasingly are. What is still essential for human life is encounters with others, with many different kinds of 'meetings'. Meeting is a crucial human property and value, the stuff of social life. Crucial to meetings is talk with others, and this may involve food, drink, music and a shared physical place, a place that becomes temporarily full of social life. Such meetings make, extend and cement social networks.

Sociologist Barry Wellman and colleagues argue that 'in networked societies: boundaries are permeable, interactions are with diverse others, connections switch between multiple networks, and hierarchies can be flatter'.[18] Such networked communities are geographically stretched out. Wellman et al. suggest that these involve the transformation to person-to-person communities. Each person, they argue, 'has become the portal'.[19] The turn to person-to-person or 'networked individualism' stems from the development of networked computers, email, mobile phones, texting, smartphones and social networking. Many of these technologies for person-to-person communications are miniaturised. They are carried close to the body, or on the body, or a person's passwords are carried in their mind (if lucky!). These are all 'miniaturised mobilities'.[20]

Each person is thus the engineer of their own ties and networks, and is so connected no matter where they are going or staying. Even on the move connections can be sustained. Social scientist Christian Licoppe reports how 'the mobile phone is portable, to the extent of seeming to be an extension of its owner, a personal object constantly there, at hand ... individuals seem to carry their network of connections which could be activated telephonically at any moment.'[21] This 'networked individualism' involves most people possessing a particular pattern of connections. And people need actively to network in order to thrive and especially to meet and to remeet from time to time.

The economic importance of this is shown in *The Wealth of Networks*, which describes the emerging nature of a 'networked information economy'.[22] Elaborate networks are involved in developing open source software or large collaborations such as Wikipedia. This reflects the process by which who you know becomes more significant than what you know.[23] Indeed, to the extent that some knowledge is tacit and informal, so success results from how people develop, access and use information gained informally. The more informal networks there are, the more opportunity there is to create, circulate and share tacit knowledge. Travelling, meeting and networking are crucial.

Meetings establish and sustain networks. Networked individualism is anything but individualistic! Establishing and maintaining ties for many social groupings is costly in terms of money, energy, personal resources and emotions. This is because of travel, a word originally derived from the French *travail* or work. In some sense people might be said only to know each other if they travel and physically meet from time to time. Such meetings are important because they enable 'tacit knowledge', the kind of knowledge that may need demonstrating face to face and is often not easily codified. This crucial form of knowledge involves 'learning through interacting', which is difficult to exchange over long distances. Meric Gertler refers to this as the 'undefinable tacitness of being (there)', with the result that key staff are often circulated between the various distributed parts of an organization.[24]

Because of the money, energy, personal resources and emotions involved in moving and meeting, people sustain networks with a limited number of others. Moreover, such networks now appear to be less coherent and overlapping. This is because people's residences and their activities, their families and their friends, are more geographically dispersed.

Within the rich North of the world this dispersal of friends, families and professional contacts results from various processes. These include an increase in the number of households worldwide and declining household size; the tendency to retire to places different from where people worked/lived; wider car ownership; airline deregulation; high-speed rail networks; the international-izing of business and professional life; the growth of large trans-national communities; the tendency for a significant proportion of a population to live abroad; the internationalizing of higher education; and the growth of weak ties between people generated by texting, emailing and social networking. Thus, as people are so spread out, more travel needs to happen in order to keep those social networks both effective and affective.

Those social groups with a high capacity to network enjoy significant advantages in making and remaking their social con-nections. The varied capacity to access 'meetings' further generates social inequality. Making and sustaining connections through 'meetings' is especially marked among 'globals'.[25] Stephen Haseler terms the super-rich 'the world's true global citizens – owing loyalty to themselves, their families and their money ... Their money is highly mobile, and so are they themselves, moving between their various homes around the world'.[26] Those unable to travel frequently over such long distances are less able to make and sustain networks and to develop and deploy tacit knowledge (such as women with small children or other dependants).

Especially significant for 'globals' is the speed of movement. According to Zygmunt Bauman, mobility 'has become today a major, perhaps the paramount factor in social stratification and the hierarchy of domination ... capital travels light with no more than cabin luggage – a briefcase, laptop computer and cellular telephone'.[27] The obligation to travel, to meet and to remeet introduces many inequalities into social life.

In any network those people with the largest number of ties will be advantaged. Meetings for them will engender more ties and hence extend their future networking capabilities. There are positive feedback mechanisms whereby the network rich get richer and the network poor poorer, so producing further social inequality.

Such networking greatly extends the need to travel and to meet. And yet it is hard to provide sufficient energy for this to happen worldwide. And where there is less meeting, then some commentators think that this reduces happiness or well-being. UK government adviser David Halpern elaborates on the importance of the 'hidden wealth of nations', that wealth which is over and above obviously measurable wealth. He concludes that 'relationships have a big impact on well-being'.[28] Especially important is what is often referred to as social capital. High social capital is more important than mere economic capital. It is the real thing as opposed to merely what can be measured within the formal economy.

However, political scientist Robert Putnam laments declining social capital and face-to-face conversation within the USA.[29] Co-present talk has seemingly reduced since the 1960s. Americans talk less frequently face to face because of television-watching and commuting. Many studies show that lengthy commuting seems generally associated with reduced happiness.[30] According to Putnam it is 'good to talk' face to face since this minimizes privatization, makes people live longer and promotes economic activity. This is borne out by research reported by economist Richard Layard into the causes of happiness. For him the growth of television seems to lower overall happiness levels through reducing the number of face-to-face meetings.[31]

Further research suggests that the typical American spends eight and a half hours each day looking at screens, often with more than one screen being watched simultaneously.[32] Each screen can interrupt the other, so there is little enduring thinking. Digital lives are lives of multitasking. And this may be a powerful system that is altering human brains. Research seems to show that screens are bad for one. Living 'on a screen' is not a satisfactory substitute for good meetings and networking. If more relationships are conducted on-screen, then this produces less conversation, poorer social interaction, a weakening of social capital and a reduction in the hidden wealth of nations.

Or, to put this the other way round, so far there are no digital encounters that effectively substitute all the affective pleasures of being present with others face to face, emotion to emotion, and sometimes body to body. Whatever digital worlds are so far developed, digital lives on screens seem less satisfying and effective than co-present meetings and networking.

Such digital experiences are critiqued by Internet sociologist Sherry Turkle. She describes such situations as being 'alone to-gether'. And as technology ramps up, so people's emotional lives ramp down. She especially criticizes the tendency for people to prefer texting to talking, for multitasking, for being connected simultaneously while in the physical company of others, and for being online rather than 'connecting with each other face-to-face'.[33] There is a tendency for digital lives to avoid the 'real consequences' of face-to-face experiences. Turkle maintains that we expect too much from digital technologies and too little from relating to each other more directly.

So there is a huge problem here. There is not enough oil to fuel sufficient meetings, especially as many of these meetings necessitate long-distance fast travel. However, digital lives are only about twenty years old. It is unclear just how they are likely to develop and change over the next two to three decades. Certainly they have taken some surprising twists and turns over even this short period, with many technology inventors getting the future dramatically wrong. Even Apple never realized just how significant 'Apps' – software applications – were to become when they introduced the first iPhone; the App Store was launched a year later. By 2010 iPhone Apps had been downloaded 6.5 billion times.

The final section examines some costs of digitizing life, although these costs will not necessarily slow down or even prevent such digitization from continuing to develop. The digital world now has much momentum. This is so even in relatively poor developing countries where mobile phones often act as an important portal for people, given the very high rates of such phone use. In Kenya 'M-Pesa' stands for 'mobile' and 'money'. Half the adult population use this mobile-based service in order to send money, to settle bills and to receive money. This service is said to operate now in a hundred countries. It is also relevant to the development of payment systems for car clubs and car sharing schemes.[34]

Major digital companies and interests compete with each other and engender powerful new developments, developments that may seem fun and fashionable but that are not good for life. In some ways there is a major contest occurring between the powers of carbon capital and those of an emerging 'digital capital' which has strong interests in deepening and extending digital lives and objects. And the likely outcomes here are more likely to result from the respective power of these capitals than from what would be socially or environmentally best, let alone decided upon through democratic deliberation.

The costs of going digital

Pervasive digital lives are not cost-free. First, analysts now suggest that the effects of widespread Internet use may be changing the very nature of mental capacity. Human brains are not, it seems, fixed in their structure and functioning but are in a constant state of flux depending upon what they are required to do. Significant historically was the transformation of the brain so that it could concentrate upon the silent reading of a printed book from the beginning to its end (such as finding out 'who did it' on the last page).[35]

The Internet by contrast encourages non-linear reading, very fast browsing and no deferred gratification in getting to the end. Research suggests that this produces poorer levels of understanding and recall. Multitasking generates a state of 'distraction', or what Nicholas Carr generally describes as the shallowing of experience. For him the Internet is irreversibly changing the way people think, read and remember, predominantly for the worse. Carr characterizes digital lives as involving hunting and gathering within an electronic data forest. He discusses how Google has in effect outsourced memory and encourages forgetfulness, allowing each person to know less. Research on academics shows that as more and more journals go online, so scholars cite fewer articles than before![36] Living digital lives flattens people's own intelligence into 'artificial intelligence'.

Neuroscientist Susan Greenfield goes on to ask how while on the Internet people can develop appropriate empathy with others, empathy she says is central to social capital and to the hidden wealth of nations. Real empathy is made very much more difficult 'if they conduct relationships via a medium which does not allow them the opportunity to gain full experience of eye contact, interpret voice tone or body language, and learn how and when to give and receive hugs?'[37] The very benefits of face-to-face contact are lost, with lives becoming predominantly digitized. This is even more marked in the case of two rapidly growing and significant elements of the Internet, online gambling and pornography.[38] Thus a rapidly reduced capacity to travel and to meet would have long-term detrimental effects upon the very formation of brains and selves if selves were to develop as predominantly digital.

The second cost here is that developing digital lives simultaneously engenders new kinds of surveillance. These are times of emerging risks, uncertain 'enemies', a new state of 'insecurity'. A terror suspect, a rioter, a protestor, can no longer be easily identified as an enemy who is easily identifiable.[39] Through digital security, the surveillance, tracking and identification of others becomes routine as people living apparently ordinary lives necessarily leave digital traces.[40] People's mundane activities are recorded and everyone is a 'digital suspect' where extensive digital worlds are to be found.

Future cities will build digital security into their infrastructures through ubiquitous computing and a 'sea of sensors'. Individuals and their behaviours will be monitored and identified, as they leave 'traces' of their movements, purchases, communications – indeed of their lives. Those lives will be digitally dependent. And, as databases are effectively interdependent, it will be possible to piece together these separate digital traces, of which there will be thousands per day. Thus the person can be remade as a reintegrated 'digital' self across different databases stemming from the billions of computers and sensors, some of which can be as small as smart dust. One future world is that there could be a network of a trillion sensors covering the globe and delivering data to anyone who 'needs' it.[41] There would be an 'Orwellization' of self and society. Indeed with many large private-sector corporations devising new 'security products', an illiberal digital future is very likely. Already digital capital and states are integrating databases containing 'private' information on each person. This further extension would link that information with data on each person's activities, automatically recorded and classified as people leave traces within cyberspace.

Such data is valuable and dangerous. In this Internet of things humans are subject to the power of vast corporations, of 'digital capital' and its almost unlimited capacity to make and remake infrastructures and environments. China with its Golden Shield programme is pioneering this digital surveillance future, with a planned database of the faces of all 1.3 billion Chinese and functioning face recognition software able to link faces and names.[42] Much of this surveillance state is being developed in alliances between American, European and Chinese companies. This may be a smart world, but we should ask whether it is smart to engender such a world.

Third, digital worlds are much more carbon energy-intensive than previously realized. There are around 1 billion computers worldwide and 4.5 billion mobile phones. It is thought that global ICTs are responsible for around 1.2 per cent of total GHG emissions. Each year the Internet releases about 300 million tons of CO_2.[43] Even humble Google searches use servers located in thirty to forty vast energy-intensive data centres spread around the world.[44]

These energy costs will be high in the future if ultra-high bandwidth is developed. Such a bandwidth would be necessary if digital lives on screens are to effectively simulate the affective qualities of meeting-ness. This would be required to induce the large-scale replacement of physical travel with extensive digital communications. Thus the energy costs of such enhanced digital lives could skyrocket and not save as much energy and GHG emissions as so far imagined.

We have thus seen that a future of digital lives has problematic neurological, surveillance and energy costs.[45] But this future is definitely possible since huge interests are building up momentum in rolling out this future. As some of the dire consequences of energy shortages and changing climates kick in, then it could be that 'digital capital' (Microsoft, Apple, Sony, Facebook, Hewlett Packard, Google and so on) begins to orchestrate a high-tech low-carbon future in opposition to the carbon interests dominant in the last century.

And this is not just a matter of connections between people being digital but of the very object world being transformed. Objects could be manufactured on demand while many other objects would only ever be 'digital' (as already with the potential disappearance of newspapers, books, DVDs, CDs and so on). This might be a future. But not inhabiting a world of material objects may also be a major problem. This is partially shown in *The Transition Companion*, which sets out how to bring about 'transition' to a low-carbon world.[46] This *Companion* establishes the importance of 'stuff', of material objects, in, of and for human life. It shows that stuff makes life as much as life makes stuff.

Trust in such a world is hard to generate when there is nothing authentic, original or enduring. Thomas Easton provocatively talks of the dangers of a 'recession in the economy of trust' that could be engendered through the widespread growth of 3D printing.[47] Clearly if the scale of material stuff was radically reduced then a digital world, essentially a world of screens, would have neuro-logical and emotional implications which are not at all neutral or benign. They may reduce carbon costs, but at the expense of significant costs arising from the loss of how humans act with and within a world of objects (what some writers call 'heterogeneous materials[48]). So this is a possible if not a desirable future, involving less trust in the materiality of the external world.

Conclusion

This future involves a radical increase in digital worlds that significantly substitute for physical travel. This future is likely to emerge if the cost of oil continues to rise, as seems likely. If oil costs rose again fifteenfold, as happened between the late 1990s and mid-2000s, then such a digital world's future would be likely.

Moreover, a digital future could result from a forceful imposi-tion, through a short-circuiting top-down action.[49] This would necessitate global science, politics and media framing a resource situation as a crisis of carbon which has to be 'dealt with' quickly, globally and without normal procedures. Shock doctrines and imposed solutions are generally bad for enduring democratic practices.

But two reasons why this future is not so likely to materialize are, first, the cost of this digital infrastructure, requiring very high levels of financing probably in a context of global austerity, at least in the next decade or so. Some of the 'hard technology' will be found in cities in the rich North over the next few years. But with increasing resource constraints the costs may make it impractical to implement on a global scale even if some prototype cities develop such a model. It is a 'first world' solution, although even here the difficulties of getting it to work are very considerable. Huge investment by private companies and large amounts of 'aid' from the rich North to the poor South would be necessary.

Second, such a 'smart solution' will be contested, especially within 'democratic' societies and where there is little 'trust' in the state or in corporations. This contestation, at a time of many other conflicts around security and population management, will make this future resisted such that it may not result in the energy savings and emissions reductions necessary to deal with a global energy crisis.

CHAPTER 10

RESOURCE FIGHTS

Recent resource wars

This chapter examines the third scenario, that since societies are massively short of oil and related resources they threaten and wage resource conflicts as the cheap energy interval in human history winds down. Previous chapters showed that there are not plentiful oilfields but dregs of oil. But these dregs have to provide sufficient oil to keep societies 'on the move' and to deal with the increased energy implications of changing climates. So oil is in short supply, much blood is spilt in extracting it, there is no plan B to replace it, and extra oil is required so as to offset changing climates. There is thus not just a local curse of oil as in the Niger Delta but a global curse. A powerful combination of interdependent consequences moves societies away from equilibrium. Michael Klare, writing of the umbilical cord between *Blood and Oil*, observes that you cannot have one without the other, but as the resource of oil winds down it is probable that more blood will be shed to extract and deliver the remaining dregs.[1]

There have been major conflicts over oil. Chapter 4 considered the power of the USA and its imposition of the doctrine of 'free trade'. The USA has often insisted that resources should be available to the highest bidder, this rule enforced through the World Bank, the IMF and the World Trade Organization. The USA also uses these and other bodies to promote and fund various exploration and pipeline developments in poorer parts of the world. Huge amounts of 'aid' are channelled to such countries. The energy resources opened up are then linked to US companies, so the oil and gas are channelled back to the USA.

From 1970 onwards an integrated 'carbon complex' developed in the USA, shaping the world to its carbon interests. This became more enhanced during the 1990s when the USA discovered that, although it had 'won' the Cold War with the Soviet Union, it did not have sufficient long-term supplies of energy. The USA deployed many tactics in order to gain the 'foreign oil' essential to continuing the high-carbon American way of life. The USA was, in the words of George W. Bush, 'addicted to oil'.

The USA developed close relations with various client states, especially in the Persian Gulf. I noted the Carter Doctrine in the late 1970s that stated that any attack on the Persian Gulf represents an attack upon the USA. The USA forged a 'lethal embrace' with Saudi Arabia despite the policies of the latter being some of the most unequal and anti-democratic in the world.[2]

The USA also engages in covert operations to destabilize regimes. In particular it funded radical Islamists to destabilize the USSR during the 1980s. However, some of the groups funded during that earlier period were then apparently responsible for attacks within the USA through a kind of boomerang effect.[3]

And when all else fails the USA uses military might. Alan Greenspan, chairman of the US Federal Reserve Board, stated that 'I am saddened that it is politically inconvenient to acknowledge what everyone knows: the Iraq war is largely about oil.'[4] Also, significantly, it was about currencies. Saddam Hussein had decided to sell Iraqi oil denominated in euros rather than US dollars and also offered drilling rights to European and Chinese companies. Iraq indeed profited as the euro rallied against the dollar. But after the Iraq War and the deposing of Saddam Hussein, Iraq's oil is once again sold only in US dollars and 'Western' companies are central to Iraqi oil exploration.

In 2011 Iran opened a new oil exchange for oil and gas where cargoes are denominated in a basket of currencies including euros and not US dollars.[5] It is likely that China will use this new exchange since Iran already provides getting on for 15 per cent of China's oil imports. China ignores the sanctions imposed by the USA and the EU on trading with Iran. Oil wars are not just about supplies of oil but also about the changing power of different currencies. There is speculation that countries such as Russia, Venezuela and India will establish oil exchanges based on currencies other than the US dollar. The potential development of the Chinese currency, the renminbi, as the world's third reserve currency is a very likely significant future development here.[6]

Historian William Engdahl shows how Washington wages resource wars, acting as a kind of global oil policeman in its imperial interests.[7] It seems that wherever there are or might be pipelines or refineries, as well as oil and gas fields, there are US military bases, of which there are hundreds around the world.

Pipelines are crucial within Afghanistan even though it is not a significant oil producer. When the countries of central Asia were part of the Soviet Union, their oil and gas flowed north through Soviet-controlled pipelines. But since the collapse of the Soviet Union in 1991, new pipelines are being developed and promoted that flow in other directions, as noted in Chapter 6. There are two key countries in the development of such pipelines, Georgia and Afghanistan, both of which lie in the way of pipelines taking oil and gas south and east from Turkmenistan and Kazakhstan. Energy economist John Foster writes how in this region 'Rivalry for pipeline routes and energy resources reflects competition for power and control ... Afghanistan is a strategic piece of real estate in the geopolitical struggle for power and dominance.'[8]

Chapter 6 showed how China is developing various strategies to secure future oil supplies. These include diversifying its sources of oil (and gas) to a much wider range of countries than previously; developing connections with countries where it is possible to send oil by pipeline rather than tanker; and deploying state-controlled companies to procure these foreign energy supplies, often with links to other national oil companies (Saudi Aramco, Gazprom) rather than Western oil corporations. The country's planned growth of oil consumption has many other countries deeply concerned, including India and Japan, as well as the USA and the EU.

Since 1991 the following pipelines have been built: the Caspian Pipeline Consortium Pipeline from the Tengiz oilfields to the Russian port of Novorossiysk on the Black Sea; the Korpezhe-Kurt Kui gas pipeline from the Turkmen fields to Iran; and, as noted above, the Kazakhstan–China pipeline from Atasu to Alataw.[9] The planned Turkmenistan–Afghanistan–Pakistan–India gas pipeline is due to proceed through some of the most dangerous areas of Afghanistan, but is delayed. Michael Klare summarizes

that, while not all the projects pursued by China will reach fruition, 'the entire region will probably be crisscrossed by pipelines
carrying Caspian oil and gas to China'.[10]

Chapter 7 documented the rise of Russia within the world
system, significantly due to increasing oil (and gas) prices after
the turn of the century. It is the world's largest oil producer,
though it possesses only 5.6 per cent of proven reserves. And
Russia has rising internal demand for oil resulting from its
own rapid growth in the past decade or so. Further, Russia's
reserves are made up of the relatively mature depleting fields in
Western Siberia, some being neglected during the Soviet period.
Russia's potential as an oil superpower could be limited over the
longer term unless it starts to extract significant oil from the
not yet exploited and controversial Arctic region.[11] And that of
course would spark huge new conflicts. The Russian flag was
contentiously planted on the seabed at the North Pole on 2
August 2007.[12]

Finally, the very recent period may be a harbinger of bleak
developments to come. Since 2005 or 2006 it has been impossible
to increase oil supplies, even though the price has been mostly
over $100 per barrel. Most Western countries have had to increase
dramatically what they spend upon imported oil. This high price
of oil is said by Murray and King to be a large contributor to the
euro crisis in 2011–12 within southern Europe, which is entirely
dependent upon imported oil.[13] We have already seen that the
economic crisis of 2007–08 was provoked by oil shortages and
price increases. Resource struggles are with us already and these
will mean that most economies will be unable to cope with
future increases in oil prices and there will be little if any rise
in production.

Future wars

It is hard to project these patterns forward and envisage a benign and peaceful future around the world. It is unlikely that societies would see that they have a *common* interest in dealing with these energy shortages even if they just might orchestrate such a future with regard to dangerously changing climates. This they have not achieved so far, although the 2011 Durban climate change conference may herald such possible agreement in the future thanks in part to the mediating role of the EU.

But most likely in the future are intense conflicts over these different and interconnected energy resources, as well as continued disagreement as to the scale and methods of reducing GHGs. But it is one thing to say that there are huge conflicts of interest and quite another to ask if these resource conflicts will lead to war. What kinds of war are likely?

Political scientist Rudolph Rummel describes how on occasion *Power Kills*. He says that democratic governments are the best way to prevent wars taking place between countries, as well as preventing violence within a society.[14] There is some evidence that 'democracies' do not go to war with each other, that less democratic regimes fight more deadly wars, that democracies are the most internally peaceful kind of regime, and that democracies do not murder their citizens. Democracy, he maintains, is the solution to war and violence. If it is true that 'power kills', then democratize societies! In this Rummel follows philosopher Immanuel Kant, who maintained that if the consent of citizens is required for war, then 'nothing is more natural than they would be very cautious in commencing such a poor game, decreeing for themselves all the calamities of war'.[15]

From this we can anticipate that Norway and Sweden will not threaten each other with war, even though Norway still possesses supplies of oil and gas that may be of interest to Sweden. Indeed for all the economic and social conflicts within the European Union, we would not expect wars between its twenty-seven members, nor probably with any of the states that are seeking to become members in the near future.

In two respects, though, Rummel's argument is unconvincing. First, he fails to notice how American and European societies have historically been war-mongering. They, after all, were the builders of the biggest of empires and this involved extensive wars and threats of war against many other societies. Their 'democracy' was founded on the violent oppression of other societies. And on occasion 'democracies' did go to war against other democracies, but they did so in locations remote from the 'West' as each sought to extend its imperial reach.

Second, Rummel ignores how energy resources have reoriented US policies over the past forty years. Along with some European allies and especially the UK, the USA has waged resource-related wars, developed new ways of torturing suspects, and invented novel means of 'security', often directed against its own citizens. Indeed for the USA 'power kills', with its high levels of militarization, its tendency to incarcerate a significant proportion of US males, and its torturing of local and foreign nationals. The US 'empire' deploys various forms of bullying in order to prevent its long-term decline from the dominant position it occupied during the 1980s, when it 'won' the Cold War against the Soviet Union and was easily the world's largest economy and most influential society.

Only a quarter of a century on, the USA is short of oil and has an economy and society locked into large supplies of 'foreign' oil; its economy is indebted, especially to China; many iconic firms declared bankruptcy as manufacturing went offshore; its political system is ineffective; there are calls by China and India for the dollar to cease being the world's reserve currency; and for the first time the country saw its credit rating downgraded by one agency from its top AAA ranking.[16] Simultaneously the USA is encountering the power of various oil 'grabbing' countries, many of which are non-democratic.

We can anticipate an upward ratcheting of both war and the threat of war in the securing of oil and gas supplies. This is partly because, as noted, oil and gas resources are only found in a narrow range of countries. The USA has waged oil wars.[17] Oil wars are likely to become more common as they may be waged by many different countries in the future. They are yet another illustration of the curse of oil, or what the former 'father of OPEC', Pérez Alfonso, dramatically describes as 'the devil's excrement' of oil. Klare writes of how 'Of all the resources … none is more likely to provoke conflict between states in the twenty-first century than oil.'[18] Indeed this seems to be a further curse of oil: that of all the world's scarce resources it is the most likely to engender conflicts and wars. This is because it is needed by all societies as a result of the mobile modernity legacy of the twentieth century; it is relatively limited in terms of where it is to be found; it generates huge rents and inequalities once it comes on stream; it directly generates economic prosperity and its opposite; and it is for almost all societies sourced from 'offshore' and hence is partially owned/controlled by 'foreign' forces.

We can anticipate that powerful societies and corporations will maximize access to scarce resources using military, diplomatic and political might. This will protect their 'global' or 'regional' warlord position.[19] In this future powerful states will deploy post-carbon policies but as a kind of misleading 'greenwash' to conceal their ruthless pursuit of oil, and especially dirty oil, as well as water, food and land. Each of these resources is increasingly subject to 'grabs' – with, it is thought, 80 million hectares of land already 'grabbed'.[20] China is by far the largest land grabber, buying or leasing twice as much as any other country. Land grabs result from strong demand from capital-exporting countries with large worries about feeding their own people and willing suppliers often persuaded to hand over land to a major power through corruption and the forcible removal of rights from indigenous populations.

Energy shortages would mean that powerful societies would focus upon short-term national security, so making longer-term global agreements impossible.[21] Each major power bloc would pull up the drawbridge and protect their fortress world. Indeed the world's two largest GHG emitters, the USA and China, are already behaving this way with regard to climate change, as shown at the 2009 Copenhagen Summit. Most analysts consider this to be a major failure that resulted from the power of the USA and China vetoing policies that would commit them to reduce their high or growing carbon economy and society. Mark Lynas summarizes: 'Copenhagen was much worse than just another bad deal, because it illustrated a profound shift in global geopolitics. This is fast becoming China's century, yet its leadership has displayed that multilateral environmental governance is not only not a priority, but is viewed as a hindrance to the new superpower's freedom of action.'[22]

This, then, is a possible emerging world of 'barbarization'. Those able to live in gated and armed encampments would do so, with much privatizing of collective functions.[23] Richer societies would break away from the poorer into fortified enclaves. Outside such enclaves there would be 'wild zones' from which the rich and powerful would exit as fast as possible, when the food, oil or water no longer flowed. In this future 'the elite retreat to protected enclaves, mostly in historically rich nations, but in favoured enclaves in poor nations, as well … Pollution is also exported outside the enclaves, contributing to the extreme environmental deterioration induced by the unsustainable practices of the desperately poor and by the extraction of resources for the wealthy.'[24] This scenario involves 'fortressed' walled cities and the extensive 'securitization' of populations, similar in some ways to cities in the medieval period, which provided protection against raiders, invaders and diseases.

A prescient 1997 report goes on to state that the 'socio-ecological system veers toward worlds of sharply declining physical amenities and erosion of the social and moral underpinnings of civilization'.[25] In this 'barbaric' future, oil, gas and water shortages and intermittent wars will undermine production, mobility, energy and communication connections and critical infrastructures.[26] Given energy shortages, many infrastructural systems would collapse, with increasing separation of production and consumption between different regions. There would be the increasingly localized recycling of bikes, cars, trucks, computer and phone systems. Much of the time they would not be working. Indeed systems of secure long-range mobility would disappear except for those used by the super-rich. As in the mediaeval epoch long-distance travel would be risky and probably only undertaken if people were armed. The rich would mainly travel in the air in armed helicopters or light aircraft, a pattern already prefigured in contemporary São Paulo.[27]

Such a de-civilizing energy-starved future would involve a falling standard of living, an ever-greater focus upon the 'products' of the increasingly privatized security industry, probable re-localization of mobility patterns, towns and cities built for visitors deteriorating into ghost towns, and an increasing frequency of resource-related wars. A major 2010 report anticipates in the case of oil: 'A severe energy crunch is inevitable without a massive expansion of production and refining capacity. While it is difficult to predict precisely what economic, political, and strategic effects such a shortfall might produce, it surely would reduce the prospects for growth in both the developing and developed worlds.'[28] It is likely to lead to various kinds of war.

First, there will be statist wars, which were most common in the nineteenth and twentieth centuries. Such wars were funded by taxation, sought to gain territory, deployed professional armies, were rule-bound, and civilian casualties were in theory minimized. Such warfare was typically subject to diplomacy, statecraft, declarations of war and complex treaties. Statist old wars will be fought over oil, as arguably the First Gulf War was. It seems likely that the two blocs of the USA and China (the G2) will 'fight' over diminishing oil reserves (and related resources of food, land and water), but probably this will not be such a statist war.[29] It is more likely to develop as a 'new war', rather like the Iraq War of 2003 turned out to be.

Second there are 'new wars'. These involve private/mercenary as well as statist military forces; de-professionalised armies (sometimes made up of 'boys'); the use of weapons bought on the market/Internet; an asymmetry of military force with no fixed 'fronts' or treaties and peace processes; the military targeting of civilians through inter alia suicide bombing, especially by women; the crucial role of warlords, who combine entrepreneurial and military skills; and the tendency for such wars to last interminable periods of time.[30] These new wars developed in this century especially in the context of failing states. Here there is no monopoly of physical coercion in the hands of legitimate national states, especially given the growth of 'private warlords'.[31] Such new wars are likely to develop particularly around energy and related resources, involving countries, corporations, NGOs, terrorists and many other non-state networks. And new wars make states more likely to fail and to render the conditions for extracting, transporting and refining oil exceptionally troublesome (hence reducing effective global oil reserves further).

We can also anticipate that states will deploy green policies as 'greenwash' which effectively conceals their pursuit of oil, water, food and territory. As climate change and energy shortages hit home, societies focus upon short-term national security, and longer-term global agreements become less likely. Indeed, given how much of the world's economy is based around war, crime and financial 'products', there is much incentive for tax-limited national states to find low-carbon innovation too troublesome and costly in this kind of future.[32] The World Bank estimates that for each of the next twenty years between $139 billion and $175 billion will be required within the developing world to pay for a transition to low-carbon energy. There is no chance of this scale of funding being provided at present by the rich North.[33]

This probably means that the energy source of coal will be increasingly used where possible instead of oil or gas, let alone low-carbon energy sources. The proportion of coal in the energy mix is now at its highest level since 1973 (27 per cent) and there are likely to be further increases in its use in many emerging and developing countries in such a new wars future scenario.[34] New wars and old energy, we might predict, are a likely cocktail.

Conclusion

This is a deeply pessimistic scenario, with about a two in five chance of being realized in many parts of the globe in the next few decades. This future assumes, first, that systems of global governance are insufficient to offset resource conflicts and violence, especially with regard to accessing sufficient energy. Second, it presumes that 'new digital technologies' do not minimize energy costs on a vast scale; and there is no magic bullet engendering a new source of transportation energy. It also holds that the institutions of global civil society, as well as a global spread of 'democracy', are ineffective at generating benign low-carbon solutions around the world. Finally, this future presumes that there is not a collapse of population, which would at least make the degree of conflict over resources less intense and significant than now appears likely. Much of this book suggests that these presumptions are likely to hold. Thus this future, although not inevitable, seems to be the most likely of the four to gain traction over the coming decades.

This is a kind of 'neo-mediaevalist' vision of the future. As in the Middle Ages there would be little democracy, limited powers on the part of states to govern legitimately, many non-state bodies with a mix of military and ideological powers, much illegal movement of peoples across borders, various empires, many new wars, and intense conflict over scarce resources. Life under this scenario would be 'solitary, poor, nasty, brutish, and short' (Thomas Hobbes). Gaia scientist James Lovelock thus asks generally about the future: 'is our civilization doomed, and will this century mark its end with a massive decline in population, leaving a few survivors in a torrid society ruled by warlords on a hostile and disabled planet?[35] Lovelock along with others thus points to the generalized 'peaking' of oil, gas and water, as well as 'Western life' more generally. These shortages will make economic production and social lives more local than appeared likely during the last century.

This dystopic future is prefigured in the contemporary world. Harbingers can be seen within what was described earlier as the 'tropic of chaos'. Violence will often be used to resolve disputes and conflicts of interest within and between societies. The past few decades point to increasingly violent conflicts, internally through riots, protests and terrorism, and externally through new wars over borders and resources. And the problem is that such relations of violence do not go away. Once a society is violent then it almost always remains violent; the violence gets locked in. This is a path-dependent pattern with which those living in 'post-conflict' zones are very familiar. The major exception to this inevitable locking in of violence has been the European Union, which uniquely made wars between its twenty-seven member countries almost impossible in the post-Second World War period.[36]

But recent wars, especially in the Middle East and in Africa, seem to engender more wars and more violence, with little effective statecraft able to bring such conflict to an effective end. The global illegal drugs industry, worth perhaps 1 per cent of world GDP, also makes this future likely since it generates many illegal and violent practices, which in turn get built into how societies operate through crime, guns and deaths.

The movies *Mad Max* and *Mad Max 2* depict this dystopic violent future. Both were conceived following the 1973 OPEC oil price rise when various doom-laden futures were being envisaged. Many corporations and states went into crisis mode, seeking to lessen their dependence upon 'foreign' oil. There were examples in the USA of the 'desperate measures individuals would take to ensure mobility. ... anyone who tried to sneak ahead in the queue [for petrol] met raw violence'.[37] These *Mad Max* movies present a vision of a bleak, dystopian, impoverished society facing breakdowns of civil order resulting from oil shortages. Power rested with those able to access oil or to improvise new mobilities, including short-term flight, as seen in *Mad Max 2*.[38]

The screenwriter of these movies, James McCausland, was also an economist. More recently he wrote of how

a report prepared for the US Department of Energy spelled it out in terms that could be plucked from Ar

mageddon: 'The world has never faced a problem like this. Without massive mitigation more than a decade before the fact, the problem will be pervasive and will not be temporary. Previous energy transitions were gradual and evolutionary. Oil peaking will be abrupt and revolutionary.'[39]

Oil does indeed seem to be the devil's excrement.

CHAPTER 11

LOW-CARBON SOCIETY

This chapter explores the fourth possible future, an organized powering down to low-carbon lives and systems. Societies are planned to cope with reduced energy supplies and yet maintain some of the pleasures and benefits of contemporary relatively wealthy societies even if measurable income falls. This future, which draws upon much innovation in thinking and practice by scientists, NGOs and think-tanks, entails developing fair and planned low-carbon economies and societies.

I noted that interesting analyses of the potential of such a powering down future were explored during the 1970s, following the oil blockade by OPEC and the fourfold increase in oil prices (modest compared with the 2000s). In the USA effects included switching to smaller European and Japanese cars; developments in carpooling and public transport; calls for a tax to subsidize mass transit; a doubling of fuel efficiency in cars; alternative energy developments such as geothermal, solar and windpower; President Jimmy Carter suggesting that homes should be maintained at lower temperatures; and limits placed on the use of oil and gas in generating electricity. Elsewhere developments included car-free days in New Zealand, government requests in the UK for households to heat only one room, violent attacks in Australia upon those queue-jumping at petrol stations, and much shifting to natural gas from coal and oil for electricity generation.[1]

But this period of experimentation was short-lived and neo-liberalism forcibly asserted itself by 1980. This 1970s opportunity was lost. Significantly these developments occurred before 'digital lives' had become an element of a possible lower carbon future.

Many suggestions are being developed around the world to engender future energy and especially future low-carbon energy. But most do not deal with how to replace oil. And changing climates over the next few decades will enhance energy require-ments.[2] Moreover, unexpected events happen which affect the vi-ability of energy developments. One example is the explosion and radioactive fallout at the Fukushima nuclear reactors in north-east Japan in early 2011. Overnight this made a worldwide nuclear energy programme less likely.[3] Likewise the Deepwater Horizon blowout in the Gulf of Mexico in 2010 reduced the probability of rapidly extending deepwater oil and gas drilling.

Significantly there are already some tiny green shoots of a powered down future, which I will now outline, before iden-tifying the preconditions and transformed practices of a more systematic and planned powering down future.

The green shoots of a powered-down future

First, it seems that globalization, which had been inexorably rising in scale and intensity, may have gone slightly into reverse. This is very difficult to assess, but an interesting Index of Globalization developed by the Swiss university ETH Zurich helps here.[4] Three dimensions of globalization are measured: the economic, the social and the political, with the Index disaggregated by continent. Figure 11.1 shows the degree of 'social globalization' over the past forty years. While globalization had been increasing up to 2003, this seems to have slowed down or ceased across all continents. In this index social globalization is measured by personal contacts, information flows and cultural proximity between people who are living within different societies.

Moreover, something similar appears to be happening with regard to the scale of consumption. Recent UK research examining the material flow accounts shows that the peak year for 'consuming' goods and services was 2001. Since then the rate

FIGURE 11.1   Social globalization across the world, 1970–2008[5]

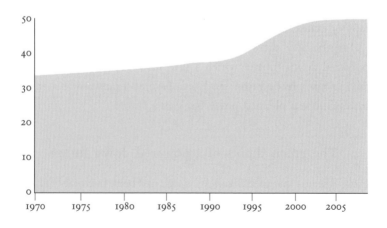

of consumption has declined. By 2009 the overall scale of material consumption had declined to match figures similar to the 1970s.[6] Since 2001 British people have been using fewer materials and generating less waste. This is shown in data reporting on the consumption of paper and cardboard, heat, power, household waste, purchases of new cars, household energy and food. Peak oil in the UK occurred in 1999.

Although the UK still uses 2 billion tons of 'stuff' each year, this has not recently increased even though income and population have risen. In other words, there might also be here the green shoots of a powering down; that is, this recent history suggests that 'prosperity' can be generated without consuming ever more goods and services.[7] There are, of course, many complexities in this argument; nevertheless the claim here is that a number of wealthy societies may be at a significant turning point.

Environmental journalist George Monbiot speculates whether this plateauing/declining resource use actually results from effective environmental campaigning and some modest transformation of people's high carbon social practices.[8] If this were so, then even a small downward shift would be of major importance.[9] There is, of course, plenty of potential here since increases in fossil fuel use have in fact been recent. While the average UK family takes only six days to use a barrel of petroleum, the figure is three days in North America and Australia, thirty days in China and India, and over a thousand days in some parts of Africa. But twenty- five years ago the UK figure was twelve days rather than six.[10] Returning to twelve days should not be so difficult for the UK economy and society, one might surmise.

Travel patterns are also interesting, with 2006 being the year when distances travelled by car in the UK started to decline. The peak in new car purchases was in 2003.[11] This pattern is similar to that in the USA, where a downturn in vehicle miles travelled can be seen in Figure 11.2, after continuous increases over the preceding fifteen years.

Connected with these reductions are large falls in the sales of new cars, especially of gas-guzzling SUVs. All US car manufacturers recently posted huge losses and sought federal government bailouts, with some European subsidiaries of American firms going 'independent'. The US car market halved in about three years, with increasing numbers of cars scrapped and a failure to

FIGURE 11.2   Vehicle miles travelled in the USA 1992–2011 (12-month average, billion miles/day)[12]

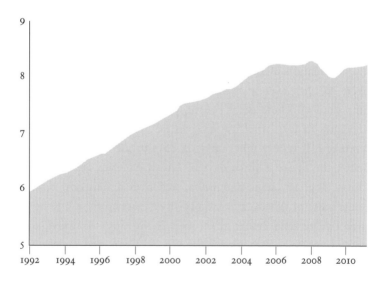

replace them with new vehicles.[13] Michael Ruppert reports the collapse of peak traffic in the USA dating from 2005, more or less as global oil supplies peaked. Americans do seem to be driving less as petrol prices have been skyrocketing. It is being reported in parts of the USA that many county roads will be allowed to return to gravel since there is no money to have them continually repaired.[14]

This peaking of car traffic is reflected in the rise and dramatic fall of Detroit. Although in the interwar years it possessed one of the best public transport systems of buses and electric streetcars, Detroit developed into the world capital of car production.[15] It was where Henry Ford built the first mass production car plant, employing 90,000 workers to produce the iconic Model T Ford. In the 1930s, car manufacturers successfully lobbied to tear up the Detroit tramlines. By the 1950s, the city was home to almost 2 million people, with many employed directly or indirectly in the car and truck industry. It was the world's 'car city'.

But Detroit's population is now less than 750,000. The film/DVD *Detroit: The Last Days* shows rusting hulks of abandoned car plants, empty freeways, blackened corpses of burnt-out houses, trees sprouting from the tops of deserted skyscrapers, half the children living below the poverty line, and almost half the adult population functionally illiterate.[16] Over a quarter of the inner city of Detroit has been reclaimed by 'nature' with many gardening projects reappropriating land for collective primitive agriculture where anyone can harvest the crops grown. Detroit is now described as a forgotten place, a striking testament to the potential end of oil itself.

Indeed this vision of Detroit is rather like the lost cities of the Mayan civilization that figure in the 'collapse of civilization' literature, discussed in the next chapter. What happens in Detroit, the historic centre of the global car industry, may provide lessons as to what might unfold more generally with powering down. I showed in Chapter 1 the role of reduced car travel in the early years of this century in undermining subprime mortgages in car-dependent suburbs and its role in the economic and financial collapse that has spread around the world since 2007–08. More generally, Jeff Rubin describes 'why your world is about to get a lot smaller', as it becomes more difficult to move about that world.[17]

And this is part of a broader peaking of travel. Transport analysts Adam Millard-Ball and Lee Schipper report that motorized travel has either levelled out (European societies) or declined (USA) in the eight industrialized countries they studied.[18] Car ownership is going up more slowly than before and these cars are being driven less and also it seems more slowly. There is also less congestion reported by UK motoring organizations. This drop in vehicle mileage began to occur before the recent rapid rise in oil prices, with some arguing that travel demand is now 'saturated'.[19] This seems implausible, but certainly oil price increases are part of a much more general process by which the vehicle miles travelled in the rich North appear to have stopped increasing and may be going slowly into reverse as 'oil civilization' slows down.

Furthermore, for young people in the developed world owning a car is now less valued than it once was and certainly less than owning a smartphone. And with their falling real incomes this also reflects the realities of a powered down and poorer future. Two-thirds of people in the UK believe the current generation of children will have a lower standard of living than their parents did; this turn to austerity is a major turnaround from even seven or eight years ago.[20] There are various predictions of the 'decline of motoring'. In the UK cash-strapped students are swapping cars for coach travel![21] Geels et al. document many small cracks in the automobility system and point to the impressive array of niche developments occurring around the world which may index a post-car system in the making.[22]

Air travel is also stable or falling away in these countries, especially with the ending of the era of cheap holiday air fares developed by budget airlines. European airlines have increased prices to cope with rapidly rising fuel costs. Leisure air travel has declined as passengers reject soaring fares. Europe has suffered the biggest decline in traffic. IATA recently stated that airlines had increased fares because the price of jet fuel jumped by more than 50 per cent over just twelve months.[23]

Millard-Ball and Schipper thus conclude that 'travel activity has reached a plateau in all eight [industrialized] countries' they studied. Thus societies seem to have reached or even passed 'peak travel'.[24] The combination of high oil prices, stagnating economic growth, an ageing population and a renaissance of walking and cycling indicate some green shoots of a powering down of fast oil-based travel within certain parts of the rich North.

Urbanist Mike Davis discusses how wartime experiences within the USA provide some significant lessons as to how to power down successfully. He suggests that the World War II home front was an important participatory green experiment (akin to Cuba since 1991).[25] The war temporarily dethroned the automobile, with Detroit assembly lines retooled to build tanks and planes. Petrol was rationed and workers were induced to share rides or adopt alternative transport. Tourism was more or less suspended. The average occupancy of cars grew through networks of neighbourhood, factory and office carpools. Car sharing was reinforced by rationing incentives, stiff fines for solo driving, and slogans such as 'When you ride ALONE, you ride with Hitler!' Hitchhiking became officially sanctioned as a form of car sharing. The next section examines how a more general powering down of societies might develop, learning the odd lesson or two from wartime societies.

Systemic powering down

Many different models explore the possibilities of low-carbon societies, or what Serge Latouche terms 'degrowth'.[26] The key questions are how to get to such a powered-down future and how to get there fast enough. It would necessitate some combination of the following features, which would need to cluster together to engineer 'systems' of low-carbon social practice. There would be no smooth progression to this possible lower carbon future.

It took something like fifty years in the rich North of the world to bring about significant reductions in tobacco smoking even though the scientific evidence for smoking's health consequences was unambiguous. In part the tobacco interests did their utmost to conceal and misrepresent the links between tobacco smoking and the increased risk of lung cancer, even though they had known for some time that there was such a relationship.[27] We can presume that a similar time would be needed to power down high-carbon societies given the enduring power of carbon capital.

The first feature required of a powered-down society would be reasonable levels of well-being, even though in terms of normal economic measures most people would be 'poorer'. I noted the difficulty of measuring this 'hidden wealth of nations', with such forms of wealth not being effectively captured by levels or growth of a society's GDP.[28] GDP is the sum of measurable market transactions within a country; it can rise even though some of what is measured is unproductive of individual well-being let alone of the environment. Such transactions do not represent what generates a good society with high levels of well-being. Indeed increases in GDP can go along with worsening emissions and reducing levels of happiness and well-being (as arguably happened in the USA over the past twenty years).

There have been various efforts to develop better measures of well-being and the environment, such as the 'Happy Planet Index' devised by the New Economics Foundation in which Costa Rica was rated number one in 2009.[29] Societies should be measured in terms of the quality of life and not only in terms of GDP or GDP per person. Significantly, societies that have high levels of economic and social well-being tend to be relatively equal with good levels of social connectivity (such as Norway).[30] The significance of what has been termed 'fraternity' is not measurable through most official statistics. Fraternity involves strong indebtedness or obligations between people within a given society spreading over generations.[31]

Research shows that after a level of income in a society has been achieved, then increasing personal incomes do not necessarily turn into more well-being. Many extra goods and services are in effect 'wasted', such as 'unnecessary' products, extra car journeys or the temperature of buildings being kept too high or too consistent.[32] Indeed some extra goods and services may engender resentment on the part of those unable to access them and actually make everyone feel worse off. More goods and services which most people cannot acquire produce resentment and less well-being. More can generate less, we can conclude.

As Richard Wilkinson and Kate Pickett document, life expectancy, the well-being of children, literacy, social mobility and trust are all higher in more equal societies.[33] Society as a whole is weaker if there is more inequality. Wilkinson and Pickett show that more equal societies almost always do better. Powering down is more or less impossible if there are exceptional levels of inequality in a society.

One consequence of inequality is that more resentment is felt by the deprived against richer people. This resentment was said to help to generate the riots that took place within neoliberal UK in August 2011. A UK Cabinet Office report argued that a materialistic culture fostered greed among young people. This was especially so because of the gap between what is represented in the media as the 'good life' for young people and what they can actually acquire. One person in Tottenham reported that 'Those people without hope, they see others with these things, and they want them, getting trainers and stuff, TVs.' Another person reported: 'This country is quite cold – greed, advertisement, money, adverts on TV, greed, greed, greed and family. Like the iPhone advert: "If you haven't got it, you haven't got IT".'[34]

Thus powering down necessitates developing not just low-carbon economies but low-carbon societies. This involves transformations across all systems, enhancing the 'capabilities for flourishing' rather than just for 'income'.[35] High status in a powered-down society would be based on not possessing connections with other people that involve travelling around the world. This means re-engineering the nature of 'success' so as to emphasize the achievements of those living 'localized' and not 'mobile' lives.

This is a challenging requirement because of the power of 'high carbon advertising and marketing'. The world's media endlessly circulate images of the good mobile life and stress the essential importance of global brands, products and services to that life. So, reducing the power and reach of the media – both old media and, especially, new media – is a crucial challenge here and at odds with a possible digital worlds future. The 'celebrity-ization' of the media is inconsistent with powering down.[36]

Thus 'post-suburban' social lives would need to develop. Part of powering down is redesigning places to lessen energy use, without vast expenditure and the use of GHG-emitting cement within new buildings. This redesign must foster higher-density living, heighten the use of slow travel alternatives and shift towards lifestyles more local and smaller in scale. This would, as Serge Latouche brings out, provide more opportunity for face-to-face talk and maintaining good relations with others.[37] Many studies following on from Jane Jacobs's *The Death and Life of Great American Cities* similarly show the attractions of neighbours living close together, residences mixing with businesses and a general lack of zoning, a high use of slow modes of travel, and an absence of extreme differences in income and wealth of those living near to each other.[38]

Research on the 1995 Chicago heatwave shows the life-saving importance of this neighbourliness.[39] In areas that afforded op-portunities for people to get out and about and to visit shops and local services, deaths from the heatwave were lower. The connectedness of houses with habitable streets, accessible parks, shops, cafés, neighbours and so on provided opportunities for walking, meeting and especially talking with others. Where opportunities were rich and diverse, then people would go out even in very high temperatures and were less likely to die from the heat. In neighbourhoods where residents rarely socialized the elderly were isolated and death rates were correspondingly higher. Ironically, wealthier neighbourhoods were less likely to have strong localism and hence experienced higher death rates.

Thus in a powering-down future, friends would have to be chosen from neighbouring streets, families would not move away at times of new household composition, and distant family members could not be visited regularly. Households would not live apart and status would be re-localized and based upon contributions made locally. In *Green Metropolis* David Owen argues that the greenest city in the USA is New York since it provides many local connections and it is made almost impossible to own and use private cars.[40] In general Owen advocates a threefold policy for promoting green metropolises: live smaller, live closer and drive less.

Some of this can be seen specifically with regard to food, which would need to be sourced more locally with long-distance transport of goods becoming uncommon. This would move against the widespread tendency for 'supermarket-ized' food, characterized by very long supply chains, vast centralized warehousing and car-dependent large-scale shopping.[41]

Dale Pfeiffer describes the potential of urban gardening, farmers' markets, the growth of allotments and related small-scale production systems.[42] Cuban agriculture after the collapse of the Soviet Union and the ending of cheap oil provides a model here. During the 1980s agriculture in Cuba was heavily mechanized and more oriented to producing a few products (sugar, tobacco, citrus) than any other Latin American country. It had developed a Soviet-style agriculture dependent upon oil, as well as food imports from the Soviet bloc. But with the collapse of the Soviet system in 1991 these food imports, fertilizers, pesticides and oil for tractors and machinery disappeared, albeit assisted by the US blockade of Cuba. Production of foodstuffs fell by more than half, calorie intake of the population dropped by over one-third, there was significant undernourishment, and a large weight loss was experienced by most Cubans.

These conditions, a 'perfect storm', provided a major case study of whether a society can respond to societal collapse through a planned and purposeful powering down which nevertheless maintains well-being. Pfeiffer argues that since the mid-1990s there has in fact been a 'Cuban miracle', with GDP actually increasing each year. Daily food intake has been more or less restored. This has been achieved not through oil-intensive agriculture, as had existed before, but through developing a low-carbon agriculture based upon diverse crops, organic principles, agroecology, small markets, permaculture, worker co-operatives, small farms and urban gardens.

The World Bank reports that by most measures of human development Cuba is now more or less the leading country within the developing world. Cuba has systematically disregarded neoliberal recommendations as to how to bring about economic and social recovery. Cuban life expectancy is almost identical to that in the USA but overall Cuba uses only about one-tenth of the USA's energy per person.[43]

Localized patterns, as pioneered in Cuban agriculture and energy, would need to be reinforced by work being located close to where people lived. Education should also be provided within local schools and colleges, with a huge scaling back of 'international students'. Many goods and services would thus need to be simpler and produced, consumed and repaired nearby.

Various analysts, such as von Hippel, increasingly emphasize the importance of 'democratizing' innovation'. He describes how many 'users' of goods and/or services engage in and develop new products and services.[44] Likewise consumer communities seem to gather around particular obsessions, sometimes 'as mere interest groups, sometimes fickle fans, sometimes hobbyists, and sometimes cults'.[45] The development of Apps for mobile phones is a good recent illustration of such widespread consumer innovation.

Low-carbon innovation would similarly require 'consumer communities' highlighting, advocating, developing and making fashionable new low-carbon actions and objects. As Jukka Gronow notes, the 'consumer is as much the heroic innovator as the entrepreneur'.[46] It would be necessary here for countless heroic consumers to innovate low-carbon, localized goods and services, with states and corporations providing the preconditions for starting up and scaling up. In the 2011 edition of *The Transition Companion* the various stages of how this can be engineered are defined as starting out, deepening, connecting, building and daring to dream alternatives. Some of the innovation features of the transition movement are that it is viral, open source, self-organizing, iterative, historic and, most importantly, fun![47]

There are examples of this. The Swedish city of Växjö is ambitiously developing a 'fossil fuel free future' in the context of a national plan in 2005 aimed at 'Making Sweden an oil-free Society'. Växjö is almost halfway there without apparently sacrificing lifestyle, comfort or economic growth. In the underground car park of the local government offices, there are no private vehicles, just a communal green-car fleet. Staff who cycle or take the local biogas buses to work book ahead for the green-car fleet. Petrol is still available but carbon emissions in Sweden are heavily taxed. The plan is to reach zero carbon emissions within the next few decades. Växjö's model of investing in bioenergy, combined heating and power systems, and district heating is repeated in other parts of Sweden, which is overall planning to make the country 'oil-free'.[48]

Also elements would need to be drawn from the digital futures examined in Chapter 9. There would be the extensive *simulating* of physical co-presence through virtual travel to reduce the frequency of physical travel by fast mobile machines. Additive manufacturing would relocalize manufacturing rather than continuing the widespread movement of goods through containerization and air freighting. Software would 'intelligently' work out the best means of undertaking tasks, whether this meant meeting up, getting to some place or event, or bringing the activity to fruition through virtual connections. We could anticipate that digital worlds would be central to work, friendship and social life.

At the same time there would be many dense forms of localized movement. This would involve small, ultra-light, smart, probably battery-based, de-privatized vehicles available on demand. Smartcards would control access to and payment for use of such vehicles. There would be a mixed flow of slow-moving micro-cars, cycles, hybrid vehicles, electric bikes and pedestrians, with mass transport integrated into networks of physical and virtual access. Vehicles would be electronically integrated through information, payment systems and physical access with collective or mass forms of transport. Such public transport requires high-density populations.[49]

Some car makers are experimenting with 'pay-as-you-go' schemes for EVs. Daimler, Peugeot and other suppliers expect such systems to be attractive to younger customers familiar with making 'access' payments for mobile phones and Internet services. The company Better Place, which is building EV infrastructures in Israel, Japan and Denmark, expects to charge by the mile.

Indeed it is considering if the 'car' as such might be highly subsidized or even free (and then more effectively recycled) while the payment from customers would be calculated by distance travelled.[50] Central to these systems would be 'near field communications'. These enable the transmitting of information quickly, simply and securely over short distances without fixed connections.[51] Such communications would enable the supply of interchangeable 'mobility services', accessed, paid for but not predominantly owned.

There would need to be policies and practices to ensure that if the main form of transportation was EVs, these were not additional to but formed a system that over time made obsolete petrol-based vehicles.[52] It is said that there are 350,000 'eco-prestige seekers' wanting to buy electric cars in addition to existing vehicles, even if more expensive.[53] What is necessary is that EVs, whether of four, three or two wheels, come to be a socio-technical system that over time makes obsolete the 'steel and petroleum' system and are not providing additional vehicles for 'eco-prestige seekers'. Although EVs may depend upon fossil-fuel-generated electricity, they can be up to four times per mile more efficient than petrol-based engines.

There are formidable technological, economic, organizational and social problems in 'engineering' an EV system that could push into the sidings the 'steel and petroleum' car system that has so far driven out all competitors.[54] Especially significant here would be preventing the rebound effect, ensuring that the fun and fashionable EVs were not so well-used that extra mileage occurs. One clear way of preventing this is to re-engineer road space so that 'cars' are less able to access housing, factories, offices and leisure sites.

It would also be a feature of powering down that societies would be prepared for surprises, and that efforts to impose *the* solution, such as a particular version of EVs, could be disastrous. Matthias Gross refers to the need for extensive experimentation, for a 'mindful openness to surprises'.[55] What seems like the right way to a low-carbon future might turn out to be a blind alley. So it is crucial not to get prematurely locked into the wrong set of possibilities. This future should mean that 'the transportation picture in the mid-twenty-first century will be very different from the fiesta of mobility we have enjoyed for the past fifty years. It will be characterized by austerity and a return to smaller scales of operation.'[56]

Reverse gear

The main problem here is the systemic nature of high-carbon worlds and the need to engender low-carbon *systems*, and not just changes of value, or belief or individual behaviour. So moving to a low-carbon economy and society necessitates 'reversing' most of the systems that were set in motion during the twentieth century. Such a reversal involves finding reverse gear while going very fast in a forward direction. There is a strong possibility of destroying the gearbox as reverse gear is sought!

There are many reasons why finding reverse gear is so troublesome. First, there is the power of carbon capital, which itself generates rising GHG emissions and is complicit in the overuse of energy. And yet that capital is expected to solve these issues. This is sometimes described as a wicked problem. In other words, the economic and social forces that generate system problems are also those that are required to generate solutions. Obviously in most cases this 'contradiction' is unresolved and the underlying problems remain.

An interesting case of trying to find a solution to a wicked problem was recently highlighted in Ecuador. Extensive oil reserves have been found under an area of rainforest which possesses greater species diversity than anywhere else in the world. Ecuador suggested a solution. If the rich countries of the world paid over a significant sum then Ecuador would leave the oil undisturbed in the ground. This is a very unusual Plan A. It is being pursued, but if the money is not forthcoming then a Chinese oil exploration company is ready to move in and this area of rainforest will be subject to the blessing/curse of oil.[57]

Further, moving to low-carbon systems reduces short-term levels of income and consumption, and this makes it difficult to induce the population to embrace low-carbon forms of life and social practice. Moreover, in the early twentieth century a cluster of high-carbon systems developed. In order to reverse such systems in this century there needs to be a simultaneous change of multiple systems to generate a new *cluster* of low-carbon systems within the next couple of decades.

In terms of developing air travel, I referred to the growth of 'airmindedness', of the role of enthusiasts, interests, media, technologies, advertisements and corporations in its systematic promotion. Something similar is now needed to develop a set of discourses and practices of what might be called 'low carbonness' or 'post-carbonness' or 'transitionness'. This too would involve enthusiasts, interests, media, technologies, advertisements and corporations seeking to develop and promote 'low carbonness'.

Overall the long-term path-dependent patterns of existing systems, including people's routines and habits, engender momentum. Such momentum makes it more difficult to reverse systems in which most of a society is strongly implicated. These systems are what constitute contemporary life.

Moreover, much societal change is slow, as is seen in the enduring car system dating from the late nineteenth century. There is also a lack of time available to make the seismic shifts that are necessary, since changes in the atmosphere and the decline in energy security are already locked 'into the system' and to some degree will happen whatever changes take place in the near future.

In addition there are also huge difficulties in organizing a global polity that can reset global agendas, especially because resources are in short supply and much contested. Serge Latouche suggests that the World Trade Organization should be replaced by the World Localization Organization! And even if there were global agreements, states are rarely able to bring about change from the top partly because of resistance and opposition to instructions for, say, developing low-carbon practices and systems.

The global media circulate stories and accounts of how corporate, political and media celebrities live ultra-high-carbon lives, which thus make them ill-suited to lecture others on how to reduce their carbon footprint. Former Labour prime minister Tony Blair regularly instructs the powerful and the powerless on the need to reduce their carbon emissions, and yet by 2010 he had acquired nine houses, many in and around London.[58] Blair apparently 'needs' an annual income of £5 million so as to 'sustain' this ultra-high-carbon lifestyle.

One central element of celebrity lives is tax limitation, or what UK Uncut terms tax dodging.[59] This occurs through the 'offshore world', which itself has a high carbon footprint. Offshoring is disastrous for reducing carbon emissions and for moderating energy use and especially oil, in part because these 'treasure islands' of tax limitation are visited by ultra-high-carbon households. But most importantly the tentacles of these treasure islands greatly limit the taxation available in societies to enable low-carbon public works and activities. A robust localism cannot develop without many activities and resources that are public and accountable and not offshored and privatized.[60]

A low-carbon world requires a very strong sense of the mutual indebtedness of people around the globe, and especially of current generations towards future generations, including those who are not yet born. This public or social indebtedness is expressed in many global documents, such as the UNESCO Declaration of 12 November 1997 on the responsibilities of the present towards future generations. However, social indebtedness has been overlain or overtaken by a financial indebtedness that ties much of the world into current systems of obligation through financial debt – of people, states and corporations. This financial indebtedness prevents 'fraternity' from developing. In the past few neoliberal decades fraternal indebtedness has been contorted by financial indebtedness, including the large-scale offshoring of taxation revenue, especially by societal leaders and celebrities.

Powering down involves taming the scale and global reach of such financial indebtedness and replacing it with social indebtedness. Elsewhere this is conceptualized as involving the replacement of neoliberal with resource capitalism.[61] This is a demanding precondition, since, as Colin Crouch recently laments, there is a 'strange non-death of neoliberalism' even after its apparent responsibility for massively damaging the world economy in 2007–08.[62]

For these various reasons, finding reverse gear is almost impossible. And this is one reason why futurist Richard Buckminster Fuller maintained that 'You never change things by fighting the existing reality. To change something, build a new model that makes the existing model obsolete.'[63] Low-carbon innovator Amory Lovins thus points out that 'saving fossil fuel is a lot cheaper than buying it'.[64] Societies would cope with reduced energy through a cluster of 'new models' that use less and yet sustain many pleasures of contemporary wealthy societies. Societies will be as 'happy', with a high life expectancy, but they will not be as rich. Societies are measured in terms of the quality of life, of 'prosperity', but not growth, to use Tim Jackson's terms.[65] So it is not so much reverse gear that is needed, but a different gear altogether. The probability of this future occurring is maybe one in five. It seems unlikely to gain traction except in relatively equal societies, of which there are depressingly few in the world.

CHAPTER 12

AFTER EASY OIL

The simple question in this book is, what is the twenty-first century going to be like? We have seen how the last century was organized around the search for, the deployment of, and the consequences of oil-based movement, manufacturing, food and water systems. But given it seems that half of that oil has gone, and gone in ways that have had such bad effects in helping to change climates, the question is: what will follow or replace that oil civilization, if anything? This concern is even shared by major corporations. The CEO of Royal Dutch Shell pronounced: 'My view is that "easy" oil has probably passed its peak';[1] while the chief economist of HSBC Bank maintains that 'Energy resources are scarce. Even if demand doesn't increase, there could be as little as 49 years of oil left'.[2] If this is the case, what will societies be like as they move into an oil dregs future?

More generally, Timothy Mitchell writes how there was a

brief episode of human time when coal miners and oil workers moved an extraordinary quantity of energy ... up to the earth's

surface ... Yet, even as the passing of this strange episode comes
into view, we seem unable to abandon the unusual practice to
which it gave rise: ways of living and thinking that treat nature
as an infinite resource.[3]

While for a century nature was treated as infinite, it is clearly not
viewed as such now and this has given rise to many 'catastrophist'
writings that imagine bleak and dystopian futures as societies
are 'de-energized'. In the next section I show how some of this
literature draws upon historical accounts of the ways in which
earlier 'dominant' civilizations collapsed. Have contemporary
societies got locked into systems of energy producing that in
turn need ever more energy, a high-carbon treadmill that they
are unable to get off? Is the only way off such a treadmill a
catastrophic societal 'collapse'? The chapter concludes with a bleak
analysis of capital's likely role in precluding a benign, planned
and democratic low-carbon future realized through what I term
a 'low-carbon civil society'. Much of this century will entail
dealing with the far from benign consequences of learning that
nature is certainly not infinite.

Catastrophism

It is increasingly argued that even rich societies could 'collapse'.
This was explored in Joseph Tainter's classic *The Collapse of Complex
Societies*, written in the late 1980s. It examines how societies come
to be organized in more complex ways often as a response to
short-term problems. This complexity then demands ever greater
amounts of high-quality energy; and yet this increased energy
involves diminishing returns. As a consequence a growing set of
energy and environmental problems unpredictably reinforce each

other across different domains. As a response to growing environmental and energy issues, Tainter observed that, 'however much we like to think of ourselves as something special in world history, in fact industrial societies are subject to the same principles that caused earlier societies to collapse.'[4]

Thus the 'collapse' of contemporary Western or global civilization is not impossible, just as it was not impossible for the Roman Empire or the Soviet Empire in 1991 to 'collapse'. A similar outpouring of doom-laden sentiment interestingly last occurred in the 1970s, coincidental with oil price increases and the intensification of the Cold War.[5]

From around 2003 many texts outline a 'collapse' thesis.[6] Analyses examine the multiple processes that seem to be generating catastrophes across environmental, climate, food, water and energy systems. This catastrophism represents a real change of zeitgeist, especially after the optimism in the rich North during the 'roaring' 1990s. Doomsday scenarios are also common among novelists and filmmakers.[7] Lord Martin Rees, former president of the UK's Royal Society, states that there is only a one in two chance of the human race surviving the twenty-first century!

Environmental problems have been responsible for the 'collapse' of societies historically, according to best-selling author Jared Diamond.[8] He lists eight key environmental processes: deforestation and habitat destruction, soil problems, water management problems, overhunting, overfishing, effects of introduced species upon native species, population growth, and the increased per capita impact of people. Populations typically grew and stretched natural resources, particularly energy resources, to their breaking point. Collapse typically occurred when societies were at the height of their powers and their carrying capacity became vastly overstretched.

One such civilization, the Mayan in the Yucatán peninsula in Central America, illustrates such collapse. This impressive civilization lasted for at least 500 years (250 to 750 CE) and developed complex technologies, mathematics, astronomy, architecture and culture. But then it all stopped, monuments were no longer built, palaces burnt, lakes silted up, cities were abandoned and the population of some millions vanished. Its population growth was like driving a car faster and faster until it blows up. Collapse happened almost overnight. Many argue that most civilizations last some hundreds of years. 'Western civilization', we might say, has survived six hundred years since the Renaissance. Like the powerful Mayan civilization, it may be coming to an end as rapidly increasing population outstrips energy resources and a tipping point is encountered.[9]

Diamond argues, along with other commentators, that human-caused climate change, the build-up of toxic chemicals in the environment and energy shortages could produce abrupt, potentially catastrophic decline for societies. Likely processes include increases in global temperatures making much plant, animal and human life impossible, the running out of oil and gas, the lack of resilience of many societies, a global failure of economy and finance, population collapse, increasing resource wars, and huge food shortages. Together these would be a 'perfect storm', analogous to the combination of system processes that produced the 'societal collapse' of the Roman Empire or of the Mayan civilization. In those cases internal contradictions working slowly over time brought down apparently dominant systems based upon the availability and use of extensive energy supplies.

Elsewhere I have reported how the lead item on a 2009 BBC News programme showed how a similarly catastrophic 'perfect storm' might develop by 2030.[10] This perfect storm would consist of runaway climate change; huge water, food and energy shortages; and mushrooming population growth. It was unusual to have this kind of analysis as a mainstream BBC News item. The item was illustrated by various reports on worldwide developments that showed how the storm was already out at sea. This BBC report suggested that without reversing various systems, the storm will soon come inshore. Various catastrophes would leave the world's population poorer, less mobile, hungrier and likely to be fighting for increasingly scarce resources, roughly along the lines examined in Chapter 8.

Decades ago Gregory Bateson critiqued the processes engendering epochal change. He maintained that 'the unit of survival is *organism* plus *environment* ... the organism that destroys its environment destroys itself'.[11] There is little doubt that many elements of the contemporary environment have been 'destroyed' and hence undermined some preconditions for continued human life. This makes 'collapse' not implausible. We might note that various societies, such as the Russian Federation and Cuba, recently experienced a significant collapse of income, life expectancy and population during the early 1990s, following the implosion of the Soviet Union.

However, this is not to argue that nature is a self-regulating system which has simply got out of equilibrium. Systems generally do not move towards equilibrium. Much economics presumes that feedbacks will only be negative and equilibrium-restoring.[12] But central to these collapse accounts of society is the importance of positive feedback mechanisms taking systems far away from equilibrium states. Systems are dynamic, processual and demonstrate the second law of thermodynamics: physical and social systems move towards entropy or disorder. Or, as Ilya Ehrenburg, a Russian journalist, dramatically wrote in 1929 about the car system: '[The automobile] can't be blamed for anything. Its conscience is as clear as Monsieur Citroen's conscience. It only fulfils its destiny: it is destined to wipe out the world.'[13]

Somewhat similarly, John Maynard Keynes pointed out in 1923 that 'In the long run we are all dead. Economists set themselves too easy, too useless a task if in tempestuous seasons they can only tell us that when a storm is past the ocean is flat again.'[14] There are many tempestuous seasons which can indeed do for societies, and there is no flat ocean to return to. Systems demonstrate a lack of proportion or 'non-linearity' between 'causes' and 'effects'. Small changes can bring about large system shifts, as well as the converse. Only certain small causes may prompt a new path of development, such as the way oil-based development took root in the early years of the twentieth century. As we have seen, systems get 'locked in' and patterns and rules can then survive for long periods.

But occasionally movement from one system state to another occurs rapidly, with almost no stage in between. For example, as a gas cools it remains a gas until it suddenly turns into a liquid. This can be seen in transformations between each ice age and the periods of relative warmth in between. There were only two states, the glacial and the interglacial, with no 'third way'. Relatively recent research on ice cores shows that there was abrupt movement from one state of the earth's system to another. Change happens with 'speed and violence'. These collapse analysts thus wonder if contemporary societies may be on the verge of tipping to such a new collapse condition also with 'speed and violence'.[15]

The importance of small changes can be described through the idea of 'black swans'. These are those rare, unexpected and highly improbable events but which have huge impacts. They are outliers not averages. These outlier events are responsible for much economic, social and political change, making history jump and not crawl. The most important events are those least predictable.[16] And when change happens it may not be gradual but at a moment, in a kind of rush. If a system passes a tipping point change occurs rapidly. The system turns over. Contemporary 'collapse' analysts examine how something similar is in prospect through current energy and environmental processes, as well as through finance.

Previous societies collapsed because systems were not in place to provide the continued energizing of their populations. Does their experience have lessons? It is important to note that before the oil age the population of the world was around 2 billion. But with the oiling of society from 1901 onwards, including the development of what we can call 'fossil foods', world population trebled over a century to 6 billion. Richard Heinberg muses on whether world population might collapse back to 2 billion during this century, given this was the population before agriculture was 'industrialized' and 'mobilized' through oil![17] That would presume a stunning scale of societal collapse, more than comparable with the collapse of the Roman or Mayan civilizations.

Moreover, the last century saw not only increases in population, resource use, incomes and inequalities, as documented in this book. The world also became much more interconnected. As population increased so connections around the world increased exponentially. And those interconnections make shocks travel faster across systems. The world might have been able to deal with this connectedness if an almost limitless and cheap supply of oil continued. But with mobility, informational and financial connections escalating beyond anyone's wildest imagination, it is hard now to see just how those connections can be sustained and deal with intermittent crises. Thomas Homer-Dixon has expressed this point clearly: 'our global system is becoming more complex, yet the abundant, cheap, high quality energy we need to cope with this complexity will be steadily less available'.[18]

This book is based upon the idea that oil matters, and oil shortages and oil price increases matter a great deal. Every time there is an oil price shock the world economy is unable to cope and there follows a significant economic and social downturn. I showed in Chapter 1 how the peaking of oil around 2006 has already contributed to the world's greatest economic downturn since 1929. As we increasingly encounter the world of dregs, then oil will be *the* pre-eminent strategic resource on the planet, whose acquisition, production and distribution will absorb senior government and military officials.[19] As noted above, oil is the most likely resource to engender conflicts and wars. It is needed by all societies, it is relatively limited in terms of where it is found, it generates huge rents, it directly generates economic prosperity, for almost all societies it is sourced from 'offshore', there is insufficient oil in the new century, and there is no global organization charged with ensuring its fair distribution (unlike the IPCC with regard to climate change).

We can consider how historians of the future will refer to the next few decades. Will they be known as the peak oil and end-of-American-hegemony years, the climate change years, the 'end of Western civilization' years, the collapse of population years, or 'business as usual' years? This debate somewhat parallels how Cubans interpret the 'Special Period' years of the early 1990s in Cuba. Will there be a new epoch across the world and if so what might this be and how will it be named? And will that era involve reversing or enhancing people's lives and livelihoods from the high-energy-consuming twentieth century?

The power of capital

We have seen how carbon capital orchestrated the last century. This capital involved giant oil and vehicle manufacturing firms dominating markets, circumventing anti-trust and tax legislation, and seizing various states to pursue policies in their interests. Markets were not dominant but giant corporations were. And those corporations seized control of the state even more energetically during the post-1980 neoliberal period. Although neoliberalism appears to free up markets, it actually involves the greatly increased domination of markets by different sections or fractions of capital. There is a heightened lobbying by corporations, the seizing of state policies and the dominance of political and policy agendas. According to Colin Crouch, neoliberalism is all about states becoming captured by capital.[20] In that capture, carbon capital was the master during the last century and can provide lessons to almost all other corporations as to how to realize such capture. Carbon capital speaks power and bends the world to its interests.[21]

This power of capital demonstrates Marx's observations that the ideas of the ruling class are in every epoch the ruling ideas, and that the executive of the modern state is but a committee for managing the common affairs of the whole bourgeoisie.[22] This is insightful except that 'capital' is more diverse and internally divided than in the mid-nineteenth century. Much of the history of Western capitalism is a history of struggle between different fractions of capital as to which is able to capture the state and run it in its interests.

For a period during part of the twentieth century the interests of the working and middle classes did hold some sway, during what Scott Lash and I term 'organized capitalism' based upon sustained conflict between national social classes.[23] This led to significant class victories, in particular the post-war development of welfare states across much of Europe. But as disorganized global capitalism or neoliberalism was unleashed from around 1980, so once again capital came to dominate, and indeed wars have become less 'statist' and are themselves more 'privatized'.

In disorganized global capitalism or neoliberalism the main issue is which fraction of capital gets to be in charge within particular societies and around the world. The power of capital is more pronounced than when Marx was writing in the 1840s. Marx himself foresaw how lower prices were the heavy artillery with which capitalism batters down 'Chinese walls', compelling all nations to adopt the bourgeois mode of production.[24] Capitalism creates a world in its own image. In particular carbon capital has pretty well made *all* the world's two hundred societies over the past hundred years. That is power.

Reversing such oil dependence is difficult. Oil and its powerful workings have seeped everywhere. There is almost no person or organization exempt from its blessing and curse, even with many cultural and arts organizations up to their armpits in oil sponsorship money.[25] Thus if we examine the possibility of reversing the power and effectiveness of carbon capital, this will not result from a planned democratic movement to bring about what might be considered desirable. There is no reason to imagine that the best or the democratic will win out. Only that which speaks effectively to power could displace carbon capital from its dominant role. According to Rawi Abdelal *Capital Rules*.[26] So the question is whether finance capital or digital capital or low-carbon capital could rule in place of or alongside carbon capital.

In this contested future, taxation is a central issue. About a quarter of global wealth is held offshore, equivalent to the entire GDP of the USA. This offshore money is mostly untaxed, and it is certainly not taxed within the countries in which that money is generated though economic activity. And without sufficient tax revenues a post-carbon future is impossible to realize. It not only requires public money but also a strong notion of public interest so as to plan and orchestrate a widespread return to the local which will involve reductions in measurable income.[27] This is not a cheap policy, and it also presumes that money and taxation are localized and in the control of those localities and nations where it is generated and not offshored. Offshoring and powering down are in strict contradiction with each other.

These secrecy jurisdictions are central to the shadow and unregulated financial system where trading is undertaken out of sight and on a scale that almost destroyed the world economy a few years ago. The reduction in the power of global finance is a precondition of a low-carbon future. A powering-down future presupposes finance being rendered relatively unimportant; there can no longer be the 'dictatorship of financial markets'.

Keynes, the most significant twentieth-century economist/social scientist, is very relevant here.[28] He noted how the Great

Depression in the 1930s followed a long period of deregulation, indebtedness, a bubble economy and huge economic inequality. There was also offshoring of finance. There are obvious similarities with the financial processes involved in the economic crash of 2007–08.[29] Keynes brings out two particular problems with finance. First, when two parties trade with each other, buying and selling goods and services, there is rough equality between the two since each wants what the other has. But with finance there is no equality. Finance is always in command and this is further reinforced when the sources and dynamic processes within finance are located outside the country in question. Keynes argues that industry is subservient to finance and often to very distant financial speculation. To avoid this he says it is necessary to bring about the 'euthanasia of the rentier, of the functionless investor'![30]

Second, most so-called investment by financial institutions is not investment in actual goods and services but rather speculation in secondary markets, gambling against companies, currencies and countries. Over 95 per cent of finance involves changes in ownership and debt but not new investment in real goods or services. These secondary markets further separate the ownership and the management of companies. According to Keynes, it is 'the remoteness between ownership and operation [that] is an evil in the relations among men'.[31] This is in part why until recently banking and finance were not viewed in national accounts as in any way 'productive'. Only over several decades has banking been moved into the category of the 'productive', even though most of it only involves transfers and not what analysts (except those in business schools?) would understand as real investment in the national economy, which is what Keynes sought to strengthen.[32]

Moreover, the growth of offshoring, with the scale of trading a hundred times greater than the volume of trade, escalates a chasm between ownership and operation through what Keynes terms 'skilful evasions'.[33] Capital in the contemporary world does not flow to where it is more 'productive' but to where it is most secret, gets the lowest tax rates, can evade as many regulations and laws as possible, and can race towards ever laxer regulation. Because of these dangers of 'capital flight' Keynes strongly argued for nationally organized exchange controls over finance. He also thought that there should be clear transparency in financial flows, and would thus regard the enormous growth in secrecy jurisdictions and the scale of financialization as counterproductive to the effective management of national economies. Simultaneously he was in favour of the free trade of goods and services.

Financialization thus runs counter to a productive low-carbon economy and society, which would be made up of mostly relatively small companies able to innovate low-carbon products and related services but on a potentially vast scale. Shaxson argues that tax havens favour large corporations and not small and medium-sized companies. The offshore world makes it hard for 'innovative minnows' to compete, and if they do prosper then they are likely to become parts of large multinational corporate bureaucracies whose income flows are then often in part offshored.[34]

So this powering-down future will not be realized unless there is a widespread reversal of offshoring income and wealth within secrecy jurisdictions beyond nation-states. Bringing monies and taxation home to where they are productive and earned is a precondition for such a future. And this is unlikely to get going even if many would consider it to be the best future. For the best is often not what wins out, especially as it would involve reducing the power and influence of Wall Street and the City of London, whose power here is paramount.

We saw in Chapter 11 the wide array of groups and organizations experimenting conceptually and practically with very many post-carbon alternatives. This emergent 'low-carbon civil society' is made up of tens of thousands of experiments, groups, networks, prototypes, laboratories, scientists, universities, designers and activists. Many involve making new connections between post-carbon practices developing around the globe, partly through new digital worlds, including the vast App economy. This low-carbon civil society is developing preparedness for changes to come and trying to limit current processes, so making eventual outcomes less dire. This civil society is helping to realize preparedness and precaution in a world of ignorance and uncertainty as to what will or could or should work.[35]

We do not know whether this 'low-carbon civil society' can generate sufficient new practices, habits, goods and services to power down societies on a global scale, offsetting contending powerful forces, especially of carbon and finance capital. Are there historical parallels which might help in thinking a way forward here?

Perhaps the best book on the history of the 'West' is E.P. Thompson's *The Making of the English Working Class*. Over 950 pages long, this book documents just how that newly forming working class in England was involved in its own 'making' over the course of the nineteenth century.[36] For Thompson such a social class is fundamentally historical and involves transforming itself over time but not in circumstances that it has itself chosen.

Can we think of low-carbon civil society developing in the same way? Can that civil society make itself and gain such traction

that in transforming its own future it in effect remakes societies worldwide? This would be analogous to the making of the
English working class. Might there be a future 950-page book
(or App) that documents a parallel making of global low-carbon
civil society which constructs a different future as it makes and
remakes itself around the world?

While civil society groups, innovation processes, the division of
labour and trade must be international, Keynes shows that finance
has to be renationalized, slowed down, onshored rather than
offshored and made transparent. Without 'nationalizing' finance
and its functioning as the handmaiden of the real economy, it
would seem to be impossible to reverse high-energy and high-
oil systems. As finance has come to form its own system, with
money begetting money as almost all domains of economy and
society are financialized, so it is unlikely that low-carbon civil
society/capital could *make* the twenty-first century.

Finance capital will not generate a planned, fair and democratic
reversal from oil.[37] Indeed Marx foresaw the capitalist capacity
for self-destruction when he described modern bourgeois society,
with its gigantic means of production and of exchange, being like
the sorcerer who is no longer able to control the powers of the
nether world that he called up by his spells.[38] The economic and
financial collapse of 2007–08 shows that no one is in charge and
understands what is going on and the powerful forces that are
being unleashed. Žižek provocatively writes that 'Capital is effectively an anonymous global machine blindly running its course,
… there is effectively no Secret Agent who animates it.'[39]

Those powers are on such a scale and developing with such
tremendous forward momentum that there are no sorcerers around
able to understand or deal with the powers unleashed by finance.

And they are certainly not up to doing so in time and on a sufficient scale worldwide. So other bleaker futures are likely given this dictatorship of global finance, which played such a dark role in those oil-dependent subprime American suburbs during what Foster and Magdoff term the 'Great Financial Crisis'.[40]

So in the end we can pose this as a choice between low carbon and high finance! We cannot have both – which is it to be and why? As oil runs down, so finance has ramped up, and it is equally detrimental to a planned powering-down future.

Conclusion

We know from Milton Friedman, the architect of neoliberalism whose ideas have been so fateful here, that there is no such thing as a free lunch.[41] This is a crucial point about energy, that there is no energy free lunch. Replacing one global system with another is an immense undertaking involving vast supplies of material resources, especially with increasing consumption, urbanization and population. Even so-called renewable energy requires minerals that are in increasingly short supply and whose manufacture generates substantial GHG emissions.[42] Again there is no free lunch – this book in no way seeks to argue for simply replacing fossil fuels with renewables.

The twentieth century operated as though that entire century was a free (liquid) lunch, especially of oil which could be burned with impunity and not even used to manufacture useful stuff. In that century oil and its carbon friends were a genie that escaped from the bottle and cannot be squeezed back in. There is no simple going back. It is a global tragedy that oil did ever seep out of the ground in the late nineteenth century and transformed twentieth-century societies in the many ways elaborated in this book. The local blessing of oil has turned into an extraordinary global curse. Oil and society formed a passionate and possibly deadly embrace.

Now we have got to the new century, we discover just how indigestible that free lunch was that came to be consumed. 'The twentieth century', according to Ian Morris, 'was both the high point of the Western age and the beginning of its end.'[43] We may well be seeing the end of the 'West' as dominant, which significantly stemmed from how it monopolized these climate-changing and non-renewable fossil fuels. Bill Spence, former vice president of Shell, writes apocalyptically that the knowledge that the next few decades require 'Twice the energy with half the carbon dioxide is a challenge for us all.'[44] How can that challenge be met given that the world is experiencing rising temperatures, oil down to its dregs, the enduring power of carbon capital, the dictatorship of financial markets and vast inequalities likely to engender bitter conflicts and opposition.

The only possible way forward is through a pervasive power-ing down to a low-carbon civil society, and as it makes itself to remake wider societies. Developing such 'a low-carbon civil society' is the pre-eminent global challenge to deal with the double whammy of rising temperatures and falling supplies of that oil which we cannot live with but will not be able to live without. The odds of this 'low-carbon civil society' making itself and hence remaking wider societies are very low, but fortunately not quite zero. This is without doubt the best of those visions of societies beyond oil. But, as noted throughout this book, what wins and what is best are often many miles apart.

NOTES

INTRODUCTION

1. Daniel Yergin, *The Quest* (London: Allen Lane, 2011), p. 4; Matthew Huber, 'Energizing historical materialism: Fossil fuels, space and the capitalist mode of production', *Geoforum* 40, 2009: 105–15.
2. See John Urry, *Climate Change and Society* (Cambridge: Polity, 2011).
3. Ian Morris, *How the West Rules – For Now* (London: Profile, 2010), p. 491. This is the same year as the Declaration of Independence by Britain's American colonies, and the publication of Adam Smith's *The Wealth of Nations*, which showed the huge economies that stem from a much marked division of labour within such factories.
4. Morris, *How the West Rules – For Now*, ch. 10.
5. Ian Carter, *Railways and Culture in Britain* (Manchester: Manchester University Press, 2001), p. 8.
6. Wolfgang Schivelbusch, *The Railway Journey* (California: University of California Press, 1986), p. 34.
7. Karl Marx, *Grundrisse* (Harmondsworth: Penguin, 1973), p. 524.
8. www.democracynow.org/2008/5/12/world_renowned_philosopher_slavoj_zizek_on, accessed 20 May 2010; on the limits of 'science' and 'policy', see Mike Hulme, *Why We Disagree About Climate Change* (Cambridge: Cambridge University Press, 2009).
9. See Morgan Downey, *Oil 101* (New York: Wooden Table Press, 2009) on the following.
10. Upton Sinclair, *Oil!* (London: Penguin, 2008 [1926]), p. 25.
11. Manraaj Singh, 'What's all the oil in the world worth?', www.fleetstreetinvest.co.uk/oil/oil-outlook/oil-world-worth-00027.html, accessed 23 June 2011.

12. See Tere Vadén, 'Oil and the regime of capitalism', *CTheory*, 23 June 2010: 1–11. There are only about 400 nuclear power stations around the world, many of which are coming to the end of their useful life.

13. Worldwide Fund for Nature, *Plugged In: The End of the Oil Age, Summary Report* (Brussels: WWF, March 2008), p. 2.

14. Thomas Homer-Dixon, *The Upside of Down* (London: Souvenir, 2006), p. 81.

15. Mark Harvey and Sarah Pilgrim, 'The new competition for land: Food, energy and climate change', *Food Policy* 36, 2011: S40–S51, p. S42. 'Industrialised farming' requires 50–100 times the energy input of 'traditional farming'.

16. In 2009, 43 per cent of CO_2 emissions from fuel combustion were produced from coal, 37 per cent from oil and 20 per cent from gas: International Energy Authority, *CO_2 Emissions from Fuel Combustion. Highlights* (Paris: IEA, 2011), p. 8.

17. See Ian Rutledge, *Addicted to Oil* (London: I.B. Tauris, 2005), pp. 1–4.

18. See Timothy Mitchell, *Carbon Democracy* (London: Verso, 2011), pp. 139–42.

19. Jeff Rubin, *Why Your World is About to Get a Whole Lot Smaller* (London: Virgin, 2009), pp. 76–7.

20. Nicholas Stern, *The Economics of Climate Change* (Cambridge: Cambridge University Press, 2007).

21. See Zygmunt Bauman, *Liquid Modernity* (Cambridge: Polity, 2000); oil is not in the index.

22. David Owen, *Green Metropolis* (London: Penguin, 2011), ch. 2.

23. Vaclav Smil, *Energy Transitions* (Santa Barbara CA: Praeger, 2010).

24. On the idea of the limits to growth, see Donella Meadows, Dennis Meadows and Jørgen Randers, *The Limits to Growth: A Report for the Club of Rome's Project on the Predicament of Mankind* (Berkeley CA: Earth Island, 1972).

25. www.energytribune.com/articles.cfm/737/The-Meek-Need-Mineral-Rights, accessed 20 December 2011.

26. See Stephen Burman, *The State of the American Empire* (London: Earthscan, 2007); Richard Heinberg, *The Party's Over* (New York: Clairview Books, 2005), pp. 30–32.

27. Julian Borger, 'Half of global car exhaust produced by US vehicles', *Guardian*, 29 June 2008; John DeCicco and Freda Fung, *Global Warming on the Road* (Washington DC: Environmental Defense, 2006).

28. Hulme, *Why We Disagree About Climate Change*, p. 261.

29. Rutledge, *Addicted to Oil*, pp. 2–3.

30. John R. McNeill, at www.theglobalist.com/StoryId.aspx?StoryId=2018, accessed 19 January 2012.

31. James Hansen, *Storms of My Grandchildren* (London: Bloomsbury, 2011), p. 176.

32. James Murray and David King, 'Climate policy: Oil's tipping point has

passed', *Nature* 481, 2012: 433–5. On energy and emissions, see International Energy Authority, *CO2 Emissions from Fuel Combustion: Highlights* (Paris: IEA, 2011).

33. Heinberg, *The Party's Over*, p. 100.

34. http://en.wiktionary.org/wiki/dregs, accessed 15 November 2011.

35. Douglas Adams, *The Hitchhikers Guide to the Galaxy* (London: Pan Macmillan, 1979).

36. Joni Mitchell, 'Big Yellow Taxi', *Ladies of the Canyon*, A&M, May 1970.

37. http://aoghs.org/did-you-know/history-of-the-42–gallon-oil-barrel; accessed 3 December 2012.

CHAPTER I

1. Antony Froggatt and Glada Lahn, *Sustainable Energy Security* (London: Lloyd's and Chatham House, 2010), pp. 13–15. Derivative markets are essentially unregulated; they contributed greatly to the economic collapse of 2007–08. There are now even 'nature' derivatives.

2. See Dan Dicker, *Oil's Endless Bid* (New York: Wiley, 2011).

3. See David Harvey, *A Brief History of Neoliberalism* (Oxford: Oxford University Press, 2005); Naomi Klein, *The Shock Doctrine* (London: Allen Lane, 2007); Colin Crouch, *The Strange Non-Death of Neo-Liberalism* (Cambridge: Polity, 2011).

4. Klein, *The Shock Doctrine*, p. 166.

5. Quoted in Nicholas Shaxson, *Treasure Islands* (London: Bodley Head, 2011), p. 230. Ridley was non-executive chairman of the toxic UK bank Northern Rock; see http://en.wikipedia.org/wiki/Matt_Ridley, accessed 31 October 2011.

6. Milton Friedman, *Capitalism and Freedom* (Chicago: University of Chicago Press, 2002).

7. Klein, *The Shock Doctrine*, pp. 3–21.

8. Ibid., p. 21.

9. Harvey, *A Brief History of Neoliberalism*, pp. 159–61.

10. Ibid., p. 3.

11. Shaxson, *Treasure Islands*, pp. 7–8, 26–7. On p. 143 he notes that one 'office' in Delaware houses 217,000 companies, in a way the world's biggest building!

12. Money laundering by criminal gangs is well described in Nick Kochan, *The Washing Machine* (London: Duckworth, 2006). See the listing of seventy or so tax havens based upon the index of financial secrecy: http://en.wikipedia.org/wiki/Financial_Secrecy_Index, accessed 28 January 2012.

13. See Joseph Stiglitz, *Making Globalization Work* (Harmondsworth: Penguin, 2007); Paul Krugman, *The Return of Depression Economics* (Harmondsworth: Penguin, 2008); George Soros, *The New Paradigm for Financial Markets* (London: Public Affairs, 2008); Hugo Radice, 'Confronting the crisis: A class analysis', *Socialist Register* 47, 2011: 21–43.

14. Saskia Sassen, 'Too big to save: The end of financial capitalism', *Open Democracy News Analysis*, 1 January 2009.

15. Serge Latouche, *Farewell to Growth* (Cambridge: Polity, 2009).

16. See Susan Strange, *Casino Capitalism* (Manchester: Manchester University Press, 1997); Nouriel Roubini and Stephen Mihm, *Crisis Economics* (London: Penguin, 2011), p. 231.

17. http://blogs.wsj.com/economics/2011/03/25/like-the-phoenix-u-s-finance-profits-soar, accessed 4 January 2012.

18. Nouriel Roubini and Stephen Mihm, *Crisis Economics* (London: Penguin, 2011), p. 82.

19. Ibid., p. 43; and see ch. 2 generally here.

20. See Andrew G. Haldane, and Robert M. May, 'Systemic risk in banking ecosystems', *Nature* 469, 2011: 351–5.

21. Richard Ingersoll, *Sprawltown* (Princeton NJ: Princeton University Press, 2006). I use the term 'petrol' rather than gasoline throughout.

22. Jeff Rubin, *Why Your World is About to Get a Whole Lot Smaller* (London: Virgin, 2009), p. 123.

23. Roubini and Mihm, *Crisis Economics*, p. 89.

24. Joseph Stiglitz, *Freefall* (London: Penguin, 2010), ch. 4.

25. These are end-of-year figures.

26. Joe Cortright, *Driven to the Brink* (Chicago: CEOs for Cities, 2008), p. 3.

27. Robert Brenner, *The Economics of Global Turbulence* (London: Verso, 2006), pp. 318–19.

28. Ibid., pp. 342–3.

29. Soros, *The New Paradigm for Financial Markets*. Gillian Tett in *Fool's Gold* (London: Little, Brown, 2009) shows how financial innovations generated at J.P. Morgan produced a global 'catastrophe' costing $2,000–4,000 billion. Roubini and Mihm, *Crisis Economics*, claim that Nouriel Roubini had seen it all coming!

30. James Murray and David King, 'Climate policy: Oil's tipping point has passed', *Nature* 481, 2012: 433–5; Roubini and Mihm, *Crisis Economics*, p. 137.

31. John Hofmeister, *Why We Hate the Oil Companies* (New York: Palgrave Macmillan, 2010), pp. 26, 48, and more generally for an oil insider's view.

32. Rubin, *Why Your World is About to Get a Whole Lot Smaller*, p. 183.

33. Mazen Labban, 'Oil in parallax: Scarcity, markets, and the financialization of accumulation', *Geoforum* 41, 2010: 541–52, p. 551. See Daniel Yergin, *The Quest* (London: Allen Lane, 2011), ch. 8, on recent oil price movement.

34. Thomas Homer-Dixon, *The Upside of Down* (London: Souvenir, 2006), p. 1.

35. See David Strahan, *The Last Oil Shock* (London: John Murray, 2007), pp. 57–60.

36. www.eia.doe.gov/oil_gas/petroleum/data_publications/wrgp/mogas_history.html, accessed 27 February 2009.

37. James Hamilton, 'The oil shock and recession of 2008: Part 2', *2009 Econbrowser*, www.econbrowser.com/archives/2009/01/the_oil_shock_a_1.html, accessed 10 March 2009.

38. Cortright, *Driven to the Brink*, p. 5. Australia too was a society whose growth in the 1990s was fuelled by cheap oil, speculative building of new tracts of car-dependent sprawltown, and increasing engine size and reduced fuel consumption: Jago Dodson and Neil Sipe, *Shocking the Suburbs* (Sydney: UNSW Press, 2008).

39. Roubini and Mihm, *Crisis Economics*, p. 95.

40. Polly Ghazi, 'Gas guzzlers and "ghostburbs"', *Guardian*, 2 July 2008; Dodson and Sipe, *Shocking the Suburbs*; Jeff Rubin, *Why Your World is About to Get a Whole Lot Smaller*, pp. 190–91.

41. Stiglitz, *Freefall*, ch. 4, on how securitizing mortgages actually made them more and not less risky.

42. Cortright, *Driven to the Brink*, p. 17.

43. www.bp.com/sectiongenericarticle.do?categoryId=9023770&contentId=7044467, accessed 20 April 2011.

44. Timothy Mitchell, *Carbon Democracy* (London: Verso, 2011), p. 233.

CHAPTER 2

1. Karl Marx, *Capital*, Volume 1 (Harmondsworth: Penguin, 1976 [1867]), p. 283. See Damian White and Chris Wilbert (eds), *Technonatures* (Waterloo, Ontario: Wilfrid Laurier University Press, 2009); Ivan Illich, *Energy and Equity* (London: Marion Boyars, 1974), p. 27.

2. Matthew Huber, 'Energizing historical materialism: Fossil fuels, space and the capitalist mode of production', *Geoforum* 40, 2009: 105–15,

3. Marx, *Capital*, Volume 1, p. 638.

4. John Urry, *Mobilities* (Cambridge: Polity, 2007), p. 14, and ch. 1 more generally.

5. Quoted in Blake Morrison, 'It was the cathedral of modern times, but the car is now a menace', *Guardian*, 26 July 2008.

6. See Morgan Downey, *Oil 101* (New York: Wooden Table Press, 2009), ch. 1.

7. Ian Rutledge, *Addicted to Oil* (London: I.B. Tauris, 2005).

8. Kingsley Dennis and John Urry, *After the Car* (Cambridge: Polity, 2009), ch. 2.

9. Jean-Pierre Bardou, Jean-Jacques Chanaron, Patrick Fridenson and James M. Laux, *The Automobile Revolution* (Chapel Hill: University of North Carolina Press, 1982).

10. Edwin Black, *Internal Combustion* (New York: St. Martin's Press, 2006), pp. 64–5.

11. See Daniel Miller (ed.), *Car Cultures* (Oxford: Berg, 2000), p. 7.

12. Andy Stern, *Who Won the Oil Wars?* (London: Conspiracy Books, 2005), p. 43; Daniel Sperling and Deborah Gordon, *Two Billion Cars* (Oxford: Oxford University Press, 2009), p. 113; Downey, *Oil 101*, p. 9.

13. Stern, *Who Won the Oil Wars?*, p. 73, as well as ch. 4 'Oil's Role in the Second World War'; John M. Greer, *The Ecotechnic Future* (Gabriola Island BC: New Society Publishers, 2009), ch. 9.

14. Fordism involves a system of economic management modelled on that employed by Henry Ford based on techniques of mass production and new kinds of mass consumption. Such Fordist firms could benefit by offering higher wages to allow workers to purchase the very products that they were producing, such as cars and other consumer goods.

15. See Paul French and Sam Chambers, *Oil on Water* (London: Zed Books, 2010).

16. Saolo Cwerner, Sven Kesselring and John Urry (eds), *Aeromobilities* (London: Routledge, 2009).

17. David Pascoe, *Airspaces* (London: Reaktion, 2001), p. 127, and more generally.

18. Peter Adey, *Aerial Life* (London: Wiley–Blackwell, 2010); Cwerner, Kesselring and Urry (eds), *Aeromobilities*.

19. See Vaclav Smil, *Oil: A Beginner's Guide* (Oxford: One World, 2008), ch. 1.

20. Mark Gottdiener, *Life in the Air* (Oxford: Rowman & Littlefield, 2001), p. 1.

21. Cited in Stern, *Who Won the Oil Wars?*, p. 30.

22. See on the importance of the *clustering* of innovation, Carlota Perez, *Technological Revolutions and Financial Capital* (Cheltenham: Edward Elgar, 2002).

23. David Nye, *Consuming Power* (Cambridge MA: MIT Press, 1998), pp. 202, 198; Thomas Hughes, *Networks of Power* (Baltimore MD: Johns Hopkins University Press, 1983), pp. 5–7, 465.

24. Mimi Sheller, 'Automotive emotions', *Theory, Culture and Society* 21, 2004: 221–42.

25. These cultural forms of autopia are elaborated in Peter Wollen and Joe Kerr (eds), *Autopia: Cars and Culture* (London: Reaktion Books, 2002). Movies include *Easy Rider*; *Rolling Stone*; *Alice Doesn't Live Here Anymore*; *American Graffiti*; *Bonnie and Clyde*; *Vanishing Point*; *Badlands*; *Thelma and Louise*; *Paris Texas*; *The Italian Job*; *Bullitt*; *Crash*.

26. Thanks to Satya Savitzky for this. See Thomas Birtchnell, '*Jugaad* as systemic risk and disruptive innovation in India', *Contemporary South Asia* 19, 2011: 357–72, on Indian cars and roads.

27. Richard Rogers, *Cities for a Small Planet* (London: Faber & Faber, 1997), p. 35.

28. Nye, *Consuming Power*, p. 251; Lewis Mumford, *Technics and Civilization* (New York: Harcourt, Brace, 1934).

29. Nye, *Consuming Power*, p. 215.

30. See Stephen Burman, *The State of the American Empire* (London: Earthscan, 2007); Richard Heinberg, *The Party's Over* (New York: Clairview Books, 2005), pp. 30–2.

31. http://en.wikipedia.org/wiki/File:Global_Carbon_Emissions.svg, accessed 20 April 2011. This figure shows the continued importance of coal emissions, as well as the significance of cement production and use, an issue relevant to the false idea that countries can *build* a green future!

32. See Burman, *The State of the American Empire*.

33. See David Strahan, *The Last Oil Shock* (London: John Murray, 2007), p. 112; David Owen, *Green Metropolis* (London: Penguin, 2011), pp. 84–5; Downey, *Oil 101*, for the science here.

34. Dale Pfeiffer, *Eating Fossil Fuels* (Gabriola Island BC: New Society, 2006), ch. 1. The Green Revolution in agriculture is the opposite of 'green'.

35. Dale Pfeiffer shows the astonishing array of deleterious effects arising from consuming even a modest cup of morning coffee: *Eating Fossil Fuels*, pp. 26–7.

36. www.opec.org/opec_web/en/index.htm, accessed 11 January 2012.

37. See Smil, *Oil: A Beginner's Guide*, ch. 1. Chapter 6 returns to these 'reserves' since their 'real' size is central to debates about peak oil.

38. See the movie *Collapse*, 2009: www.collapsemovie.com/; and see Michael C. Ruppert, *Confronting Collapse* (Vermont: Chelsea Green, 2009).

39. David Owen, *Green Metropolis* (London: Penguin, 2011), pp. 72–4.

40. See Bruno Latour, *We Have Never Been Modern* (Hemel Hempstead: Harvester Wheatsheaf, 1993).

CHAPTER 3

1. David Owen, *Green Metropolis* (London: Penguin, 2011), pp. 96–9.

2. See Dale Pfeiffer, *Eating Fossil Fuels* (Gabriola Island BC: New Society Publishers, 2006), p. 25 and throughout.

3. Michael C. Ruppert, *Confronting Collapse* (Vermont: Chelsea Green, 2009), p. 86.

4. Marc Levinson, *The Box* (Princeton NJ: Princeton University Press, 2006).

5. See Jonas Larsen, John Urry and Kay Axhausen, *Mobilities, Networks, Geographies* (Aldershot: Ashgate, 2006). I draw the concept of 'romance miles' from Anthony Elliott.

6. Anthony Elliott and John Urry, *Mobile Lives* (London: Routledge, 2010).

7. See the witty Karl Georg Høyer, 'Epilogue: The travelling circus of climate change', in Roy Bhaskar et al. (eds), *Interdisciplinarity and Climate Change* (London: Routledge, 2010).

8. Steffan Mau, *Social Transnationalism* (London: Routledge, 2010).

9. Adrian Favell, *Eurostars and Eurocities* (Oxford: Blackwell, 2008), pp. 9, 3.

10. Mattias Junemo, '"Let's build a palm island": Playfulness in complex times', in Mimi Sheller and John Urry (eds), *Tourism Mobilities* (London: Routledge, 2004), p. 184.

11. Jim Krane, *City of Gold* (London: Picador, 2010), ch. 13.

12. See www.burj-al-arab.com. See Christopher Davidson, *Dubai: The Vulnerability of Success* (London: Hurst, 2008); Heiko Schmid, *Economy of Fascination* (Berlin: Gebrüder Borntraeger, 2009); Krane, *City of Gold*.

13. Mike Davis, 'Sand, fear, and money in Dubai', in Mike Davis and Daniel Bertrand Monk (eds), *Evil Paradises* (New York: New Press, 2007), p. 52.

14. Umberto Eco, *Travels in Hyper-Reality* (London: Pan, 1987).

15. See Krane, *City of Gold*, ch. 6.

16. Davis, 'Sand, fear, and money in Dubai', pp. 64–6.

17. Krane, *City of Gold*, p. 117.

18. Richard Hoggart, *The Uses of Literacy* (London: Penguin, 2009), p. 49.

19. See Barry Smart, *Consumer Society* (London: Sage, 2010), one of the few books systematically linking consumerism and environmental issues.

20. See John Urry and Jonas Larsen, *The Tourist Gaze 3.0* (London: Sage, 2011).

21. David Nye, *Consuming Power* (Cambridge MA: MIT Press, 1998), p. 182; Ben Fine, *The World of Consumption* (London: Routledge, 2002), chs 5, 6.

22. See Daniel Miller, *A Theory of Shopping* (New York: Cornell University Press, 1998).

23. Smart, *Consumer Society*, pp. 160–61.

24. Amory Lovins et al., *Winning the Oil Endgame* (London: Earthscan, 2004), p. 17.

25. Caren Kaplan, *Questions of Travel* (Durham NC: Duke University Press, 1996), p. ix.

26. Ibid., p. ix.

27. Fred Hirsch, *Social Limits to Growth* (London: Routledge & Kegan Paul, 1977), pp. 39–40.

28. Barry Schwartz, *The Paradox of Choice* (New York: Harper, 2004), p. 191; John Urry, *Reference Groups and the Theory of Revolution* (London: Routledge, 1973).

29. John Meyrowitz, *No Sense of Place* (New York: Oxford University Press, 1985).

30. www.sfnblog.com/industry_trends/2009/09/sfn_report_global_ad_expenditure_to_reac.php, accessed 18 January 2012.

31. Worldwatch Institute, *2010 State of the World* (New York: W.W. Norton, 2010), p. 13; Smart, *Consumer Society*, pp. 45–6.

32. John Perkins, *Confessions of an Economic Hit Man* (London: Ebury Press, 2005), p. xiii.

33. Joseph Stiglitz, *Making Globalization Work* (Harmondsworth: Penguin, 2007).

34. Naomi Klein, *No Logo* (London: Flamingo, 2000).

35. Worldwatch Institute, *2010 State of the World*, p. 14; Smart, *Consumer Society* (London: Sage, 2010), p. 67; personal communication from Anthony Elliott re the cosmetics industry.

36. Smart, *Consumer Society*, ch. 4.

37. http://www.guardian.co.uk/commentisfree/2007/oct/16/comment.health, accessed 16 October 2007.

38. Avner Offer, *The Challenge of Affluence* (Oxford: Oxford University Press, 2006); Smart, *Consumer Society*, pp. 149–51.

39. Anthony Elliott, *Making the Cut* (London: Reaktion Books, 2007), p. 145.

40. See Clive Hamilton, *Requiem for a Species* (London: Earthscan, 2010), ch. 3.

41. These consuming addictions are wittily dissected in Michael Moore's 2009 movie *Capitalism: A Love Story*. It is not clear if there is more addiction now than in previous eras. And see the 2011 George Clooney movie *The Ides of March* where the presidential candidate promises to lead the USA into new world leadership through low-carbon technologies enabling the country finally to break with the addictive sands of Saudi Arabia.

42. Worldwatch Institute, *2010 State of the World*, p. 6.

43. Kenneth Gould, 'The ecological costs of militarization', *Peace Review* 19: 331–4, p. 331.

44. Andrew Jorgenson, Brett Clark and Jeffrey Kentor, 'Militarization and the environment: A panel study of carbon dioxide emissions and the ecological footprint of nations', *Global Environmental Politics* 10, 2010: 7–28, p. 9; Michael Klare, *Rising Powers, Shrinking Planet* (Oxford: One World, 2008), p. 11.

45. See John Urry, *Mobilities* (Cambridge: Polity, 2007).

46. Mimi Sheller and John Urry (eds), *Tourism Mobilities* (London: Routledge, 2004); Machiel Lamers, *The Future of Tourism in Antarctica* (Maastricht: Universitaire Press Maastricht, 2009); Mike Robinson and Marina Novelli (eds), *Niche Tourism* (Oxford: Elsevier, 2005).

47. Mike Davis and Daniel Bertrand Monk (eds), *Evil Paradises* (New York: New Press, 2007); Tim Simpson, 'Macao, capital of the 21st century', *Environment and Planning D: Society and Space* 26, 2008: 1053–79. See Chapter 6 below.

48. http://granscalablog.com/gran-scala, accessed 8 June 2009.

49. Mimi Sheller, *Consuming the Caribbean* (London: Routledge, 2003).

50. Mimi Sheller, 'Infrastructures of the imagined island: Software, mobilities, and the new architecture of cyberspatial paradise', *Environment and Planning A* 41, 2008: 1386–1403, p. 1396.

51. Mimi Sheller, 'The new Caribbean complexity: Mobility systems and the re-scaling of development', *Singapore Journal of Tropical Geography* 14, 2008: 373–84.

52. www.avidcruiser.com/cruise-line-profiles/big-ship/royal-caribbean-cruise-line, accessed 10 November 2011.

53. Rowland Atkinson and Sarah Blandy, 'A picture of the floating world: Grounding the secessionary affluence of the residential cruise liner', *Antipode* 41: 92–110, p. 105.

54. See Steve Graham and Simon Marvin, *Splintering Urbanism* (London: Routledge, 2001).
55. Atkinson and Blandy, 'A picture of the floating world', pp. 92–110, p. 96.
56. Gilberto Gallopin, Al Hammond, Paul Raskin and Rob Swart, *Branch Points: Global Scenarios and Human Choice* (Stockholm: Stockholm Environment Institute, Global Scenario Group, 1997); Mike Hulme, *Why We Disagree About Climate Change* (Cambridge: Cambridge University Press, 2009), pp. 269–71. Danny Dorling hypothesizes that world population may also be peaking: 'Possible "peak population": A world without borders', *Open Democracy*, 18 October 2011.
57. Clive Hamilton, *Requiem for a Species* (London: Earthscan, 2010), p. 43.
58. Other estimates suggest that this occurred earlier around 2000; see www.themobilecity.nl/2009/04/24/telecom-transport-and-unequal-time-space-compression, accessed 4 December 2011.
59. Richard Rogers, *Cities for a Small Planet* (London: Faber & Faber, 1997).
60. See Mike Davis, *Planet of Slums* (London: Verso, 2007), on the 200,000 or so slums mostly located on the edge of huge cities.
61. Suzana Kahn Ribeiro, Shigeki Kobayashi et al., 'Transport and its infrastructure', in *Climate Change 2007: Mitigation. Contribution of Working Group III to the Fourth Assessment Report of the Intergovernmental Panel on Climate Change* (Cambridge: Cambridge University Press, 2007), p. 328.
62. See Ian Roberts with Phil Edwards, *The Energy Glut* (London: Zed Books, 2010).
63. Thomas Homer-Dixon, *The Upside of Down* (London: Souvenir, 2006), p. 198.
64. See the map at www.themobilecity.nl/2009/04/24/telecom-transport-and-unequal-time-space-compression, accessed 4 December 2011.
65. www.cnn.com/2009/business/12/14/dubai.10.billion.bailout/index.html, accessed 5 March 2010.

CHAPTER 4

1. See Stephen Burman, *The State of the American Empire* (London: Earthscan, 2007); Richard Heinberg, *The Party's Over* (Forest Row, East Sussex: Clairview Books, 2005), pp. 30–32.
2. Jeremy Leggett, *Half Gone* (London: Portobello Books, 2005), p. 12; see Tom Bower, *The Squeeze* (London: Harper Press, 2009).
3. One can suggest that the twentieth century saw a more general 'carbon military–industrial complex' develop.
4. Quoted in Edward Platt, *Leadville* (London: Picador, 2000), p. 194.
5. See Peter Wollen and Joe Kerry (eds), *Autopia* (London: Reaktion Books, 2002); Heathcote Williams, *Autogeddon* (London: Jonathan Cape, 1991).
6. Each company was fined $5,000 plus court costs of $4,220.78, and each individual was ordered to pay $1 for 'his role in the conspiracy'. See Edwin Black, *Internal Combustion* (New York: St. Martin's Press, 2006).

7. Quoted in Ian Rutledge, *Addicted to Oil* (London: I.B. Tauris, 2005), p. 13.

8. Wolfgang Sachs, *For Love of the Automobile* (Berkeley: University of California Press, 1992).

9. See Peter Merriman's account of making the new 'driving space' of the M1, *Driving Spaces* (Malden MA: Blackwell, 2007).

10. Earth Day is observed on 22 April each year by more than 500 million people and 175 governments.

11. Eugene Linden, *Winds of Change* (New York: Simon & Schuster, 2007), p. 101.

12. Kenneth E. Boulding, *Earth as a Space Ship* (Washington: Washington State University, Committee on Space Sciences, 10 May 1965).

13. Cited in UNDP, *Human Development Report 2007/8* (New York: UNDP, 2007), p. 21.

14. James Lovelock, *The Revenge of Gaia* (London: Allen Lane, 2006).

15. Joni Mitchell, 'Big Yellow Taxi', *Ladies of the Canyon*, A&M, May 1970.

16. See Donella Meadows, Dennis Meadows and Jørgen Randers, *The Limits to Growth: A Report for the Club of Rome's Project on the Predicament of Mankind* (Berkeley CA: Earth Island, 1972); E.F. Schumacher, *Small is Beautiful* (London: Blond & Briggs, 1973); and see André Gorz (Michel Bosquet), *Ecologie et Politique* (Paris: Galilée, 1975); Ivan Illich, *Energy and Equity* (London: Marion Boyars, 1974); Theodor Roszak, *Where the Wasteland Ends* (New York: Doubleday, 1973).

17. Timothy Mitchell, *Carbon Democracy* (London: Verso, 2011), ch. 7.

18. See Sharon Beder, *Global Spin* (London: Green Books, 2002); Naomi Oreskes and Erik Conway, *Merchants of Doubt* (New York: Bloomsbury, 2010), on how corporations cast 'doubt' on science.

19. Aaron McCright and Riley Dunlap, 'Anti-reflexivity: The American Conservative movement's success in undermining climate change science and policy', *Theory, Culture and Society* 27, 2010: 100–133; Timothy Mitchell, *Carbon Democracy* (London: Verso, 2011), ch. 7.

20. See John Hofmeister, *Why We Hate the Oil Companies* (New York: Palgrave Macmillan, 2010).

21. On the 1980s return to guilt-free 'spending, driving, wasting', see Heinberg, *The Party's Over*, pp. 78–9.

22. Beder, *Global Spin*, p. 21; Arthur Mol, 'The environmental movement in an era of ecological modernisation', *Geoforum* 31, 2000: 45–56, p. 52.

23. www.margaretthatcher.org/document/107346, accessed 16 May 2011.

24. Beder, *Global Spin*; Oreskes and Conway, *Merchants of Doubt*.

25. Aaron McCright and Riley Dunlap, 'Anti-reflexivity: The American Conservative movement's success in undermining climate change science and policy', *Theory, Culture and Society* 27, 2010: 100–33.

26. www.guardian.co.uk/politics/2009/dec/01/hugh-muirs-diary-john-prescott, accessed 28 December 2009; see Nigel Lawson, *An Appeal to Reason: A Cool Look at Global Warming* (London: Gerald Duckworth, 2008).

27. Nick Davies, *Flat Earth News* (London: Vintage, 2009), p. 188.

28. See Beder, *Global Spin*.

29. Heinberg, *The Party's Over*, p. 75.

30. http://en.wikipedia.org/wiki/Three_Days_of_the_Condor, accessed 10 November 2011.

31. Heinberg, *The Party's Over*, p. 43; and see David Strahan, *The Last Oil Shock* (London: John Murray, 2007), pp. 185–6.

32. See the 2005 film documentary *Enron: The Smartest Guys in the Room* (dir. Alex Gibney).

33. See Michael Klare, *Rising Powers, Shrinking Planet* (Oxford: One World, 2008), pp. 176, 180.

34. Andy Stern, *Who Won the Oil Wars?* (London: Conspiracy Books, 2005), pp. 159–60.

35. See MichaelMoore.com website and the movie *Fahrenheit 9/11*.

36. This conspiracy account linking September 11th to peak oil is found in Michael C. Ruppert's *Crossing the Rubicon* (Gabriola Island BC: New Society, 2004).

37. This speech was made on 9 December 1999: www.sustainableabq.com/peakoil.htm, accessed 27 May 2011. See Rutledge, *Addicted to Oil*, on how American foreign policy has been formed around the interlocking interests of oil and vehicle manufacturing.

38. William Engdahl, *A Century of War* (London: Pluto, 2004), on the place of oil in the dark history of the twentieth century.

39. See Klare, *Rising Powers, Shrinking Planet*, p. 187; http://en.wikipedia.org/wiki/United_States_armed_forces, accessed 28 September 2011.

40. IPCC www.ipcc.ch/ (2007), accessed 2 June 2008; Nicholas Stern, *The Economics of Climate Change* (Cambridge: Cambridge University Press, 2007); UNDP, *Human Development Report 2007/8* (New York: UNDP, 2007).

41. Kirstin Dow and Thomas Downing, *The Atlas of Climate Change* (London: Earthscan, 2011), p. 38; on the widespread agreement between scientists as to the significance of anthropogenic climate change, see: www.sciencemag.org/content/306/5702/1686.full, accessed 24 November 2011.

42. Kathryn Yusoff, 'Biopolitical economies and the political aesthetics of climate change', *Theory, Culture and Society* 27, 2010: 73–99.

43. See Dow and Downing, *The Atlas of Climate Change*, ch. 1.

44. James Hansen, *Storms of My Grandchildren* (London: Bloomsbury, 2011), ch. 11.

45. Peter Newell and Matthew Paterson, *Climate Capitalism* (Cambridge: Cambridge University Press, 2010).

46. See the UK government's http://actonco2.direct.gov.uk/actonco2/home.html, accessed 28 December 2009.

47. Kim Humphrey, *Excess* (Cambridge: Polity, 2010), especially ch. 2.

48. www.transitiontowns.org, accessed 8 January 2010. See Shaun Chamberlin, *The Transition Timeline* (Totnes: Green Books, 2009).

49. http://transitionculture.org/wp-content/uploads/KinsaleEnergyDescent ActionPlan.pdf, accessed 22 May 2011. Transition Towns has featured in the plot line of the long-running BBC Radio 4 series *The Archers*.

50. See the illuminating map at www.transitionnetwork.org/map, accessed 14 January 2012.

51. Raquel Pinderhughes, *Alternative Urban Futures* (New York: Rowman & Littlefield, 2004), p. 137.

52. Oreskes and Conway, *Merchants of Doubt*, p. 213. Only one climate-change-sceptic book appeared in 2001, while eighteen were published in 2009.

52. See McCright and Dunlap, 'Anti-reflexivity', pp. 100–33. The Koch brothers are large-scale funders of climate-change denial foundations and think-tanks: Christian Parenti, *Tropic of Chaos* (New York: Nation Books, 2011), ch. 15.

54. Office of Senator James Inhofe ('Inhofe Delivers Major Speech on the Science of Climate Change', 28 July 2003). Press release: http://inhofe. senate.gov/pressapp/record.cfm?id=206907, accessed 23 December 2009.

55. www.lcv.org/images/client/pdfs/LCV_2006_Scorecard_final.pdf, accessed 30 December 2009.

56. Suzanne Goldenberg, 'Republicans attack Obama's green agenda across multiple fronts', *Guardian*, 5 March 2011.

57. http://en.wikipedia.org/wiki/Top_gear, accessed 12 March 2010.

58. Matthew Paterson, *Automobile Politics* (Cambridge: Cambridge University Press, 2007), ch. 3.

59. Worldwide Fund for Nature, *Plugged In: The End of the Oil Age, Summary Report* (Brussels: WWF, March 2008), p. 7.

60. Klare, *Rising Powers, Shrinking Planet*, p. 72.

61. Hofmeister, *Why We Hate the Oil Companies*, p. 221. On his last occasion at a global summit, former oilman President George W. Bush signed off with this unforgettable comment on the USA's emissions legacy to the world: 'Goodbye from the world's biggest polluter.' It is now the second largest in terms of GHG emissions.

CHAPTER 5

1. David Strahan, *The Last Oil Shock* (London: John Murray, 2007), ch. 2; Stephen Burman, *The State of the American Empire* (London: Earthscan, 2007), pp. 26–9; Amory Lovins et al., *Winning the Oil Endgame* (London: Earthscan, 2004), p. 12.

2. See Robert Hirsch, *Peaking of World Oil Production: The Timetable* (Washington DC: Atlantic Council of the United States, 2005), on how peak oil especially impacts upon the USA. See special issues on peak oil in *Geoforum*, 2010, and *Futures*, 2011.

3. Kjell Aleklett, *Peak Oil and the Evolving Strategies of Oil Importing and Exporting Countries*, OECD Discussion Paper 2007–17, Stockholm, December 2007, and generally on peak oil.

4. In 1956, M. King Hubbert, a Shell Oil geologist, predicted the peaking of US oil in 1965–70 (the actual peak was 1970; the level was somewhat higher than Hubbert predicted): see http://peakoil.com, accessed 30 May 2010. On 'peak gas', see Julian Darley *High Noon for Natural Gas* (Vermont: Chelsea Green, 2004).

5. Colin Campbell and Siobhan Heapes, *An Atlas of Oil and Gas Depletion* (London: Jeremy Mills, 2009).

6. Report cited in Michael C. Ruppert, *Confronting Collapse* (Vermont: Chelsea Green, 2009), p. 19.

7. www.energybulletin.net/node/11621, accessed 28 December 2010.

8. Colin Campbell of the Association for the Study of Peak Oil and Gas (ASPO); and Kenneth Deffeyes, *Beyond Oil – the View from Hubbert's Peak* (New York: Hill & Wang, 2005).

9. '2020 vision', *The Economist*, 10 December 2009; Jeremy Leggett, *Half Gone* (London: Portobello Books, 2005).

10. www.good.is/post/international-energy-agency-s-top-economist-says-oil-peaked-in-2006, accessed 27 December 2011; Minqi Li, 'Peak oil, the rise of China and India, and the Global Energy Crisis', *Journal of Contemporary Asia* 37, 2007: 449–71, p. 452; www.youtube.com/watch?v=-bbAJ5dk6y8, accessed 27 December 2011.

11. www.irishtimes.com/newspaper/world/2011/0429/1224295673147.html, accessed 30 May 2011.

12. Antony Froggatt and Glada Lahn, *Sustainable Energy Security: Strategic Risks and Opportunities for Business* (London: Lloyd's and Chatham House, 2010), p. 13; see the authoritative UKERC Report, www.ukerc.ac.uk/support/tiki-index.php?page=0910GlobalOilRelease, accessed 3 June 2012.

13. Jeff Rubin, *Why Your World is About to Get a Whole Lot Smaller* (London: Virgin, 2010), p. 11; James Murray and David King, 'Climate policy: Oil's tipping point has passed', *Nature* 481, 2012: 433–5.

14. 'Peak oil alarm revealed by secret official talks', *Observer*, 22 August 2010; see George Monbiot at www.guardian.co.uk/environment/george monbiot/2011/jun/16/peak-oil-labour-government, accessed 10 November 2011. See Murray and King, 'Climate policy', pp. 433–5; David King was a former UK Government Chief Scientist.

15. http://earlywarn.blogspot.com/2011/07/update-on-north-sea-oil-production.html, accessed 30 December 2011. This figure treats the UK as a single entity. It thus conceals the issue of 'Scottish oil', oil derived from the Scottish continental shelf. The significance of this underlies the growth of recent Scottish nationalism and a possible referendum on Scottish independence that might be held in 2013/14.

16. www.bbc.co.uk/news/business-15462923, accessed 12 April 2012.

17. Peter Maass, *Crude World* (London: Allen Lane, 2009), p. 19.

18. Michael C. Ruppert, *Crossing the Rubicon* (Gabriola Island BC: New Society Publishers, 2004), pp. 44–5.

19. See www.ifandp.com/article/009585.html (accessed 23 June 2011) on recent doubts about the real size of Saudi oil reserves. See *Guardian*, 8 February 2011 and 10 February 2011.

20. Cited in Maass, *Crude World*, p. 12. See Matthew Simmons, *Twilight in the Desert* (New York: John Wiley, 2005).

21. See the salutary analysis in William Freudenberg and Robert Gramling, *Blowout in the Gulf* (Cambridge MA: MIT Press, 2011).

22. See Ruppert, *Confronting Collapse*, ch. 3. Recent drilling off Greenland by Cairn Energy cost $1 billion but resulted in no significant finds: www.heraldscotland.com/business/corporate-sme/greenland-woe-puts-pressure-on-cairn-energy-1.1137470, accessed 2 December 2011.

23. Industry Taskforce on Peak Oil and Energy Security, *Briefing Note on Deepwater Oil Production* (London: ITPOES, November 2010).

24. See the campaigning group Platform, *BP and Shell: Rising Risks in Tar Sands Investments* (London: Platform, 2008), as well as www.platformlondon.org/aboutplatform.asp, accessed 14 August 2010. See Morgan Downey, *Oil 101* (New York: Wooden Table Press, 2009), pp. 43–6, as well as *Fubar 2*, a comedy film set in the Canadian tar sands.

25. Murray and King, 'Climate policy', pp. 433–5.

26. See analysis in Richard Heinberg, *The Party's Over* (New York: Clearview Books, 2005), p. 127, who discusses this in the context of Bjørn Lomborg's climate change scepticism.

27. The *BP Statistical Review of World Energy* (London: BP, 2012) shows oil production in 2010 was 88 million barrels per day.

28. See Shaun Chamberlin, *The Transition Timeline* (Totnes: Green Books, 2009), pp. 119–21.

29. Daniel Sperling and Deborah Gordon, *Two Billion Cars* (Oxford: Oxford University Press, 2009), ch 5; Robert Hirsch, *The Inevitable Peaking of World Oil Production* (Washington DC: Atlantic Council of the United States, October 2005), p. 7. For a comprehensive rejoinder, see Daniel Yergin, *The Quest* (London: Allen Lane, 2011), who argues that at worst there will be a plateauing of oil supplies, especially because new technologies will permit novel energy resources to be accessed in the future.

30. See http://makewealthhistory.org/2010/06/11/how-much-oil-is-there-left-really, accessed 25 June 2011; www.appgopo.org.uk, accessed 8 January 2012.

31. Jeremy Rifkin, *The Hydrogen Economy* (New York: Penguin Putnam, 2002), p. 174.

32. See UN–Habitat, *Cities and Climate Change* (London: Earthscan, 2011).

33. Suzana Ribeiro and Shigeki Kobayashi, 'Transport and its infrastructure', in B. Metz, O.R. Davidson, P.R. Bosch, R. Dave and L.A. Meyer (eds),

Climate Change 2007: Mitigation of Climate Change (Cambridge: Cambridge University Press, 2007), p. 328. See Karen Lucas et al. (eds), *Auto Motives* (London: Emerald, 2010).

34. Heinberg, *The Party's Over*, p. 1.

35. Amory Lovins et al., *Winning the Oil Endgame* (London: Earthscan, 2004), pp. 8–12.

36. See Paul French and Sam Chambers, *Oil on Water* (London: Zed Books, 2010), ch. 5, on the security dangers of transporting oil through the Malacca Straits, the Straits of Hormuz and past Somalia.

37. Sperling and Gordon, *Two Billion Cars*, pp. 120–21.

38. See Nicholas Shaxson, *Treasure Islands* (London: Bodley Head, 2011).

39. www.guardian.co.uk/business/2011/dec/14/iea-high-oil-prices-global-economy, accessed 27 December 2011.

40. Froggatt and Lahn, *Sustainable Energy Security*, pp. 13–5; Lovins et al., *Winning the Oil Endgame*, pp. 8–12.

41. See Mazen Labban, 'Oil in parallax: Scarcity, markets, and the financialization of accumulation', *Geoforum* 41, 2010: 541–52.

42. See Thomas Homer-Dixon, *The Upside of Down* (London: Souvenir, 2006); Anthony Giddens, *The Politics of Climate Change* (Cambridge: Polity, 2009); John Urry, *Climate Change and Society* (Cambridge: Polity, 2011).

43. John Vidal, 'Warning: Extreme weather ahead', *Guardian*, 14 June 2011; see documentation at www.heatisonline.org/weather.cfm, accessed 24 December 2011.

44. Mike Davis, 'Who will build the ark?' *New Left Review* 61, 2010: 29–46, p. 17.

45. Chris Abbott, *An Uncertain Future* (Oxford: Oxford Research Group, 2008).

46. Davis, 'Who will build the ark?', p. 17.

47. See Christian Parenti, *Tropic of Chaos* (New York: Nation Books, 2011), pp. 7–9, and throughout.

48. See extensive documentation in www.un.org/womenwatch/feature/climate_change, accessed 8 January 2012.

49. James Kunstler, *The Long Emergency* (London: Atlantic Books, 2006), p. 65.

50. See Strahan, *The Last Oil Shock*, p. 123; Thomas Homer-Dixon (ed.), *Carbon Shift* (Canada: Random House, 2009), p. 13.

51. See Urry, *Climate Change and Society*, ch. 3. See Gavin Bridge, 'Geographies of peak oil: The other carbon problem', *Geoforum* 41, 2010: 523–30.

CHAPTER 6

1. William Engdahl, *A Century of War* (London: Pluto, 2004), pp. 250–55.

2. Ian Morris, *How the West Rules – For Now* (London: Profile, 2010); Martin Jacques, *When China Rules the World* (London: Penguin, 2012), ch. 1.

3. J. Timmons Roberts, 'Multipolarity and the new world (dis)order: US hegemonic decline and the fragmentation of the global climate regime', *Global Environmental Change* 21, 2011: 776–84; on reduced defence expenditure, see www.voanews.com/english/news/usa/Obama-to-Unveil-New-Military-Shaped-by-Budget-Cuts-136728598.html, accessed 8 January 2012.

4. See the influential *Joint Operating Environment Report 2010*, www.peakoil.net/files/JOE2010.pdf, accessed 31 October 2011.

5. http://en.wikipedia.org/wiki/List_of_countries_by_population, accessed 8 January 2012.

6. Minqi Li, 'Peak oil, the rise of China and India, and the Global Energy Crisis', *Journal of Contemporary Asia* 37, 2007: 449–71; Perry Anderson, 'Two revolutions', *New Left Review* 61, 2010: 59–96. My thinking on China has been greatly assisted by collaborating with David Tyfield.

7. http://en.wikipedia.org/wiki/Joseph_Needham, accessed 10 November 2011; Matthew Huber, 'Energizing historical materialism: Fossil fuels, space and the capitalist mode of production', *Geoforum* 40, 2009: 105–15, fig. 2. See Julia Lovell, *The Great Wall* (London: Atlantic, 2006), on presumed Chinese superiority.

8. See www.bbc.co.uk/news/business-12427321, accessed 30 June 2011; and Jacques, *When China Rules the World*, on the debates when, and not if, China will overtake the USA as the world's largest economy.

9. Jacques, *When China Rules The World*. See Giovanni Arrighi, *Adam Smith in Beijing* (London: Verso, 2007).

10. Michael Klare, *Rising Powers, Shrinking Planet* (Oxford: One World, 2008), pp. 66–7; Jean Daubier, *A History of the Chinese Cultural Revolution* (New York: Vintage, 1974).

11. www.imf.org/external/pubs/ft/weo/2011/02/weodata/index.aspx, accessed 12 January 2012. See Sylvia Walby, *Globalization and Inequalities* (London: Sage, 2009) p. 230, on the alternative purchasing power parity measure of GDP. By early 2012 some commentators were predicting a dramatic slowdown in Chinese growth.

12. See David Tyfield, Yongguan Zhu and Jinghua Cao, 'The importance of the "international dividend": The case of China', *Science and Public Policy* 36, 2009: 723–35. Citation rates of Chinese papers remain relatively low.

13. On this paragraph, see www.businessinsider.com/china-is-worlds-largest-energy-consumer-2011-6#ixzz1QkyWJVpI, accessed 30 June 2011.

14. On comparative energy efficiency, see Tom Bower, *The Squeeze* (London: HarperPress, 2009), pp. 343–4; Klare, *Rising Powers, Shrinking Planet*, ch. 3.

15. James Kunstler, *The Long Emergency* (London: Atlantic Books, 2006), p. 84; www.bbc.co.uk/news/10311029, accessed 30 June 2011.

16. http://seekingalpha.com/article/130258-peak-oil-china-vs-usa, accessed 30 June 2011).

17. David Strahan, *The Last Oil Shock* (London: John Murray, 2007), pp. 178–9.

18. Klare, *Rising Powers, Shrinking Planet*, pp. 73–7; Peter Maass, *Crude World* (London: Allen Lane, 2009), ch. 2.

19. See Bill Brugger, *Contemporary China* (London: Croom Helm, 1977).

20. See Pál Nyíri, *Mobility and Cultural Authority in Contemporary China* (Seattle: University of Washington Press, 2010), ch. 1.

21. Ibid., pp. 11–12.

22. David Owen, *Green Metropolis* (London: Penguin, 2011), ch. 6.

23. See www.guardian.co.uk/world/2010/may/27/foxconn-suicide-tenth-iphone-china, accessed 31 October 2011.

24. Nyíri, *Mobility and Cultural Authority in Contemporary China*, p. 17.

25. Klare, *Rising Powers, Shrinking Planet*, p. 69.

26. Jonathan Watts, *When a Billion Chinese Jump* (London: Faber & Faber, 2011), p. 166.

27. See Tim Simpson, 'Neoliberalism with Chinese characteristics: Consumer pedagogy in Macao', in Heiko Schmid, Wolf-Dietrich Sahr and John Urry (eds), *Cities and Fascination* (Aldershot: Ashgate, 2011).

28. Quoted in Tim Simpson, 'Macao, capital of the 21st century', *Environment and Planning D* 26, 2008: 1053–79.

29. Ibid., pp. 1053–79, p. 1057. The rates of consumer spending in China are still very low and hence China generates extraordinary surpluses.

30. Explored in Nyíri, *Mobility and Cultural Authority in Contemporary China*.

31. www.chinadialogue.net/article/show/single/en/297–Which-way-China-, accessed 11 April 2007.

32. Jacques, *When China Rules the World*, p. 539.

33. www.iht.com/articles/2007/05/30/asia/letter.php, accessed 4 June 2007.

34. See www.spiked-online.com/index.php/site/article/7330, accessed 8 July 2011.

35. Eric Thun, *Changing Lanes in China* (Cambridge: Cambridge University Press, 2006), p. 54.

36. Daniel Sperling and Deborah Gordon, *Two Billion Cars* (Oxford: Oxford University Press, 2009), p. 4; Li, 'Peak oil, the rise of China and India, and the Global Energy Crisis', pp. 449–71.

37. See projections in Marcos Chamon, Paolo Mauro and Yohei Okawa, 'Mass car ownership in the emerging market giants', *Economic Policy* (Washington DC: IMF, 2008), pp. 243–96.

38. See Ian Roberts with Phil Edwards, *The Energy Glut* (London: Zed Books, 2010), p. 46, on the exceptional obesity growth in China. See Klare, *Rising Powers, Shrinking Planet*, pp. 66–73, on the resource implications of 'urban mobilization' in China.

39. Jonathan Porritt, 'China: The most important story in the world', *China Dialogue*, 11 September 2006.

40. Jacques, *When China Rules The World*, pp. 212, 542–3.

41. See Paul French and Sam Chambers, *Oil on Water* (London: Zed Books, 2010), p. 39 and more generally.

42. Marc Levinson, *The Box* (Princeton NJ: Princeton University Press, 2008). It is said that one in every two containers in the world spends time in China during each of its journeys; see French and Chambers, *Oil on Water*, p. 43.

43. I am grateful to Satya Savitzky for his observations here.

44. Klare, *Rising Powers, Shrinking Planet*, p. 247.

45. Thomas Friedman, 'The new sputnik', *International Herald Tribune*, 28 September 2009. See Watts, *When a Billion Chinese Jump*.

46. On 2010, see Kirstin Dow and Thomas Downing, *The Atlas of Climate Change* (London: Earthscan, 2011), p. 38.

47. See Watts, *When a Billion Chinese Jump*, ch. 3.

48. See ibid.

49. Porritt, 'China'.

50. Giovanni Arrighi, *Adam Smith in Beijing* (London: Verso, 2007), pp. 388–9.

51. Watts, *When a Billion Chinese Jump*, ch. 3.

52. See Jonathan Watts, 'China tries to jump-start green car market', *Guardian*, 3 April 2009; and *When a Billion Chinese Jump*.

53. http://en.wikipedia.org/wiki/High-speed_rail_in_China#The_.22Speed_Up.22_campaigns, accessed 23 November 2011.

54. See www.publications.parliament.uk/pa/cm201012/cmselect/cmtran/writev/rail/m63.htm (accessed 18 December 2011) for UK debates.

55. Li, 'Peak oil, the rise of China and India, and the Global Energy Crisis', pp. 449–71, pp. 465–7.

56. Peter Maass, *Crude World* (London: Allen Lane, 2009); Andy Stern, *Who Won the Oil Wars?* (London: Conspiracy Books, 2005), p. 246. See Jacques, *When China Rules the World* for the best analysis of a China-dominated economic, social and cultural world.

CHAPTER 7

1. *There Will Be Blood*, 2007, dir. Paul Thomas Anderson.

2. Ivan Illich, *Energy and Equity* (London: Marion Boyars, 1974), p. 17.

3. Norman Dennis, Fernando Henriques and Clifford Slaughter, *Coal is Our Life* (London: Tavistock, 1956).

4. Timothy Mitchell, *Carbon Democracy* (London: Verso, 2011).

5. Ibid., ch. 1.

6. Daniel Sperling and Deborah Gordon, *Two Billion Cars* (Oxford: Oxford University Press, 2009), pp. 122–3.

7. Amory Lovins et al., *Winning the Oil Endgame* (London: Earthscan, 2004), p. 19. See Sperling and Gordon, *Two Billion Cars*, p. 122, on oil's curse.

8. Terry Lynn Karl, *The Paradox of Plenty* (Berkeley: University of California Press, 1997).

9. *BP Statistical Review of World Energy*, June 2011, pp. 6–8.

10. This is well documented in Timothy Mitchell, *Carbon Democracy* (London: Verso, 2011), chs 2, 3, 4. See ch. 8 on the history of Saudi Arabia and of the dominance of Wahhabism.

11. Peter Maass, *Crude World* (London: Allen Lane, 2009), p. 170.
12. http://hdrstats.undp.org/en/indicators/161.html, accessed 29 July 2011.
13. See Maass, *Crude World*, p. 169.
14. See the long list of bases at www.globemaster.de/regbases.html, accessed 29 July 2011.
15. www.hrw.org/en/world-report-2011/saudi-arabia, accessed 29 July 2011.
16. http://english.aljazeera.net/indepth/opinion/2011/06/201161694746333674. html, accessed 28 July 2011.
17. Maass, *Crude World*, p. 176.
18. www.guardian.co.uk/global-development/poverty-matters/2011/may/11/ most-dangerous-roads, accessed 28 July 2011.
19. www.saudiaramcoworld.com/issue/199206/the.discovery.principle-.touch. think.and.explore..htm, accessed 28 July 2011.
20. Maass, *Crude World*, p. 181.
21. Ibid., ch. 9; William Engdahl, *A Century of War* (London: Pluto, 2004), p. 202.
22. *BP Statistical Review of World Energy*, June 2011, pp. 6–8. Russia does not possess the largest reserves, though, so this position is unsustainable in the longer term.
23. Maass, *Crude World*, pp. 191–2.
24. Dominic Midgley and Chris Hutchins, *Abramovich: The Billionaire from Nowhere* (London: HarperCollins, 2005); http://en.wikipedia.org/wiki/ Roman_Abramovich, accessed 28 July 2011.
25. www.imdb.com/title/tt1733525, accessed 11 November 2011.
26. See documentation and mapping of oil in the Gulf of Guinea, in Andy Rowell, James Marriott and Lorne Stockman, *The Next Gulf* (London: Constable, 2005); Nicholas Shaxson, *Poisoned Wells* (London: Palgrave, 2008).
27. Rowell, Marriott and Stockman, *The Next Gulf*, p. 75.
28. Okey Ibeanu and Robin Luckman, 'Nigeria: Political violence, governance and corporate responsibility in a petro-state', in Mary Kaldor, Terry Lynn Karl and Yahia Said (eds), *Oil Wars* (London: Pluto, 2007), argue against the thesis that Nigeria would inevitably collapse into petro-violence.
29. See documentation in Tom Bower, *The Squeeze* (London: HarperPress, 2010), ch. 4; http://blog.platformlondon.org/2011/10/03/counting-the-cost-corporations-and-human-rights-abuses-in-the-niger-delta, accessed 21 November 2011.
30. Shaxson, *Poisoned Wells*, p. 17.
31. http://hdrstats.undp.org/en/countries/profiles/NGA.html, accessed 29 July 2011.
32. See documentation in Cyril Obi and Siri Aas Rustad (eds), *Oil and Insurgency in the Niger Delta* (London: Zed Books, 2011).
33. See ibid.; Rowell, Marriott and Stockman, *The Next Gulf*, ch. 3; Ibeanu and Luckman, 'Nigeria'.

34. Helon Habila, *Oil on Water* (London: Penguin, 2010); on Shell's recent major oil spill 75 miles off the Niger Delta, see www.guardian.co.uk/environment/2011/dec/22/nigerian-shell-oil-spill (accessed 27 December 2011).

35. See Tom O'Neill, 'Curse of the Black Gold: Hope and betrayal on the Niger Delta', *National Geographic*, February 2007.

36. Shaxson, *Poisoned Wells*, pp. 2, 228, and throughout.

37. Ibid., p. 235.

38. http://hdrstats.undp.org/en/countries/profiles/NOR.html, accessed 29 July 2011.

39. *BP Statistical Review of World Energy*, June 2011, pp. 6–8; www.cia.gov/library/publications/the-world-factbook/geos/no.html, accessed 29 July 2011.

40. www.foreignpolicy.com/articles/2011/06/17/2011_failed_states_index_interactive_map_and_rankings, accessed 29 July 2011.

41. www.transparency.org/policy_research/surveys_indices/cpi/2010/results, accessed 29 July 2011.

42. https://www.cia.gov/library/publications/the-world-factbook/rankorder/2172rank.html?countryName=Norway&countryCode=no&regionCode=eur&rank=134#no, accessed 29 July 2011.

43. The killing spree of anti-Muslim Anders Behring Breivik in 2011 thus traumatized Norway; see http://digitalgroup.info/wordpress/index.php/archives/136703, accessed 11 November 2011.

44. http://en.wikipedia.org/wiki/Sovereign_wealth_fund#Largest_sovereign_wealth_funds, accessed 29 July 2011.

45. Paul French and Sam Chambers, *Oil on Water* (London: Zed Books, 2010), p. 160.

46. Vaclav Smil, *Oil: A Beginner's Guide* (Oxford: Oneworld, 2008), p. 38.

47. Maass, *Crude World*, p. 125.

48. Cited in Andy Stern, *Who Won the Oil Wars?* (London: Conspiracy Books, 2005), p. 172.

49. Karl, *The Paradox of Plenty*.

50. See Timothy Mitchell, *Carbon Democracy* (London: Verso, 2011).

51. Maass, *Crude World*, p. 125; Ian Rutledge, *Addicted to Oil* (London: I.B. Tauris, 2005), p. 3.

52. Kaldor et al. (eds), *Oil Wars*, pp. 3–5.

53. See Michael Ross, *Oil and Democracy Revisited* (Los Angeles: UCLA Department of Political Science, 2009); Karl, *The Paradox of Plenty*.

CHAPTER 8

1. David Strahan, *The Last Oil Shock* (London: John Murray, 2007), p. 85.

2. See a similar set of futures in Robert Costanza, 'Four visions of the century ahead', *The Futurist*, February 1999: 23–8.

3. See Mike Hulme, *Why We Disagree About Climate Change* (Cambridge: Cambridge University Press, 2009), pp. 348–53.

4. www.youtube.com/watch?v=wa2DUe2vJew, accessed 16 December 2008. The German insurance giant Allianz is even preparing to launch space travel insurance policies; see www.thelocal.de/national/20111118–38951. html, accessed 21 November 2011.

5. Jeremy Rifkin, *The Hydrogen Economy* (New York: Penguin Putnam, 2002), p. 177.

6. www.worldwatch.org/node/4664, accessed 9 January 2012.

7. Tim Flannery, *The Weather Makers* (London: Penguin, 2007), p. 262.

8. See for detail, Kingsley Dennis and John Urry, *After the Car* (Cambridge: Polity, 2009), ch. 4.

9. UK Parliament, House of Commons, *Cars of the Future: Seventeenth Report of Session 2003–04 (HC 319–I)*, House of Commons Transport Committee, London, 2004, pp. 1–54.

10. Richard Heinberg, *PowerDown* (London: Clairview, 2004), p. 129.

11. Joseph Romm, *The Hype about Hydrogen* (New York: Island Press, 2005).

12. Brian Arthur, *The Nature of Technology* (New York: Free Press, 2009); Frank Geels and Wim Smit, 'Failed technology futures: Pitfalls and lessons from a historical survey', *Futures* 32, 2000: 867–85.

13. David Edgerton, 'The contradictions of techno-nationalism and techno-globalism: A historical perspective', *New Global Studies* 1, 2007: 1–32.

14. Frank Geels, 'The dynamics of transitions in socio-technical systems: A multi-level analysis of the transition pathway from horse-drawn carriages to automobiles (1860–1930)', *Technology Analysis & Strategic Management* 17, 2005: 445–76. The kinds of socio-technical transitions involved here are well analysed in Frank Geels, René Kemp, Geoff Dudley and Glenn Lyons (eds), *Automobility in Transition?* (London: Routledge, 2012).

15. US National Intelligence Council, *US Global Trends 2025: A Transformed World* (Washington DC: US National Intelligence Council, 2008).

16. See http://ec.europa.eu/research/science-society/document_library/pdf_06/ european-knowledge-society_en.pdf, accessed 8 December 2011.

CHAPTER 9

1. See Nigel Thrift and Sean French, 'The automatic production of space', *Transactions of the Institute of British Geographers*, NS, 27, 2002: 309–35.

2. Manuel Castells, 'Informationalism, networks, and the network society: A theoretical blueprint', in Manuel Castells (ed.), *The Network Society* (Cheltenham: Edward Elgar, 2004), p. 7; and *Communication Power* (Oxford: Oxford University Press, 2009).

3. Anthony Elliott and John Urry, *Mobile Lives* (London: Routledge, 2010), ch. 2.

4. See www.ted.com/talks/pattie_maes_demos_the_sixth_sense.html, accessed 30 May 2010.

5. Frank Geels and Wim Smit, 'Lessons from failed technology futures: Potholes in the road to the future', in Nik Brown, Brian Rappert and Andrew Webster (eds), *Contested Futures* (Aldershot: Ashgate, 2000).

6. Lucy Suchman, *Human–Machine Reconfigurations* (Cambridge: Cambridge University Press, 2007).

7. Harvey Molotch, *Where Stuff Comes From* (New York: Routledge, 2003).

8. David Edgerton, *The Shock of the Old* (London: Profile Books, 2006).

9. This account draws on ESRC-funded research conducted by Thomas Birtchnell and myself (ES/J007455/1). See Thomas Birtchnell and John Urry, 'Fabricated futures and the Transportation of Objects', in *Mobilities* (forthcoming).

10. See www.economist.com/node/18114221, accessed 16 August 2011.

11. www.bbc.co.uk/news/technology-14946808, accessed 21 November 2011.

12. www.economist.com/node/21541382, accessed 18 January 2012.

13. www.guardian.co.uk/technology/2011/nov/17/3d-printing-throwaway-culture, accessed 21 November 2011.

14. Jeremy Rifkin, *The Age of Access* (London: Penguin, 2000). Of course much downloading of files is illegal.

15. See http://dsi.dhl-innovation.com/en/node/256 (accessed 16 August 2011) on how logistics giant DHL is concerned about the implications of this possible post-container future.

16. Frank Geels, 'Multi-level perspective on system innovation: Relevance for industrial transformation', in Xander Olsthoorn and Anna Wieczorek (eds), *Understanding Industrial Transformation* (New York: Springer, 2006), p. 165.

17. See Ken Green, Simon Shackley, Paul Dewick and Marcela Miozzo, 'Long-wave theories of technological change and the global environment', *Global Environment Change* 12, 2002: 79–81.

18. Barry Wellman, 'Physical place and cyber place: The rise of networked individualism', *International Journal of Urban and Regional Research* 25, 2001: 227–52, p. 227.

19. Ibid., pp. 227–52, p. 238.

20. Elliott and Urry, *Mobile Lives*.

21. Christian Licoppe, '"Connected" presence: The emergence of a new repertoire for managing social relationships in a changing communication technoscape', *Environment and Planning D: Society and Space* 22, 2004: 135–56, p. 139.

22. Yochai Benckler, *The Wealth of Networks* (New Haven CT: Yale University Press, 2006); David Grewal, *Network Power* (New York: Caravan, 2008).

23. Charlie Leadbetter, *We-Think* (London: Profile Books, 2008).

24. Meric Gertler, 'Tacit knowledge and the economic geography of context, or the undefinable tacitness of being (there)', *Journal of Economic Geography* 3, 2003: 75–99.

25. Elliott and Urry, *Mobile Lives*.

26. Stephen Haseler, *The Super-Rich* (London: Macmillan, 2000), p. 3.

27. Zygmunt Bauman, *The Individualized Society* (Cambridge: Polity, 2002), pp. 26–7.

28. David Halpern, *The Hidden Wealth of Nations* (Cambridge: Polity, 2010), p. 43.

29. Robert Putnam, *Bowling Alone* (New York: Simon & Schuster, 2000).

30. Halpern, *The Hidden Wealth of Nations*, p. 9.

31. Richard Layard, *Happiness: Lessons from a New Science* (London: Allen Lane, 2005), p. 78.

32. Nicholas Carr, *The Shallows* (New York: W.W. Norton, 2010), p. 87.

33. Sherry Turkle, *Alone Together* (New York: Basic Books, 2011), p. 11. See Elliott and Urry, *Mobile Lives*, on some emotional pleasures and costs of moving and communicating.

34. www.bbc.co.uk/news/business-11793288, accessed 21 November 2011.

35. See Carr, *The Shallows*, ch. 4.

36. Ibid., p. 217.

37. Susan Greenfield, 'Computers may be altering our brains – we must ask how', *Independent*, 12 August 2011.

38. See John Farnsworth and Terry Austrin, 'The ethnography of new media worlds? Following the case of global poker', *New Media & Society* 12, 2010: 1120–36.

39. Greg Noble, *Bin Laden in the Suburbs* (Sydney: Sydney Institute of Criminology, 2004).

40. See White House, *The National Strategy for Physical Protection of Critical Infrastructures and Key Assets*, National Infrastructure Advisory Council (NIAC), February 2003, pp. 1–96.

41. See *The Economist*, 6 November 2010, p. 6.

42. See Naomi Klein, 'Police state 2.0', *Guardian*, 3 June 2008.

43. www.guardian.co.uk/environment/2010/aug/12/carbon-footprint-internet, accessed 16 August 2011.

44. See www.eweek.com/c/a/Search-Engines/Greenminded-Google-Gets-Redfaced-Over-Search-Energy-Consumption-Claims, accessed 4 November 2009.

45. There are also very significant costs with e-waste, which often gets exported from richer to poorer countries while much is never recycled. See http://en.wikipedia.org/wiki/E-waste, accessed 8 December 2011.

46. Rob Hopkins, *The Transition Companion* (Totnes: Green Books, 2011). On stuff, see Harvey Molotch, *Where Stuff Comes From* (New York: Routledge, 2003).

47. Thomas Easton, 'A recession in the economy of trust', in Gabriel Ricci (ed.), *Values and Technology* (Piscataway NJ: Transaction Publishers, 2011).

48. On actor-networks of humans and nonhumans, see Bruno Latour, *Reassembling the Social* (Oxford: Oxford University Press, 2005).

49. Naomi Klein, *The Shock Doctrine*, (London: Allen Lane, 2007).

CHAPTER 10

1. Michael Klare, *Blood and Oil* (New York: Holt, 2005).
2. See ibid., ch. 2.
3. See ibid., pp. 54–5.
4. www.timesonline.co.uk/tol/news/world/article2461214.ece, accessed 3 August 2011.
5. www.tehrantimes.com/index.php/economy-and-business/1041–irans-oil-bourse-a-new-pressure-on-us-dollar, accessed 4 August 2011.
6. Martin Jacques, *When China Rules the World* (London: Penguin, 2012), pp. 600–603.
7. See William Engdahl, *A Century of War* (London: Pluto, 2004), and Ian Rutledge, *Addicted to Oil* (London: I.B. Tauris, 2005), both of which show carbon capital's role in the dark history of the last century.
8. www.commondreams.org/view/2009/08/13–6, accessed 4 August 2011.
9. www.sras.org/geopolitics_of_oil_pipelines_in_central_asia, accessed 4 August 2011.
10. Michael Klare, *Rising Powers, Shrinking Planet* (Oxford: Oneworld, 2008), p. 137.
11. See Jeff Rubin, *Why Your World is About to Get a Whole Lot Smaller* (London: Virgin, 2010), pp. 80–81; Tom Bower, *The Squeeze* (London: HarperPress, 2009), ch. 6.
12. Klare, *Rising Powers, Shrinking Planet*, p. 113.
13. James Murray and David King, 'Climate policy: Oil's tipping point has passed', *Nature* 481, 2012: 433–5.
14. Rudolph Rummel, *Power Kills* (Piscataway NJ: Transaction Publishers, 2006).
15. Ibid., p. 129.
16. This is written the day after the US credit rating was reduced by Standard & Poor's (5 August 2011). See Jacques, *When China Rules the World*.
17. See Mary Kaldor, Terry Lynn Karl and Yahia Said (eds), *Oil Wars* (London: Pluto, 2007).
18. Michael Klare, *Resource Wars* (New York: Metropolitan Books, 2001), p. 27; Ian Rutledge, *Addicted to Oil* (London: I.B. Tauris, 2005).
19. The BBC drama *Spooks* (5:10) involves a document *Aftermath* that sets out how the UK and the USA would in future operate entirely in their own resource interests within a warlord-dominated world.
20. See documentation in *The Economist*, www.economist.com/node/18648855, accessed 5 August 2011. See Leo Lewis, 'Fears of violence as world's water begins to run out', *The Times*, 22 January 2009.
21. See Michael C. Ruppert, *Crossing the Rubicon* (Gabriola Island BC: New Society Publishers, 2004).
22. Mark Lynas, 'How do I know China wrecked the Copenhagen deal? I was in the room', *Guardian*, 22 December 2009, www.guardian.co.uk,

environment/2009/dec/22/copenhagen-climate-change-mark-lynas, accessed 11 February 2010. And see J. Timmons Roberts, 'Multipolarity and the new world (dis)order: US hegemonic decline and the fragmentation of the global climate regime', *Global Environmental Change* 21, 2011: 776–84.

23. See Robin Leichenko, Adelle Thomas and Mark Baines, 'Vulnerability and adaptation to climate change', in Constance Lever-Tracy (ed.), *Routledge Handbook on Climate Change and Society* (London: Routledge, 2010), p. 142.

24. Gilberto Gallopin, Al Hammond, Paul Raskin and Rob Swart, *Branch Points* (Stockholm: Stockholm Environment Institute, Global Scenario Group, 1997), p. 34.

25. Ibid., p. 29.

26. Antony Froggatt and Glada Lahn, *Sustainable Energy Security: Strategic Risks and Opportunities for Business* (London: Lloyd's and Chatham House, 2010), ch. 4.

27. Saulo Cwerner, 'Helipads, heliports and urban air space: Governing the contested infrastructure of helicopter travel', in Saulo Cwerner, Sven Kesselring and John Urry (eds), *Aeromobilities* (London: Routledge, 2009).

28. JOE, *Joint Operating Environment Report 2010*, at www.peakoil.net/files/JOE2010.pdf , p. 30, accessed 15 November 2011.

29. See Kaldor et al. (eds), *Oil Wars*, on various kinds of oil wars.

30. See Herfried Münkler, *The New Wars* (Cambridge: Polity, 2005); Kaldor et al. (eds), *Oil Wars*.

31. Roy Woodbridge, *The Next World War* (Toronto: Toronto University Press, 2005), p. 207.

32. See Ruppert, *Crossing the Rubicon*.

33. www.opendemocracy.net/shruti-mehrotra-benedick-bowie/energy-and-peace-dangers-of-our-slow-energy-transition, note 2, accessed 27 November 2011.

34. www.opendemocracy.net/shruti-mehrotra-benedick-bowie/energy-and-peace-dangers-of-our-slow-energy-transition, accessed 27 November 2011.

35. James Lovelock, *The Revenge of Gaia* (London: Allen Lane, 2006), p. 151; also see Slavoj Žižek, *Living in the End Times*, updated new edn (London: Verso, 2011), on the West's 'bereavement'.

36. As strongly argued in Sylvia Walby, *Globalization and Inequalities* (London: Sage, 2009).

37. www.couriermail.com.au/business/scientists-warnings-unheeded/story-e6freqmx-111111263I991, accessed 7 August 2011. See Robert Costanza, 'Four visions of the century ahead', *The Futurist*, February 1999: 23–8.

38. See the movies *Mad Max* (1979) and *Mad Max 2* (1982). A similar recent example is the 2007 Mexican film *La Zona* (dir. Rodrigo Plá). See Paul Tranter and Scott Sharpe, 'Escaping Monstropolis: Child-friendly cities, peak oil and *Monsters Inc*', *Children's Geographies* 6, 2008: 295–308.

39. www.couriermail.com.au/business/scientists-warnings-unheeded/story-e6freqmx-1111112631991, accessed 7 August 2011.

CHAPTER 11

1. Jeff Rubin, *Why Your World is About to Get a Whole Lot Smaller* (London: Virgin, 2009), ch. 3.

2. Mike Davis, 'Who will build the ark?' *New Left Review* 61, 2010: 29–46, p. 17; William Engdahl, *A Century of War* (London: Pluto, 2004); Michael Klare, *Rising Powers, Shrinking Planet* (Oxford: Oneworld, 2008).

3. See www.miamiherald.com/2011/10/16/2454502/fukushima-disaster-can-happen.html (accessed 2 November 2011) on the implications of Fukushima for nuclear energy expansion in Miami.

4. http://globalization.kof.ethz.ch, accessed 2 November 2011. A similar pattern to this can be identified for economic globalization, although political globalization, the degree of cooperation between countries, has continued to increase, according to ETH data.

5. http://globalization.kof.ethz.ch, accessed 2 November 2011.

6. Duncan Clark, 'The only way is down', *Guardian* G2, 1 November 2011.

7. Tim Jackson, *Prosperity without Growth* (London: Earthscan, 2009).

8. As George Monbiot points out in 'Peak Stuff?', at www.monbiot.com/2011/11/03/peak-stuff, accessed 4 November 2011.

9. Incidentally the UK has produced more GHG emissions per person than any other country because of its 'cumulative historical emissions'. The UK got in first and has been using fossil fuels for longest! See James Hansen, *Storms of My Grandchildren* (London: Bloomsbury, 2011), p. 178.

10. http://lornegifford.webs.com/sixdays.htm p. 3, accessed 27 November 2011).

11. Clark, 'The only way is down'.

12. http://earlywarn.blogspot.com/2011/05/us-vehicle-miles-travelled.html, accessed 3 November 2011.

13. Rubin, *Why Your World is About to Get a Whole Lot Smaller*, pp. 124–6.

14. Michael C. Ruppert, *Confronting Collapse* (Vermont: Chelsea Green, 2009), pp. 54–5; www.postcarbon.org/article/299173–fight-of-our-lives-moores-law#, accessed 8 December 2011.

15. Rubin, *Why Your World is About to Get a Whole Lot Smaller*, pp. 117–18.

16. See Julian Temple, *Guardian*, 11 March 2010, www.guardian.co.uk/film/2010/mar/10/detroit-motor-city-urban-decline, accessed 3 November 2011. And see the photographic essay, www.guardian.co.uk/artanddesign/2011/jan/02/detroit-ruins-marchand-meffre-photographs-ohagan, accessed 11 November 2011.

17. Rubin, *Why Your World is About to Get a Whole Lot Smaller*, ch. 7. It should be noted that most of these observations on the 'green shoots' only apply to the rich North. Energy consumption and emissions seem to be rising

as ever in emerging economies: www.nature.com/nclimate/journal/vaop/ncurrent/full/nclimate1332.html, accessed 8 December 2011.

18. See Adam Millard-Ball and Lee Schipper, 'Are we reaching peak travel? Trends in passenger transport in eight industrialized countries', *Transport Reviews* 31, 2011: 357–78.

19. Ibid., pp. 357–78, pp. 364–5; and on the UK, see www.bbc.co.uk?news/magazine-12664047, accessed 3 November 2011.

20. John Reed, 'Carmakers put the mobile into automobile', *Financial Times*, 7 May 2010; www.guardian.co.uk/society/2011/dec/03/britons-children-lives-parents-poll, accessed 4 December 2011.

21. www.guardian.co.uk/politics/2011/sep/25/end-of-motoring, accessed 26 January 2012; Gwyn Topham, 'Cash-strapped students swap car for coach', *Guardian*, 27 February 2012.

22. Frank Geels, René Kemp, Geoff Dudley and Glenn Lyons (eds), *Automobility in Transition?* (London: Routledge, 2012), ch. 16.

23. www.independent.co.uk/news/business/news/soaring-fuel-costs-and-taxes-spell-the-end-for-cheap-flights-2294309.html, accessed 3 November 2011.

24. Millard-Ball and Schipper, 'Are we reaching peak travel?', pp. 373–4. In 2011 forty-one travel firms went out of business in the UK.

25. See www.sierraclub.org/sierra/200707/ecology.asp, accessed 8 December 2011.

26. See National Intelligence Council, *Global Trends 2025* (Washington DC: National Intelligence Council, 2008); Rob Hopkins, *The Transition Handbook* (Totnes: Green Books, 2008); Shaun Chamberlin, *The Transition Timeline* (Totnes: Green Books, 2009); John M. Greer, *The Ecotechnic Future* (Gabriola Island BC: New Society Publishers, 2009); Serge Latouche, *Farewell to Growth* (Cambridge: Polity, 2009); David Holmgren, *Future Scenarios* (Vermont: Green Books, 2009); Richard Heinberg and Daniel Lerch (eds), *The Post-Carbon Reader* (Healdsburg CA: Watershed Media, 2010); Forum for the Future, *Megacities on the Move* (London: Forum for the Future, 2010); John Grin et al., *Transitions to Sustainable Development* (New York: Routledge, 2011); John Urry, *Climate Change and Society* (Cambridge: Polity, 2011); Rob Hopkins, *The Transition Companion* (Totnes: Green Books, 2011); Frank Geels, René Kemp, Geoff Dudley and Glenn Lyons (eds), *Automobility in Transition?* (London: Routledge, 2012).

27. See Naomi Oreskes and Erik Conway, *Merchants of Doubt* (New York: Bloomsbury, 2010).

28. David Halpern, *The Hidden Wealth of Nations* (Cambridge: Polity, 2010).

29. www.happyplanetindex.org/public-data/files/happy-planet-index-first-global.pdf, accessed 3 November 2011.

30. See Tim Jackson, *Prosperity without Growth* (London: Earthscan, 2009), p. 155.

31. See Richard Dienst, *The Bonds of Debt* (London: Verso, 2011).

32. On heating comfort, see Elizabeth Shove, Heather Chappells and Loren Lutzenhiser (eds), *Comfort in a Lower Carbon Society* (London: Routledge, 2009); Avner Offner, *The Challenge of Affluence* (Oxford: Oxford University Press, 2006).

33. Richard Wilkinson and Kate Pickett, *The Spirit Level: Why More Equal Societies Almost Always Do Better* (London: Allen Lane, 2009); and see www.equalitytrust.org.uk, accessed 27 November 2011.

34. Gareth Morrell, Sara Scott, Di McNeish and Stephen Webster, *The August Riots in England* (London: Cabinet Office, 2011).

35. Jackson, *Prosperity without Growth*.

36. See Offner, *The Challenge of Affluence*, on the many challenges of affluence, albeit not in the context of powering down.

37. Latouche, *Farewell to Growth*, p. 70.

38. Jane Jacobs, *The Death and Life of Great American Cities* (New York: Vintage, 1992 [1961]); David Owen, *Green Metropolis* (London: Penguin, 2011), ch. 1.

39. See Eric Klinenberg, *Heatwave* (Chicago: Chicago University Press, 2002); and discussion in Jane Jacobs, *Dark Age Ahead* (New York: Random House, 2004).

40. See Owen, *Green Metropolis*.

41. See ibid., ch. 6, on the complexities of 'locavourism' and the dangers of high energy cost localism!

42. Dale Pfeiffer, *Eating Fossil Fuels* (Gabriola Island BC: New Society Publishers, 2006), p. 71; see chapter 7 on the Cuban 'miracle' as well as the 2007 DVD *The Power of Community: How Cuba Survived Peak Oil*.

43. See www.renewableenergyworld.com/rea/news/article/2009/04/la-revolucion-energetica-cubas-energy-revolution (accessed 5 March 2012), which sets out some elements of the energy programme in Cuba, including some efforts to effect 'demand reduction'.

44. Eric von Hippel, *Democratizing Innovation* (Cambridge MA: MIT Press, 2006).

45. Nigel Thrift, *Non-Representational Theory* (London: Routledge, 2008), pp. 41, 54.

46. Jukka Gronow, 'Fad, fashions and 'real' innovations', in Elizabeth Shove, Frank Trentmann and Richard Wilk (eds), *Time, Consumption and Everyday Life* (Oxford: Berg, 2009), p. 133.

47. Hopkins, *The Transition Companion*.

48. http://vaxjo.se/upload/www.vaxjo.se/Kommunledningsf%C3%B6rvaltn ingen/Planeringskontoret/Fossil%20Fuel%20Free%20V%C3%A4xj%C3% B6%20-%20the%20story_2010.pdf, accessed 27 November 2011; http://en.wikipedia.org/wiki/Making_Sweden_an_Oil-Free_Society, accessed 31 December 2011.

49. Owen, *Green Metropolis*, ch. 3.

50. www.ft.com/cms/s/0/dba162ba-5980-11df-99ba-00144feab49a.html

#axzz1facGGRwO, accessed 4 December 2011; John Reed, 'Carmakers put the mobile into automobile', *Financial Times*, 7 May 2010.

51. www.nfc-forum.org/aboutnfc, accessed 3 December 2011.

52. See Kingsley Dennis and John Urry, *After the Car* (Cambridge: Polity, 2009); William Mitchell, Christopher Borroni-Bird and Lawrence Burns, *Reinventing the Automobile* (Cambridge MA: MIT Press, 2010); Geels et al. (eds), *Automobility in Transition?*

53. http://web.hbr.org/email/archive/dailystat.php?date=021110, accessed 4 December 2011.

54. Worldwide Fund for Nature, *Plugged In: The End of the Oil Age*, Summary Report (Brussels: WWF, March 2008), p. 6; Royal Academy of Engineering, *Electric Vehicles: Charged with Potential* (London: RAE, 2010).

55. Matthias Gross, *Ignorance and Surprise* (Cambridge MA: MIT Press, 2010), p. 5.

56. James Kunstler, *The Long Emergency* (London: Atlantic Books, 2006), p. 270.

57. See John Vidal, 'Ecuador asks: How much is the rainforest worth?' *Observer* The New Review, 14 August 2011, pp. 18–19.

58. www.telegraph.co.uk/news/politics/tony-blair/7968858/Blair-home-number-nine-1m-house-for-student-daughter.html, accessed 5 November 2011; www.telegraph.co.uk/earth/environment/climatechange/7054986/Tony-Blairs-climate-change-project-paid-for-by-Oleg-Deripaska-oligarch-who-entertained-Lord-Mandelson-and-George-Osborne.html, accessed 5 November 2011.

59. See www.ukuncut.org.uk, accessed 27 January 2012. The terms 'dodging' and 'limitation' do not distinguish between tax avoidance (legal) and evasion (illegal).

60. Nicholas Shaxson, *Treasure Islands* (London: Bodley Head, 2011); and the research reported in www.taxjustice.net/cms/front_content.php?idcat=2, accessed 26 November 2011.

61. Richard Dienst, *The Bonds of Debt* (London: Verso, 2011); John Urry, *Climate Change and Society* (Cambridge: Polity, 2011).

62. Colin Crouch, *The Strange Non-Death of Neo-Liberalism* (Cambridge: Polity, 2011); Andrew G. Haldane and Robert M. May, 'Systemic risk in banking ecosystems', *Nature* 469, 2011: 351–5.

63. http://challenge.bfi.org/movie, accessed 4 November 2011.

64. Amory Lovins, 'More profit with less carbon', *Scientific American*, September 2005, p. 74.

65. Jackson, *Prosperity without Growth*.

CHAPTER 12

1. www.ft.com/cms/s/1/fb775ee8-8d0e-11da-9daf-0000779e2340.html#axzz1frosHakH, accessed 8 December 2011.

2. Karen Ward, HSBC, cited in www.cnbc.com/id/42224813/Oil_Will_Be_
Gone_in_50_Years_HSBC, accessed 28 December 2011.

3. Timothy Mitchell, *Carbon Democracy* (London: Verso, 2011), p. 231.

4. Joseph Tainter, *The Collapse of Complex Societies* (Cambridge: Cambridge
University Press, 1988), p. 216; see Richard Heinberg, *The Party's Over*
(New York: Clearview Books, 2005), pp. 34–6.

5. Andy Beckett, 'The economy's bust, the climate's on the brink and even
the arts are full of gloom', *Guardian* G2, 19 December 2011, pp. 6–9. See
discussion of *Mad Max* in ch. 11.

6. English-language examples include Martin Rees, *Our Final Century* (London:
Arrow Books, 2003); Jane Jacobs, *Dark Age Ahead* (New York: Random
House, 2004); Roy Woodbridge, *The Next World War* (Toronto: Toronto
University Press, 2005); Jared Diamond, *Collapse* (London: Allen Lane, 2005);
Bill McGuire, *Global Catastrophes* (Oxford: Oxford University Press, 2006);
Charles Perrow, *The Next Catastrophe* (Princeton NJ: Princeton University
Press, 2007); Sing Chew, *The Recurring Dark Ages* (Lanham MD: AltaMira
Press, 2007); Elizabeth Kolbert, *Field Notes from a Catastrophe* (London:
Bloomsbury, 2007); Fred Pearce, *With Speed and Violence* (Boston MA:
Beacon Press, 2007); Eugene Linden, *Winds of Change* (New York: Simon
& Schuster, 2007); Meyer Hillman, Tina Fawcett, Sudhir Raja, *The Suicidal
Planet* (New York: Thomas Dunne Books, 2007); Allan Stoekl, *Bataille's
Peak* (Minneapolis: University of Minneapolis Press, 2007); Kurt Campbell
(ed.), *Climatic Cataclysm:* (Washington DC: Brookings, 2008); Vaclav Smil,
Global Catastrophes and Trends (Cambridge MA: MIT Press, 2008); Dmitry
Orlov, *Reinventing Collapse* (Gabriola Island BC: New Society Publishers,
2008); David Orr, *Down to the Wire* (New York: Oxford University Press,
2009); Thomas Friedman, *Hot, Flat and Crowded* (London: Penguin, 2009);
Clive Hamilton, *Requiem for a Species* (London: Earthscan, 2010); James
Lovelock, *The Vanishing Face of Gaia* (London: Penguin, 2010); Slavoj Žižek,
Living in the End Times (London: Verso, 2011).

7. See Sarah Hall, *The Carhullan Army* (London: Faber & Faber, 2007); Marcel
Theroux, *Far North* (London: Faber & Faber, 2009); Ian McEwan, *Solar*
(London: Jonathan Cape, 2010). Movies include *28 Days Later, Burn Up, I
am Legend, Syriana, The Day After Tomorrow, The Age of Stupid, Melancholia,
Take Shelter* and *The Road*.

8. Diamond, *Collapse*.

9. Rory Carroll, 'The temples of doom', *Guardian* G2, 28 October 2008,
pp. 6–9; Andy Beckett, 'The economy's bust, the climate's on the brink
and even the arts are full of gloom', *Guardian* G2, 19 December 2011, pp.
6–9.

10. BBC News, 24 August 2009. UK Government Chief Scientist John
Beddington was the source of this material: John Urry, *Climate Change
and Society* (Cambridge: Polity, 2011), p. 1.

11. Cited in Ian Welsh, 'Climate change: Complexity and collaboration between the sciences', in Constance Lever-Tracy (ed.), *Routledge Handbook on Climate Change and Society* (London: Routledge, 2010), p. 34.

12. Brian Arthur, *Increasing Returns and Path Dependence in the Economy* (Michigan: University of Michigan Press, 1994); Eric Beinhocker, *The Origin of Wealth* (London: Random House, 2006), ch. 3.

13. Ilya Ehrenburg, *The Life of the Automobile* (London: Serpent's Tail, 1999 [1929]), p. 175.

14. Cited in Bryan Lovell, *Challenged by Carbon* (Cambridge: Cambridge University Press, 2010), p. 163.

15. Fred Pearce, *With Speed and Violence* (Boston MA: Beacon Press, 2007).

16. Nassim Taleb, *The Black Swan* (London: Penguin, 2007), pp. 166–7.

17. Richard Heinberg, *The Party's Over* (New York: Clearview Books, 2005), p. 196.

18. Thomas Homer-Dixon, 'Prepare today for tomorrow's breakdown', *Toronto Globe and Mail*, 14 May 2006, p. 2.

19. See Michael Klare, *Rising Powers, Shrinking Planet* (Oxford: Oneworld, 2008), p. 7.

20. See Colin Crouch, *The Strange Non-Death of Neo-Liberalism* (Cambridge: Polity, 2011).

21. See the forthcoming US movie on the destructive power of carbon capital *Greedy Lying Bastards*. See http://greedylyingbastards.com, accessed 20 January 2012.

22. Karl Marx and Friedrich Engels, *The Manifesto of the Communist Party* (Moscow: Foreign Languages, 1888 [1848]), pp. 85, 52.

23. Scott Lash and John Urry, *The End of Organized Capitalism* (Cambridge: Polity, 1987).

24. Marx and Engels, *The Manifesto of the Communist Party*, p. 55.

25. See documentation of the 'carbon web' at www.platformlondon.org/aboutplatform.asp, accessed 20 January 2012.

26. Rawi Abdelal, *Capital Rules* (Cambridge MA: Harvard University Press, 2007). My analysis here mostly deals with the (once?) rich North; see William Robinson, *Latin America and Global Capitalism* (Baltimore MD: Johns Hopkins University Press, 2008), on Latin American debates.

27. Nicholas Shaxson, *Treasure Islands* (London: Bodley Head, 2011), pp. 26–7.

28. See discussions of Keynes in Shaxson, *Treasure Islands*, ch. 4; and Timothy Mitchell, *Carbon Democracy* (London: Verso, 2011), ch. 5.

29. See Paul Krugman, *The Return of Depression Economics* (Harmondsworth: Penguin, 2008).

30. John Maynard Keynes, *The General Theory of Employment, Interest and Money* (London: Macmillan, 1961 [1936]), p. 376.

31. John Maynard Keynes, 'National Self-Sufficiency', *Yale Review* 22, 1933: 755–69, p. 756.

32. Brett Christophers, 'Making finance productive', *Economy and Society* 40, 2011: 112–40. Investment banking involves almost anything but investment! See the upfront Lee Hadnum, *The World's Best Tax Havens* (Kirkcaldy: Taxcafé, 2011)!

33. Keynes, *The General Theory of Employment, Interest and Money*, p. 372.

34. Shaxson, *Treasure Islands*, pp. 190–91.

35. Thanks to Bron Szerszynski for some distinctions about different ways of preparing for futures.

36. Edward P. Thompson, *The Making of the English Working Class* (Harmondsworth: Penguin, 1968).

37. Timothy Mitchell, *Carbon Democracy* (London: Verso, 2011), pp. 139–41.

38. Marx and Engels, *The Manifesto of the Communist Party*, p. 58.

39. Slavoj Žižek, 'Multiculturalism, or the cultural logic of multinational capitalism', *New Left Review* 225, 1997: 28–51, p. 45.

40. On especially American finance, see John Bellamy Foster and Fred Magdoff, *The Great Financial Crisis* (New York: Monthly Review Press, 2009).

41. See Milton Friedman on YouTube, www.youtube.com/watch?v=YmqoCHR 14n8, accessed 15 November 2011.

42. On shortages of rare minerals, see: www.guardian.co.uk/environment/2012/jan/27/rare-minerals-global-renewables-industry, accessed 28 January 2012.

43. Ian Morris, *How the West Rules – For Now* (London: Profile, 2010), p. 554. See William Robinson, *Latin America and Global Capitalism* (Baltimore MD: Johns Hopkins University Press, 2008), for parallel scenarios of Latin American developments.

44. Cited in Bryan Lovell, *Challenged by Carbon* (Cambridge: Cambridge University Press, 2010), p. 171.

Bibliography

Abbott, Chris, *An Uncertain Future* (Oxford: Oxford Research Group, 2008).

Abdelal, Rawi, *Capital Rules* (Cambridge MA: Harvard University Press, 2007).

Adams, Douglas, *The Hitchhikers Guide to the Galaxy* (London: Pan Macmillan, 1979).

Adey, Peter, *Aerial Life* (London: Wiley–Blackwell, 2010).

Aleklett, Kjell, *Peak Oil and the Evolving Strategies of Oil Importing and Exporting Countries*, OECD Discussion Paper 2007–17, December 2007.

Anderson, Perry, 'Two revolutions', *New Left Review* 61, 2010: 59–96.

André Gorz, *Ecologie et Politique* (Paris: Galilée, 1975).

Arrighi, Giovanni, *Adam Smith in Beijing* (London: Verso, 2007).

Arthur, Brian, *Increasing Returns and Path Dependence in the Economy* (Michigan: University of Michigan Press, 1994).

Arthur, Brian, *The Nature of Technology* (New York: Free Press, 2009).

Atkinson, Rowland, and Sarah Blandy, 'A picture of the floating world: Grounding the secessionary affluence of the residential cruise liner', *Antipode* 41: 92–110.

Bardou, Jean-Pierre, Jean-Jacques Chanaron, Patrick Fridenson and James M. Laux, *The Automobile Revolution* (Chapel Hill: University of North Carolina Press, 1982).

Bauman, Zygmunt, *Liquid Modernity* (Cambridge: Polity, 2000).

Bauman, Zygmunt, *The Individualized Society* (Cambridge: Polity, 2002).

Beckett, Andy, 'The economy's bust, the climate's on the brink and even the arts are full of gloom', *Guardian* G2, 19 December 2011, pp. 6–9.

Beder, Sharon, *Global Spin* (London: Green Books, 2002).

Beinhocker, Eric, *The Origin of Wealth* (London: Random House, 2006).

Benckler, Yochai, *The Wealth of Networks* (New Haven CT: Yale University Press, 2006).

Birtchnell, Thomas, '*Jugaad* as systemic risk and disruptive innovation in India', *Contemporary South Asia* 19, 2011: 357–72.

Birtchnell, Thomas, and John Urry, 'Fabricated futures and the Transportation of Objects', *Mobilities* (forthcoming).

Black, Edwin, *Internal Combustion* (New York: St. Martin's Press, 2006).

Borger, Julian, 'Half of global car exhaust produced by US vehicles', *Guardian*, 29 June 2008.

Boulding, Kenneth E., *Earth as a Space Ship* (Washington: Washington State University, Committee on Space Sciences), 10 May 1965.

Bower, Tom, *The Squeeze* (London: Harper Press, 2009).

Brenner, Robert, *The Economics of Global Turbulence* (London: Verso, 2006).

Bridge, Gavin, 'Geographies of peak oil: The other carbon problem', *Geoforum* 41, 2010: 523–30.

Brugger, Bill, *Contemporary China* (London: Croom Helm, 1977).

Burman, Stephen, *The State of the American Empire* (London: Earthscan, 2007).

Campbell, Colin, and Siobhan Heapes, *An Atlas of Oil and Gas Depletion* (London: Jeremy Mills, 2009).

Campbell, Kurt (ed.), *Climatic Cataclysm:* (Washington DC: Brookings, 2008).

Carr, Nicholas, *The Shallows* (New York: W.W. Norton, 2010).

Carter, Ian, *Railways and Culture in Britain* (Manchester: Manchester University Press, 2001).

Castells, Manuel, 'Informationalism, networks, and the network society: A theoretical blueprint', in Manuel Castells (ed.), *The Network Society* (Cheltenham: Edward Elgar, 2004).

Castells, Manuel, *Communication Power* (Oxford: Oxford University Press, 2009).

Chamberlin, Shaun, *The Transition Timeline* (Totnes: Green Books, 2009).

Chamon, Marcos, Paolo Mauro and Yohei Okawa, 'Mass car ownership in the emerging market giants', *Economic Policy* (Washington DC: IMF, 2008).

Chew, Sing, *The Recurring Dark Ages* (Lanham MD: AltaMira Press, 2007).

Christophers, Brett, 'Making finance productive', *Economy and Society* 40, 2011: 112–40.

Clark, Duncan, 'The only way is down', *Guardian* G2, 1 November 2011.

Cortright, Joe, *Driven to the Brink* (Chicago: CEOs for Cities, 2008).

Costanza, Robert, 'Four visions of the century ahead', *The Futurist*, February 1999: 23–8.

Crouch, Colin, *The Strange Non-Death of Neo-Liberalism* (Cambridge: Polity, 2011).

Cwerner, Saolo, Sven Kesselring and John Urry (eds), *Aeromobilities* (London: Routledge, 2009).

Darley, Julian, *High Noon for Natural Gas* (Vermont: Chelsea Green, 2004).

Daubier, Jean, *A History of the Chinese Cultural Revolution* (New York: Vintage, 1974).

Davidson, Christopher, *Dubai: The Vulnerability of Success* (London: Hurst, 2008).

Davies, Nick, *Flat Earth News* (London: Vintage, 2009).

Davis, Mike, *Planet of Slums* (London: Verso, 2007).

Davis, Mike, 'Sand, fear, and money in Dubai', in Mike Davis and Daniel Bertrand Monk (eds), *Evil Paradises* (New York: New Press, 2007).

Davis, Mike, 'Who will build the ark?' *New Left Review* 61, 2010: 29–46.

Davis, Mike, and Daniel Bertrand Monk (eds), *Evil Paradises* (New York: New Press, 2007).

DeCicco, John, and Freda Fung, *Global Warming on the Road* (Washington DC: Environmental Defense, 2006).

Deffeyes, Kenneth, *Beyond Oil – the View from Hubbert's Peak* (New York: Hill & Wang, 2005).

Dennis, Kingsley, and John Urry, *After the Car* (Cambridge: Polity, 2009).

Dennis, Norman, Fernando Henriques and Clifford Slaughter, *Coal is Our Life* (London: Tavistock, 1956).

Diamond, Jared, *Collapse* (London: Allen Lane, 2005).

Dicker, Dan, *Oil's Endless Bid* (New York: Wiley, 2011).

Dienst, Richard, *The Bonds of Debt* (London: Verso, 2011).

Dodson, Jago, and Neil Sipe, *Shocking the Suburbs* (Sydney: UNSW Press, 2008).

Dorling, Danny, 'Possible "peak population": A world without borders', *Open Democracy*, 18 October 2011.

Dow, Kirstin, and Thomas Downing, *The Atlas of Climate Change* (London: Earthscan, 2011).

Downey, Morgan, *Oil 101* (New York: Wooden Table Press, 2009).

Easton, Thomas, 'A recession in the economy of trust', in Gabriel Ricci (ed.), *Values and Technology* (Piscataway NJ: Transaction, 2011).

Eco, Umberto, *Travels in Hyper-Reality* (London: Pan, 1987).

The Economist, '2020 vision', 10 December 2009.

Edgerton, David, *The Shock of the Old* (London: Profile Books, 2006).

Edgerton, David, 'The contradictions of techno-nationalism and techno-globalism: A historical perspective', *New Global Studies* 1, 2007: 1–32.

Ehrenburg, Ilya, *The Life of the Automobile* (London: Serpent's Tail, 1999 [1929]).

Elliott, Anthony, *Making the Cut* (London: Reaktion Books, 2007).

Elliott, Anthony, and John Urry, *Mobile Lives* (London: Routledge, 2010).

Engdahl, William, *A Century of War* (London: Pluto, 2004).

Farnsworth, John, and Terry Austrin, 'The ethnography of new media worlds?' in Greg Noble, *Bin Laden in the Suburbs* (Sydney: Sydney Institute of Criminology, 2004).

Favell, Adrian, *Eurostars and Eurocities* (Oxford: Blackwell, 2008).

Fine, Ben, *The World of Consumption* (London: Routledge, 2002).

Flannery, Tim, *The Weather Makers* (London: Penguin, 2007), p. 262.

Forum for the Future, *Megacities on the Move* (London: Forum for the Future, 2010).

Foster, John Bellamy, and Fred Magdoff, *The Great Financial Crisis* (New York: Monthly Review Press, 2009).

French, Paul, and Sam Chambers, *Oil on Water* (London: Zed Books, 2010).

Freudenberg, William, and Robert Gramling, *Blowout in the Gulf* (Cambridge MA: MIT Press, 2011).

Friedman, Milton, *Capitalism and Freedom* (Chicago: University of Chicago Press, 2002).

Friedman, Thomas, *Hot, Flat and Crowded* (London: Penguin, 2009).

Friedman, Thomas, 'The new sputnik', *International Herald Tribune*, 28 September 2009.

Froggatt, Antony, and Glada Lahn, *Sustainable Energy Security: Strategic Risks and Opportunities for Business* (London: Lloyd's and Chatham House, 2010).

Gallopin, Gilberto, Al Hammond, Paul Raskin and Rob Swart, *Branch Points: Global Scenarios and Human Choice* (Stockholm: Stockholm Environment Institute, Global Scenario Group, 1997).

Geels, Frank, 'The dynamics of transitions in socio-technical systems: A multi-level analysis of the transition pathway from horse-drawn carriages to automobiles (1860–1930)', *Technology Analysis & Strategic Management* 17, 2005: 445–76.

Geels, Frank, 'Multi-level perspective on system innovation: Relevance for industrial transformation', in Xander Olsthoorn and Anna Wieczorek (eds), *Understanding Industrial Transformation* (New York: Springer, 2006).

Geels, Frank, and Wim Smit, 'Failed technology futures: Pitfalls and lessons from a historical survey', *Futures* 32, 2000: 867–85.

Geels, Frank, and Wim Smit, 'Lessons from failed technology futures: Potholes in the road to the future', in Nik Brown, Brian Rappert and Andrew Webster (eds), *Contested Futures* (Aldershot: Ashgate, 2000).

Geels, Frank, René Kemp, Geoff Dudley and Glenn Lyons (eds), *Automobility in Transition?* (London: Routledge, 2012).

Gertler, Meric, 'Tacit knowledge and the economic geography of context, or the undefinable tacitness of being (there)', *Journal of Economic Geography* 3, 2003: 75–99.

Ghazi, Polly, 'Gas guzzlers and "ghostburbs"', *Guardian*, 2 July 2008.

Giddens, Anthony *The Politics of Climate Change* (Cambridge: Polity, 2009).

Gillian Tett, *Fool's Gold* (London: Little, Brown, 2009).

Goldenberg, Suzanne, 'Republicans attack Obama's green agenda across multiple fronts', *Guardian*, 5 March 2011.

Gottdiener, Mark, *Life in the Air* (Oxford: Rowman & Littlefield, 2001).

Gould, Kenneth, 'The ecological costs of militarization', *Peace Review* 19: 331–4.

Graham, Steve, and Simon Marvin, *Splintering Urbanism* (London: Routledge, 2001).

Green, Ken, Simon Shackley, Paul Dewick and Marcela Miozzo, 'Long-wave theories of technological change and the global environment', *Global Environment Change* 12, 2002: 79–81.

Greenfield, Susan, 'Computers may be altering our brains – we must ask how', *Independent*, 12 August 2011.

Greer, John M., *The Ecotechnic Future* (Gabriola Island BC: New Society Publishers, 2009).

Grewal, David, *Network Power* (New York: Caravan, 2008).

Grin, John, et al., *Transitions to Sustainable Development* (New York: Routledge, 2011).

Gronow, Jukka, 'Fad, fashions and 'real' innovations', in Elizabeth Shove, Frank Trentmann and Richard Wilk (eds), *Time, Consumption and Everyday Life* (Oxford: Berg, 2009).

Gross, Matthias, *Ignorance and Surprise* (Cambridge MA: MIT Press, 2010).

Habila, Helon, *Oil on Water* (London: Penguin, 2010).

Hadnum, Lee, *The World's Best Tax Havens* (Kirkcaldy: Taxcafé, 2011).

Haldane, Andrew G., and Robert M. May, 'Systemic risk in banking ecosystems', *Nature* 469, 2011.

Hall, Sarah, *The Carhullan Army* (London: Faber & Faber, 2007).

Halpern, David, *The Hidden Wealth of Nations* (Cambridge: Polity, 2010).

Hamilton, Clive, *Requiem for a Species* (London: Earthscan, 2010).

Hamilton, James, 'The oil shock and recession of 2008: Part 2', *Econbrowser*, www.econbrowser.com/archives/2009/01/the_oil_shock_a_1.html.

Hansen, James, *Storms of My Grandchildren* (London: Bloomsbury, 2011).

Harvey, David, *A Brief History of Neoliberalism* (Oxford: Oxford University Press, 2005).

Harvey, Mark, and Sarah Pilgrim, 'The new competition for land: Food, energy and climate change', *Food Policy* 36, 2011: S40–S51.

Haseler, Stephen, *The Super-Rich* (London: Macmillan, 2000).

Heinberg, Richard, *PowerDown* (London: Clairview, 2004).

Heinberg, Richard, *The Party's Over* (New York: Clearview Books, 2005).

Heinberg, Richard, and Daniel Lerch (eds), *The Post-Carbon Reader* (Healdsburg CA: Watershed Media, 2010).

Hillman, Meyer, Tina Fawcett, Sudhir Raja, *The Suicidal Planet* (New York: Thomas Dunne Books, 2007).

Hirsch, Fred, *Social Limits to Growth* (London: Routledge & Kegan Paul, 1977).

Hirsch, Robert, *The Inevitable Peaking of World Oil Production* (Washington DC: Atlantic Council of the United States, October 2005).

Hofmeister, John, *Why We Hate the Oil Companies* (New York: Palgrave Macmillan, 2010).

Hoggart, Richard, *The Uses of Literacy* (London: Penguin, 2009 [1957]).

Holmgren, David, *Future Scenarios* (Vermont: Green Books, 2009).

Homer-Dixon, Thomas, *The Upside of Down* (London: Souvenir, 2006).

Homer-Dixon, Thomas, 'Prepare today for tomorrow's breakdown', *Toronto Globe and Mail*, 14 May 2006, p. 2.

Homer-Dixon, Thomas (ed.), *Carbon Shift* (Canada: Random House, 2009).

Hopkins, Rob, *The Transition Handbook* (Totnes: Green Books, 2008).

Hopkins, Rob, *The Transition Companion* (Totnes: Green Books, 2011).

Høyer, Karl Georg, 'Epilogue: The travelling circus of climate change', in Roy Bhaskar et al. (eds), *Interdisciplinarity and Climate Change* (London: Routledge, 2010).

Huber, Matthew, 'Energizing historical materialism: Fossil fuels, space and the capitalist mode of production', *Geoforum* 40, 2009: 105–15.

Hughes, Thomas, *Networks of Power* (Baltimore MD: Johns Hopkins University Press, 1983).

Hulme, Mike, *Why We Disagree About Climate Change* (Cambridge: Cambridge University Press, 2009).

Humphrey, Kim, *Excess* (Cambridge: Polity, 2010).

Ibeanu, Okey, and Robin Luckman, 'Nigeria: Political violence, governance and corporate responsibility in a petro-state', in Mary Kaldor, Terry Lynn Karl and Yahia Said (eds), *Oil Wars* (London: Pluto, 2007).

Illich, Ivan, *Energy and Equity* (London: Marion Boyars, 1974).

Industry Taskforce on Peak Oil and Energy Security, *Briefing Note on Deepwater Oil Production* (London: ITPOES, November 2010).

Ingersoll, Richard, *Sprawltown* (Princeton NJ: Princeton University Press, 2006).

International Energy Authority, CO_2 *Emissions from Fuel Combustion: Highlights* (Paris: IEA, 2011).

Jackson, Tim, *Prosperity without Growth* (London: Earthscan, 2009).

Jacobs, Jane, *The Death and Life of Great American Cities* (New York: Vintage, 1992).

Jacobs, Jane, *Dark Age Ahead* (New York: Random House, 2004).

Jacques, Martin, *When China Rules the World* (London: Penguin, 2012).

Jorgenson, Andrew, Brett Clark and Jeffrey Kentor, 'Militarization and the environment: A panel study of carbon dioxide emissions and the ecological footprint of nations', *Global Environmental Politics* 10, 2010: 7–28.

Junemo, Mattias, '"Let's build a palm island": Playfulness in complex times', in Mimi Sheller and John Urry (eds), *Tourism Mobilities* (London: Routledge, 2004).

Kaldor, Mary, Terry Lynn Karl and Yahia Said (eds), *Oil Wars* (London: Pluto, 2007).

Kaplan, Caren, *Questions of Travel* (Durham NC: Duke University Press, 1996).

Karl, Terry Lynn, *The Paradox of Plenty* (Berkeley: University of California Press, 1997).

Keynes, John Maynard, 'National Self-Sufficiency' *Yale Review* 22, 1933: 755–69.

Keynes, John Maynard, *The General Theory of Employment, Interest and Money* (London: Macmillan, 1961 [1936]).

Klare, Michael, *Resource Wars* (New York: Metropolitan Books, 2001).

Klare, Michael, *Blood and Oil* (New York: Holt, 2005).

Klare, Michael, *Rising Powers, Shrinking Planet* (Oxford: Oneworld, 2008).

Klein, Naomi, *No Logo* (London: Flamingo, 2000).

Klein, Naomi, *The Shock Doctrine*, (London: Allen Lane, 2007).

Klein, Naomi, 'Police state 2.0', *Guardian*, 3 June 2008.

Klinenberg, Eric, *Heatwave* (Chicago: Chicago University Press, 2002).

Kochan, Nick, *The Washing Machine* (London: Duckworth, 2006).

Kolbert, Elizabeth, *Field Notes from a Catastrophe* (London: Bloomsbury, 2007).

Krane, Jim, *City of Gold* (London: Picador, 2010).

Krugman, Paul, *The Return of Depression Economics* (Harmondsworth: Penguin, 2008).

Kunstler, James, *The Long Emergency* (London: Atlantic Books, 2006).

Labban, Mazen, 'Oil in parallax: Scarcity, markets, and the financialization of accumulation', *Geoforum* 41, 2010: 541–52.

Lamers, Machiel, *The Future of Tourism in Antarctica* (Maastricht: Universitaire Press Maastricht, 2009).

Larsen, Jonas, John Urry and Kay Axhausen, *Mobilities, Networks, Geographies* (Aldershot: Ashgate, 2006).

Lash, Scott, and John Urry, *The End of Organized Capitalism* (Cambridge: Polity, 1987).

Latouche, Serge, *Farewell to Growth* (Cambridge: Polity, 2009).

Latour, Bruno, *We Have Never Been Modern* (Hemel Hempstead: Harvester Wheatsheaf, 1993).

Latour, Bruno, *Reassembling the Social* (Oxford: Oxford University Press, 2005).

Lawson, Nigel, *An Appeal to Reason: A Cool Look at Global Warming* (London: Duckworth, 2008).

Layard, Richard, *Happiness: Lessons from a New Science* (London: Allen Lane, 2005).

Leadbetter, Charlie, *We-Think* (London: Profile Books, 2008).

Leggett, Jeremy, *Half Gone* (London: Portobello Books, 2005).

Leichenko, Robin, Adelle Thomas and Mark Baines, 'Vulnerability and adaptation to climate change', in Constance Lever-Tracy (ed.), *Routledge Handbook on Climate Change and Society* (London: Routledge, 2010).

Levinson, Marc, *The Box* (Princeton NJ: Princeton University Press, 2006).

Lewis, Leo, 'Fears of violence as world's water begins to run out', *The Times*, 22 January 2009.

Li, Minqi, 'Peak oil, the rise of China and India, and the Global Energy Crisis', *Journal of Contemporary Asia* 37, 2007: 449–71.

Licoppe, Christian, '"Connected" presence: The emergence of a new repertoire for managing social relationships in a changing communication technoscape', *Environment and Planning D: Society and Space* 22, 2004: 135–56.

Linden, Eugene, *Winds of Change* (New York: Simon & Schuster, 2007).

Lovell, Bryan, *Challenged by Carbon* (Cambridge: Cambridge University Press, 2010).

Lovell, Julia, *The Great Wall* (London: Atlantic, 2006).

Lovelock, James, *The Revenge of Gaia* (London: Allen Lane, 2006).

Lovelock, James, *The Vanishing Face of Gaia* (London: Penguin, 2010).

Lovins, Amory, 'More profit with less carbon', *Scientific American*, September 2005.

Lovins, Amory, et al., *Winning the Oil Endgame* (London: Earthscan, 2004).

Lucas, Karen, et al. (eds), *Auto Motives* (London: Emerald, 2010).

Lynas, Mark, 'How do I know China wrecked the Copenhagen deal? I was in the room', *Guardian*, 22 December 2009, www.guardian.co.uk, environment/ 2009/dec/22/copenhagen-climate-change-mark-lynas.

Maass, Peter, *Crude World* (London: Allen Lane, 2009).

Marx, Karl, *Grundrisse* (Harmondsworth: Penguin, 1973).

Marx, Karl, *Capital*, Volume 1 (Harmondsworth: Penguin, 1976).

Marx, Karl, and Friedrich Engels, *The Manifesto of the Communist Party* (Moscow: Foreign Languages, 1888 [1848]).

Mau, Steffan, *Social Transnationalism* (London: Routledge, 2010).

McCright, Aaron, and Riley Dunlap, 'Anti-reflexivity: The American Conservative movement's success in undermining climate change science and policy', *Theory, Culture and Society* 27, 2010: 100–133.

McEwan, Ian, *Solar* (London: Jonathan Cape, 2010).

McGuire, Bill, *Global Catastrophes* (Oxford: Oxford University Press, 2006).

Meadows, Donella, Dennis Meadows and Jørgen Randers, *The Limits to Growth: A Report for the Club of Rome's Project on the Predicament of Mankind* (Berkeley CA: Earth Island, 1972).

Merriman, Peter, *Driving Spaces* (Malden MA: Blackwell, 2007).

Meyrowitz, John, *No Sense of Place* (New York: Oxford University Press, 1985).

Midgley, Dominic, and Chris Hutchins, *Abramovich: The Billionaire from Nowhere* (London: HarperCollins, 2005).

Millard-Ball, Adam, and Lee Schipper, 'Are we reaching peak travel? Trends in passenger transport in eight industrialized countries', *Transport Reviews* 31, 2011: 357–78.

Miller, Daniel, *A Theory of Shopping* (New York: Cornell University Press, 1998).

Miller, Daniel (ed.), *Car Cultures* (Oxford: Berg, 2000).

Mitchell, Timothy, *Carbon Democracy* (London: Verso, 2011).

Mitchell, William, Christopher Borroni-Bird and Lawrence Burns, *Reinventing the Automobile* (Cambridge MA: MIT Press, 2010).

Mol, Arthur, 'The environmental movement in an era of ecological modernisation', *Geoforum* 31, 2000: 45–56.

Molotch, Harvey, *Where Stuff Comes From* (New York: Routledge, 2003).

Monbiot, George, 'Peak Stuff?', www.monbiot.com/2011/11/03/ peak-stuff.

Morrell, Gareth, Sara Scott, Di McNeish and Stephen Webster, *The August Riots in England* (London: Cabinet Office, 2011).

Morris, Ian, *How the West Rules – For Now* (London: Profile, 2010).

Morrison, Blake, 'It was the cathedral of modern times, but the car is now a menace', *Guardian*, 26 July 2008.

Mumford, Lewis, *Technics and Civilization* (New York: Harcourt, Brace, 1934).

Münkler, Herfried, *The New Wars* (Cambridge: Polity, 2005).

Murray, James, and David King, 'Climate policy: Oil's tipping point has passed', *Nature* 481, 2012: 433–5.

National Intelligence Council, *Global Trends 2025* (Washington DC: National Intelligence Council, 2008).

Newell, Peter, and Matthew Paterson, *Climate Capitalism* (Cambridge: Cambridge University Press, 2010).

Nye, David, *Consuming Power* (Cambridge MA: MIT Press, 1998).

Nyíri, Pál, *Mobility and Cultural Authority in Contemporary China* (Seattle: University of Washington Press, 2010).

O'Neill, Tom, 'Curse of the Black Gold: Hope and betrayal on the Niger Delta', *National Geographic*, February 2007.

Obi, Cyril, and Siri Aas Rustad (eds), *Oil and Insurgency in the Niger Delta* (London: Zed Books, 2011).

Offer, Avner, *The Challenge of Affluence* (Oxford: Oxford University Press, 2006).

Oreskes, Naomi, and Erik Conway, *Merchants of Doubt* (New York: Bloomsbury, 2010).

Orlov, Dmitry, *Reinventing Collapse* (Gabriola Island BC: New Society Publishers, 2008).

Orr, David, *Down to the Wire* (New York: Oxford University Press, 2009).

Owen, David, *Green Metropolis* (London: Penguin, 2011).

Parenti, Christian, *Tropic of Chaos* (New York: Nation Books, 2011).

Pascoe, David, *Airspaces* (London: Reaktion, 2001).

Paterson, Matthew, *Automobile Politics* (Cambridge: Cambridge University Press, 2007).

Pearce, Fred, *With Speed and Violence* (Boston MA: Beacon Press, 2007).

Perez, Carlota, *Technological Revolutions and Financial Capital* (Cheltenham: Edward Elgar, 2002).

Perkins, John, *Confessions of an Economic Hit Man* (London: Ebury Press, 2005).

Perrow, Charles, *The Next Catastrophe* (Princeton NJ: Princeton University Press, 2007).

Pfeiffer, Dale, *Eating Fossil Fuels* (Gabriola Island BC: New Society, 2006).

Pinderhughes, Raquel, *Alternative Urban Futures* (New York: Rowman & Littlefield, 2004).

Platform, *BP and Shell: Rising Risks in Tar Sands Investments* (London: Platform 2008).

Platt, Edward, *Leadville* (London: Picador, 2000).

Porritt, Jonathan, 'China: The most important story in the world', *China Dialogue*, 11 September 2006.

Putnam, Robert, *Bowling Alone* (New York: Simon & Schuster, 2000).

Radice, Hugo, 'Confronting the crisis: A class analysis', *Socialist Register* 47, 2011: 21–43.

Reed, John, 'Carmakers put the mobile into automobile', *Financial Times*, 7 May 2010.

Rees, Martin, *Our Final Century* (London: Arrow Books, 2003).

Ribeiro, Suzana, and Shigeki Kobayashi, 'Transport and its infrastructure', in B. Metz, O.R. Davidson, P.R. Bosch, R. Dave and L.A. Meyer (eds), *Climate Change 2007: Mitigation of Climate Change* (Cambridge: Cambridge University Press, 2007).

Rifkin, Jeremy, *The Age of Access* (London: Penguin, 2000).

Rifkin, Jeremy, *The Hydrogen Economy* (New York: Putnam, 2002).

Roberts, Ian, with Phil Edwards, *The Energy Glut* (London: Zed Books, 2010).

Roberts, J. Timmons, 'Multipolarity and the new world (dis)order: US hegemonic decline and the fragmentation of the global climate regime', *Global Environmental Change* 21, 2011: 776–84.

Robinson, Mike, and Marina Novelli (eds), *Niche Tourism* (Oxford: Elsevier, 2005).

Robinson, William, *Latin America and Global Capitalism* (Baltimore MD: Johns Hopkins University Press, 2008).

Rogers, Richard, *Cities for a Small Planet* (London: Faber & Faber, 1997).

Romm, Joseph, *The Hype about Hydrogen* (New York: Island Press, 2005).

Rory Carroll, 'The temples of doom', *Guardian* G2, 28 October 2008, pp. 6–9.

Ross, Michael, *Oil and Democracy Revisited* (Los Angeles: UCLA Department of Political Science, 2009).

Roszak, Theodor, *Where the Wasteland Ends* (New York: Doubleday, 1973).

Roubini, Nouriel, and Stephen Mihm, *Crisis Economics* (London: Penguin, 2011).

Rowell, Andy, James Marriott and Lorne Stockman, *The Next Gulf* (London: Constable, 2005).

Royal Academy of Engineering, *Electric Vehicles: Charged with Potential* (London: RAE, 2010).

Rubin, Jeff, *Why Your World is About to Get a Whole Lot Smaller* (London: Virgin, 2009).

Rummel, Rudolph, *Power Kills* (Piscataway NJ: Transaction, 2006).

Ruppert, Michael C., *Crossing the Rubicon* (Gabriola Island BC: New Society Publishers, 2004).

Ruppert, Michael C., *Confronting Collapse* (Vermont: Chelsea Green, 2009).

Rutledge, Ian, *Addicted to Oil* (London: I.B. Tauris, 2005).

Sachs, Wolfgang, *For Love of the Automobile* (Berkeley: University of California Press, 1992).

Sassen, Saskia, 'Too big to save: The end of financial capitalism', *Open Democracy News Analysis*, 1 January 2009.

Schivelbusch, Wolfgang, *The Railway Journey* (California: University of California Press, 1986).

Schmid, Heiko, *Economy of Fascination* (Berlin: Gebrüder Borntraeger, 2009).

Schumacher, E.F., *Small is Beautiful* (London: Blond & Briggs, 1973).

Schwartz, Barry, *The Paradox of Choice* (New York: Harper, 2004).

Shaxson, Nicholas, *Poisoned Wells* (London: Palgrave, 2008).

Shaxson, Nicholas, *Treasure Islands* (London: Bodley Head, 2011).

Sheller, Mimi, *Consuming the Caribbean* (London: Routledge, 2003).

Sheller, Mimi, 'Automotive emotions', *Theory, Culture and Society* 21, 2004: 221–42.

Sheller, Mimi, 'Infrastructures of the imagined island: Software, mobilities, and the new architecture of cyberspatial paradise', *Environment and Planning A* 41, 2008: 1386–1403.

Sheller, Mimi, 'The new Caribbean complexity: Mobility systems and the re-scaling of development', *Singapore Journal of Tropical Geography* 14, 2008: 373–84.

Sheller, Mimi, and John Urry (eds), *Tourism Mobilities* (London: Routledge, 2004).

Shove, Elizabeth, Heather Chappells and Loren Lutzenhiser (eds), *Comfort in a Lower Carbon Society* (London: Routledge, 2009).

Simmons, Matthew, *Twilight in the Desert* (New York: John Wiley, 2005).

Simpson, Tim, 'Macao, capital of the 21st century', *Environment and Planning D: Society and Space* 26, 2008: 1053–79.

Simpson, Tim, 'Neoliberalism with Chinese characteristics: Consumer pedagogy in Macao', in Heiko Schmid, Wolf-Dietrich Sahr and John Urry (eds), *Cities and Fascination* (Aldershot: Ashgate, 2011).

Sinclair, Upton, *Oil!* (London: Penguin, 2008 [1926]).

Singh, Manraaj, 'What's all the oil in the world worth?', www.fleetstreetinvest.co.uk/oil/oil-outlook/oil-world-worth-00027.html.

Smart, Barry, *Consumer Society* (London: Sage, 2010).

Smil, Vaclav, *Global Catastrophes and Trends* (Cambridge MA: MIT Press, 2008).

Smil, Vaclav, *Oil: A Beginner's Guide* (Oxford: Oneworld, 2008).

Smil, Vaclav, *Energy Transitions* (Santa Barbara CA: Praeger, 2010).

Soros, George, *The New Paradigm for Financial Markets* (London: Public Affairs, 2008).

Sperling, Daniel, and Deborah Gordon, *Two Billion Cars* (Oxford: Oxford University Press, 2009).

Stern, Andy, *Who Won the Oil Wars?* (London: Conspiracy Books, 2005).

Stern, Nicholas, *The Economics of Climate Change* (Cambridge: Cambridge University Press, 2007).

Stiglitz, Joseph *Making Globalization Work* (Harmondsworth: Penguin, 2007).

Stiglitz, Joseph, *Freefall* (London: Penguin, 2010).

Stoekl, Allan, *Bataille's Peak* (Minneapolis: University of Minneapolis Press, 2007).

Strahan, David, *The Last Oil Shock* (London: John Murray, 2007).

Strange, Susan, *Casino Capitalism* (Manchester: Manchester University Press, 1997).

Suchman, Lucy, *Human–Machine Reconfigurations* (Cambridge: Cambridge University Press, 2007).

Tainter, Joseph, *The Collapse of Complex Societies* (Cambridge: Cambridge University Press, 1988).

Taleb, Nassim, *The Black Swan* (London: Penguin, 2007).

Theroux, Marcel, *Far North* (London: Faber & Faber, 2009).

Thompson, Edward P., *The Making of the English Working Class* (Harmondsworth: Penguin, 1968).

Thrift, Nigel, *Non-Representational Theory* (London: Routledge, 2008).

Thrift, Nigel, and Sean French, 'The automatic production of space', *Transactions of the Institute of British Geographers*, New Series, 27, 2002: 309–35.

Thun, Eric, *Changing Lanes in China* (Cambridge: Cambridge University Press, 2006).

Topham, Gwyn, 'Cash-strapped students swap car for coach', *Guardian*, 27 February 2012.

Tranter, Paul, and Scott Sharpe, 'Escaping Monstropolis: Child-friendly cities, peak oil and *Monsters Inc*', *Children's Geographies* 6, 2008: 295–308.

Turkle, Sherry, *Alone Together* (New York: Basic Books, 2011).

Tyfield, David, Yongguan Zhu and Jinghua Cao, 'The importance of the "international dividend": The case of China', *Science and Public Policy* 36, 2009: 723–35.

UK Parliament, House of Commons, *Cars of the Future: Seventeenth Report of Session 2003–04 (HC 319–I)*, House of Commons Transport Committee, London, 2004, pp. 1–54.

UN–Habitat, *Cities and Climate Change* (London: Earthscan, 2011).

UNDP, *Human Development Report 2007/8* (New York: UNDP, 2007).

Urry, John, *Reference Groups and the Theory of Revolution* (London: Routledge, 1973).

Urry, John, *Mobilities* (Cambridge: Polity, 2007).

Urry, John, *Climate Change and Society* (Cambridge: Polity, 2011).

Urry, John, and Jonas Larsen, *The Tourist Gaze 3.0* (London: Sage, 2011).

US National Intelligence Council, *US Global Trends 2025: A Transformed World* (Washington DC: US National Intelligence Council, 2008).

Vadén, Tere, 'Oil and the regime of capitalism', *CTheory*, 23 June 2010: 1–11.

Vidal, John, 'Warning: Extreme weather ahead', *Guardian*, 14 June 2011.

Vidal, John, 'Ecuador asks: How much is the rainforest worth?' *Observer*, 14 August 2011.

von Hippel, Eric, *Democratizing Innovation* (Cambridge MA: MIT Press, 2006).

Walby, Sylvia, *Globalization and Inequalities* (London: Sage, 2009).

Watts, Jonathan, 'China tries to jump-start green car market', *Guardian*, 3 April 2009.

Watts, Jonathan, *When a Billion Chinese Jump* (London: Faber & Faber, 2011).

Wellman, Barry, 'Physical place and cyber place: The rise of networked individualism', *International Journal of Urban and Regional Research* 25, 2001: 227–52.

Welsh, Ian, 'Climate change: Complexity and collaboration between the sciences', in Constance Lever-Tracy (ed.), *Routledge Handbook on Climate Change and Society* (London: Routledge, 2010).

White, Damian, and Chris Wilbert (eds), *Technonatures* (Waterloo, Ontario: Wilfrid Laurier University Press, 2009).

White House, *The National Strategy for Physical Protection of Critical Infrastructures and Key Assets*, National Infrastructure Advisory Council (NIAC), February 2003.

Wilkinson, Richard, and Kate Pickett, *The Spirit Level: Why More Equal Societies Almost Always Do Better* (London: Allen Lane, 2009).

Williams, Heathcote, *Autogeddon* (London: Jonathan Cape, 1991).

Wollen, Peter, and Joe Kerr (eds), *Autopia: Cars and Culture* (London: Reaktion Books, 2002).

Woodbridge, Roy, *The Next World War* (Toronto: Toronto University Press, 2005).

Worldwatch Institute, *2010 State of the World* (New York: W.W. Norton, 2010).

Worldwide Fund for Nature, *Plugged In: The End of the Oil Age, Summary Report* (Brussels: WWF, March 2008).

Yergin, Daniel, *The Quest* (London: Allen Lane, 2011).

Yusoff, Kathryn, 'Biopolitical economies and the political aesthetics of climate change', *Theory, Culture and Society* 27, 2010: 73–99.

Žižek, Slavoj, 'Multiculturalism, or the cultural logic of multinational capitalism', *New Left Review* 225, 1997: 28–51.

Žižek, Slavoj, *Living in the End Times* (London: Verso, 2011).

INDEX